VIOLENT UTOPIA

VIOLENT UTOPIA

DISPOSSESSION & BLACK RESTORATION IN TULSA

Jovan Scott Lewis

Duke University Press   *Durham and London*   2022

© 2022 DUKE UNIVERSITY PRESS

Project editor: Lisa Lawley
Designed by Courtney Leigh Baker
Typeset in Minion Pro and Trade Gothic by
Westchester Publishing Services.

Library of Congress Cataloging-in-Publication Data
Names: Lewis, Jovan Scott, author.
Title: Violent utopia : dispossession and Black restoration in
Tulsa / Jovan Scott Lewis.
Description: Durham : Duke University Press, 2022. | Includes
bibliographical references and index.
Identifiers: LCCN 2021052092 (print)
LCCN 2021052093 (ebook)
ISBN 9781478016014 (hardcover)
ISBN 9781478018568 (paperback)
ISBN 9781478023265 (ebook)
Subjects: LCSH: Tulsa Race Massacre, Tulsa, Okla., 1921. | African
Americans—Violence against—Oklahoma—Tulsa—History—20th
century. | Greenwood (Tulsa, Okla.)—Race relations—History—
20th century. | Greenwood (Tulsa, Okla.)—History—20th century.
| Tulsa (Okla.)—Race relations—History—20th century. | BISAC:
SOCIAL SCIENCE / Ethnic Studies / American / African American &
Black Studies | SOCIAL SCIENCE / Anthropology / Cultural & Social
Classification: LCC F704.T92 L48 2022 (print) | LCC F704.T92
(ebook) | DDC 305.8009766/86—dc23/eng/20220126
LC record available at https://lccn.loc.gov/2021052092
LC ebook record available at https://lccn.loc.gov/2021052093

Cover art: *In the Shadow of the Highway*. A man walks under Interstate 244 where it passes over Greenwood Avenue on the last day of the Legacy Festival commemorating the one-hundred-year anniversary of the 1921 Tulsa Race Massacre. © Joseph Rushmore. Courtesy of the photographer.

As with everything that I do, this book is for Rhys. This book is also in memory of his grandpa, Vincent Edman. Walk good, Mas' Vinny.

CONTENTS

ACKNOWLEDGMENTS

I first went to Tulsa in August 2014, a mere couple of weeks after defending my dissertation at the London School of Economics. Still, months before, I had already begun immersing myself in the complicated circumstances of the city's residents. I had been hired by Tulsa native Charles Stafford and his colleague Rita Astuti, both anthropology professors at the London School of Economics, to join their team researching the relationship between cooperation and inequality. We were joined by another recent LSE graduate, Ana Garza-Gutierrez. Ana, Charles, and I together tried to understand the dynamic of poverty and race among Black, Mexican American, and White Tulsans. I provide this background here, as opposed to in the book's main text, because while my research extended past that summer, these individuals deserve more than serving as a background for my time in Tulsa. These colleagues helped establish the intellectual basis of my interests as material, historical, and ethical concerns, anchored by an explicit commitment to the empirics that only considerate and considerable ethnography can command. I am incredibly thankful to Charles for encouraging me throughout and for opening to me his family in Tulsa, who in turn introduced me to their city in ways that I might not have otherwise had the opportunity or privilege to experience.

The hospitality and generosity of Tulsa's residents can be credited with any success that this work might achieve. Starting with Joseph Grzywacz and his staff at the Center for Family Resilience of Oklahoma State University–Tulsa, my network in Tulsa opened exponentially, with Shameca Brown at the center of it all. Shameca has been a constant partner in my research over the past seven years, from the beginning until my last visit to Tulsa for this project to observe the 1921 massacre centennial commemoration. Through Shameca, I became familiar with North Tulsa, so she is owed the greatest gratitude.

In North Tulsa the list of interlocutors, friends, and outright characters who made research a pleasure is long. I am incredibly thankful to DJ Mercer,

Anthony Marshall, Billie Parker, Reverend, Roberta Clardy, Dewayne Dickens, Philip Abode, Joseph Rushmore, Kerrye Woods, Chris Terrell, and Uwa Anwari. This list does not comprehensively represent everyone who shared with me, even briefly, the stories of their lives and North Tulsa. I interviewed several more people who do not appear in this list because listing their pseudonyms would fail to account for their impact. I am grateful for every conversation that appears in this text (and for the many more that do not). I have sought to honor those individuals by retaining as comprehensive an account of their experiences as possible.

A broad community of scholars and friends supported the work. I am thankful to Peter James Hudson for reading and commenting on an early draft of the book and for his commitment to critical and material Black study. Karla Slocum went above and beyond in reviewing this book on multiple occasions. I am grateful for her generosity of both time and care. Karla's devotion to Black Oklahomans' history and contemporary lived experience has been an inspiration and model for this work. Karla's work is instrumental to my argument and invaluable to expanding the narrative and possibilities of the Black experience.

I thank Joel Wanek and Joseph Rushmore for helping me to visually articulate the experiences of Black Tulsans, and I am even more grateful to those who generously and graciously allowed us to frame their lives. I always appreciate my colleagues in the Department of Geography at the University of California, Berkeley, for the comradeship and support that I've received there since the very beginning. Thanks to Jake Kosek, Nathan Sayre, and Shard Chari. Gillian Hart has been a constant source of support in this work. I want to especially thank Brandi Thompson Summers for her feedback, encouragement, and friendship.

I am grateful to my graduate students: Kaily Heitz, Jane Henderson, Bobby Moeller, Morgan Vickers, April L. Graham, William Carter, Annie Lloyd, Franchesca Araujo, and Zein Dahir. You each are such brilliant examples of what it means to do scholarship that is devoted to community, especially when what is at stake is the sacred relationship that community has to Blackness and belonging. I want to thank Elizabeth Ault at Duke University Press for her instant enthusiasm, motivation, and steady support in getting this book published but most of all for understanding the work's importance and timeliness.

I want to thank my wife, Zaviear, and our remarkable and beautiful child, Rhys, for their love and support. Zaviear and Rhys both demonstrated the kind of resilience and compassion that strengthens and grows any family. I cannot find adequate words to show my love and appreciation for what they do for me daily. All I know is that their love sustains me. They each understood the gravity of North Tulsa's story. Having their love, companionship, care, and investment throughout the completion of this project was a blessing. I owe them a debt that I will forever work to pay. To my mother, Susan, thank you for your steadfast love and support and for being a reminder of what's important in this life (calling one's mother, of course).

This book was completed mainly during the height of the COVID-19 pandemic and primarily written from my apartment's linen closet. Amid the anxiety of the period and the complications of the daily choreography of work and first grade teaching (Rhys, know that you were my greatest teacher), I found so much joy in the intimacy of being with my family. Though my family has lost much in the pandemic, we gained more of each other. It is for that reason that I want to acknowledge all the unknown individuals during that period who helped make this work possible. I want to show my appreciation for the essential workers who could not stay home with their families and who, through their sacrifice—undoubtedly greater than was asked of me—enabled me to be home with my own.

Throughout my research North Tulsa's story has gone from relatively undiscussed to a global phenomenon. In telling its story here, I hope to provide a holistic and genuine narrative that contributes to North Tulsans' aspirations on their terms. As the hip-hop group Fire in Little Africa has noted, "North Tulsa's got something to say!" Theirs is a vast story that stretches back to emancipation and is an example of multifaceted humanity that continues to search for its fullest manifestation. This text is a very humble attempt to pay homage to that journey as a universal story, a journey to which I will forever be committed.

I arrived in Tulsa just a few days after Officer Darren Wilson murdered Mike Brown in Ferguson, Missouri, on August 9, 2014. Ferguson had erupted and was burning in anger and grief. Only five hours' drive away, there were no protests in Tulsa. However, the moment brought up another—and, in a way, a closer—moment of racial violence. What loomed over many of the conversations I had in Tulsa that summer was the specter of the 1921 Tulsa Race Riot, now known as the Tulsa Race Massacre. Over two days in 1921, after a Black man, Dick Rowland, was accused of assaulting a White woman, Sarah Page, unabashed White violence razed the Black community of Greenwood and murdered scores of its residents. Black Tulsans recounted in hushed conversations how police officers had left Greenwood's dead in the street, as Brown had been. We talked about how the price that Greenwood paid for Page's claim—which she ultimately dropped—was not merely the razing of the city and the murder of hundreds of its citizens but Greenwood's ultimate dispossession. Despite their displacement, injuries, and mourning for their dead, Greenwood rebuilt.

From early on, I sensed hesitation in these discussions about the riot. To the community members, it was almost not worth mentioning—perhaps, I thought, because their riot was one of many during the early decades of the twentieth century. Indeed, the Tulsa Race Riot was preceded by riots and massacres in Evansville, Indiana, in 1903; Atlanta in 1906; Springfield, Illinois, in 1908; East St. Louis in 1917; and Macon, Mississippi, and Chicago in 1919. The Rosewood massacre in Florida followed in 1923. I realized that these quiet conversations with North Tulsa's residents revealed how violence is buried within ordinary, everyday life and ongoing relationships, as Veena Das has noted.[1] Maybe the violence of the riot was too deep to recover through casual conversation. I found the riot's violence less in the words of North Tulsans and more in the archive that was the landscape they inhabited, which made it clear that the Greenwood riot was just the beginning of the assault on Black Tulsa.

Despite the sheer horror of that violence and the trauma of its recollection, it did not seem to define North Tulsa or its residents. Before the riot, Greenwood's commercial productivity had earned it the moniker Negro Wall Street, given it by Booker T. Washington, later becoming Black Wall Street. Following the riot, the survivors then rebuilt Greenwood back into an active Black community. It became clear over time that Black Tulsans had a deep and diverse historical and ethical reservoir from which they drew their sense of worth and the promise of their future. It was a kind of confidence that I understood was firmly rooted in a broader sense of their history.

Although Tulsa is a small city, its geographical sense is complex. I could see the effects of the highway and the racism that produced it on the city's neighborhoods, which I would learn had so much history behind that complexity. Navigating Tulsa was a disorienting experience, spatially, historically, and ethically. But the flatness of the geography provided a constant, ever-present horizon wherever I turned. Over time, I realized that the notion of the horizon would explain Tulsa, especially its Black residents' experience. The contemporary landscape of North Tulsa was like many other Black spaces throughout the country ravaged by urban renewal and Jim Crow before it.

Greenwood's commercial diversity and activity were replaced by a lack of grocery stores and poor access to everyday services, which, where available, were provided by various nonprofit organizations. Greenwood's population had been displaced further north, with the Black community no longer referenced as Greenwood but North Tulsa. The "difficult entanglements of racial encounter" that Katherine McKittrick calls the "Black sense of place" were evident everywhere.[2] *Vacant* was the only word that came to mind. I had always known Black neighborhoods as populated, active, and visible. At first, I assumed it had to do with it being mid-August, when the temperatures would reach into the high nineties but feel even hotter owing to the humidity. After getting to know many of North Tulsa's Black residents, I learned that this was the norm.

North Tulsa

When I first visited North Tulsa, I was invested in exploring what contemporary Blackness might look like given the history of Black people's material and psychological displacement from land, oppression as a people, and exclusion from the benefits of citizenship during and following the Reconstruction era. Structural violence has prevented a collective recognition of Black humanity and has resulted in an alienated sense of Black individuality. Yet North Tulsa's history and geography worked to limit the effects of that form of oppression, which played out in the community's discourses.

Indeed, this Black community was like most but was also distinctly determined and defined by its geography. The ways Black people coped with repeated assaults on their being were often couched in terms of community, and that community was read through geographic frameworks. Thus, from the ethical resources that were Greenwood and Black Wall Street, Black people in North Tulsa drew strength, grounded their community identity, and secured the terms of their humanity. North Tulsa's residents had long struggled to resist external assault and remain self-sufficient through forms of community, understood as an ethical responsibility to one another. This resistance produced a palpable sense of pride in what they had achieved. Being able to locate that achievement, they sought to reproduce it. In other words, to paraphrase Ruth Wilson Gilmore, for North Tulsans, "freedom was a place," and as a place, it could be defined and defended.[3]

I wanted to understand how the historical processes of social and structural violence, the politics of North Tulsa's abandonment, and the resulting lack of material resources were reimagined at the community level as a struggle against these processes and as the basis of North Tulsans' relationships. I wanted to understand how they learned to cope with the challenges before them. I wanted to know how they sustained a sense of pride despite their circumstances. With these questions in mind, I met with North Tulsa residents to fully appreciate this process.

"If you really wanna see people, you have to visit a church or a Booker T. [High School] football game," Shameca Brown told me. Shameca was a young Black Tulsan who worked with the Center for Family Resilience at Oklahoma State University–Tulsa (OSU–Tulsa). The center was established in 2009 to serve as "a community resource focused on equipping every family to support its members in achieving their fullest personal and social potential," according to its website.[4] In practical terms, the center studies local families and translates that knowledge into programs that are driven by a commitment to fostering resilience. These programs were affiliated with or administered by local human and social service agencies. Some of these programs were staffed entirely by the center. Shameca was one of the staff members whom the center hired to work in its Promotora program. The Promotora program initially focused on the needs of the Hispanic farmworking community, providing lessons on health and safety as part of a research program at the center. It expanded slightly to cover the learning-gap concerns of African American families, and this was the community in which Shameca worked.

Through an affiliation with the center, facilitated by the director, Joseph Grzywacz, I quickly developed a network through the Promotoras. Moreover, through the center I got a firsthand understanding of how prevalent social programs were in the everyday life of North Tulsans, as I accompanied Shameca on her visits to several Black families in North Tulsa. Through Shameca and the Tulsans who shared their time with me, I would come to know so much more about North Tulsa's Black community than could have been gleaned from public view. I would come to know intimately the intersections of poverty, race, and gender and the way they formed from this town's history. I would see the sheer weight of the theme of resilience, which, given the postmassacre history of Greenwood, is as essential an inquiry as any if one is to understand the circumstances of Black life in Tulsa and the forces that worked to make those circumstances so.

Darrell, a master's student at OSU-Tulsa whom I met through the center, told me, "This used to be considered Greenwood where we are." We were near downtown Tulsa, at a location that straddles the border between historic Greenwood and the Brady District. The district was renamed the Tulsa Arts District in 2019, given that its namesake, Tate Brady, one of Tulsa's founders, had belonged to the Ku Klux Klan. As the Brady District became the Tulsa Arts District, the wave of regeneration that saw the former turn into a chic art and cultural zone has seen the latter fall victim to pernicious gentrification. "If you go straight that way, that's where the race riot happened. You could walk three blocks, two blocks even, that way, and that's Greenwood. It's hard to believe that right over there was Black Wall Street. . . . That's where it was."

The famed Greenwood Avenue runs alongside the ONEOK Field, the home of the Tulsa Drillers baseball team. North of Interstate 244, which callously and with much consequence cut across the Greenwood District, much of historic Greenwood is occupied by OSU-Tulsa's campus—land made available through urban renewal policies. The site houses the Greenwood Cultural Center, the landmark Vernon AME Church, and Mt. Zion Baptist Church. I had to meditate on what it meant to experience such history mediated through such mundanity. Without Vernon, the Greenwood Cultural Center, and the nearly hundred-year-old Greenwood Chamber of Commerce as landmarks, historic Greenwood would appear indistinct from any other small-city downtown district. The adjacent area that is the Tulsa Arts District is dotted with bars and restaurants, which over the years have become increasingly hip and chic to attract the nearby students of OSU-Tulsa, the growing workforce of an ever-increasing downtown, and the patrons of the developing art scene.

Perhaps for these reasons, to Darrell, the geographic boundaries of Black Tulsa were "kinda weird. And depending on who you talk to, it changes," he added. "So, if you're talking to someone from Fifty-Sixth Street North, deep North Tulsa, it feels far. Like it's probably a twenty-minute drive; it's not that far, but for North Tulsa it's far." So much of what was considered Greenwood had changed over the years. This transformation had everything to do with not only the shifts produced by the race massacre but the history of racial dispossession that followed in its wake. There was a sense of geographic recession by which Greenwood had become North Tulsa. The area and the culture had become a repository for Black Tulsa's history, which had been evacuated from Greenwood. Still, of Greenwood, Darrell shared, "We are very emotionally attached to it, and rightfully so," continuing, "Younger people . . . the kids who actually grew up here, are not always very familiar with its history, but it's definitely left a significant mark on Tulsa's history, and the other things that have happened since." The past of Greenwood now served to articulate and validate the present's concerns, needs, and hopes, albeit slightly further north. And so, although largely absent in a material sense, Greenwood was still present in the way that mattered most: as a geography of memory and aspiration.

North Tulsans lived within the double wake of material privation through urban renewal and the semiotic dispossession represented in the narrative of the massacre. Today community members navigate an underdeveloped space where nonprofits provide many everyday services, and residents struggle for adequate access to quality food. But within that context, North Tulsans do what Black people have always done when deprived of their freedom, which is to plan, build, and thrive.

Public discourse on the riot was relatively quiet when I first arrived in Tulsa but has since become a flash point for thinking about the broader experience of anti-Black violence. If the murder of Mike Brown resulted in little public response among North Tulsans, the murder of George Floyd six years later saw Black Tulsans, like much of the world, respond with open revolt. Floyd's murder by Minnesota police officer Derek Chauvin occurred on the ninety-ninth-anniversary weekend of the Tulsa Race Massacre, which added a more potent and poignant sense of Tulsa's relevance. The massacre was perhaps most publicly revived and put to use in 2019 with the release of the HBO series *Watchmen*, which used the massacre as a narrative backdrop.

Through the various forms by which Greenwood's story was mobilized and even celebrated, a nuanced appreciation is needed for how both the violence and the prosperity reflected in that story are intertwined with the history of the massacre as an event. Moreover, it must be understood how each finds its way into the structures of Black life in Tulsa and how they are at play in the broader experience of Blackness. Neglect, dispossession, and deterioration are central to the longer-term exclusion of Black Tulsans, and so an emphasis on the 1921 massacre as an exceptional event belies the fact that the massacre was but one act of disruption of Greenwood's social order. Still, it was a critical and foundational act of violence, and Greenwood's history, which became North Tulsa's, suggests that the massacre's legacy has profoundly altered the terms and conditions of Black life in Tulsa. What has been left to those who live in Greenwood today is a complicated sense of that legacy.

North Tulsans live with this past as a sense of place that, while distant in many ways, is constitutional to their present. As I show in this book, this history, as the preservation of the collective memory, has been the only mooring of North Tulsans to the promise of what Greenwood was and what North Tulsa can be. That promise has been held on to despite the city's refusal to provide compensation for damages, even though Greenwood's destruction and its recovery are increasingly becoming recognized as part of Tulsa's broader legacy, from which entities outside of North Tulsa have sought to benefit. Few surviving structures stand as material testaments to North Tulsa's past prosperity. Still, their memorialization has discursively been etched into North Tulsa's streets to stand as monuments to the community's prospects. And to fully appreciate the contemporary meaning of Greenwood, one must understand how history and memory are themselves fraught with ambivalent meanings and contested narratives when deployed as resources for collective social-political action.

Indian Territory

That history began with the failure of Reconstruction in 1877, when many southern Blacks who hadn't already fled the region as refugees during the Civil War became early expatriates following emancipation. In the early years, many remained on the plantation lands where they once toiled as unfree laborers. However, some sought to exercise their new freedom elsewhere. One of those places was Indian Territory, which would later become the state of Oklahoma. The first African American arrivals in Oklahoma preceded this period, starting with Indian Removal. Indeed, to fully understand Tulsa and the possibilities for freedom that Black people would make for themselves, one needs an understanding of that particular geography, the so-called Five Civilized Tribes, the Dawes Commission, and its impact on them and Indian Territory.

The Five Civilized Tribes comprised the Cherokee, Chickasaw, Choctaw, Muscogee, and Seminole peoples, who settled in Indian Territory following the Indian Removal Act of 1830, which dispossessed the groups of their lands in the American Southeast. At this same time, the first Black people arrived in Indian Territory, as removal included the Freedmen (former slaves who held tribal membership) and Black slaves who were brought by their Native owners. To be sure, Indian Territory was never a plantation society. Indian Territory should be understood as a "society with slaves" rather than a "slave society" like the antebellum South. For both Native and Black people, removal, which Claudio Saunt calls *expulsion*, had been a transformation of a "geographical relationship" that produced a "geographical segregation," whose consequences would long play out in later Oklahoma as the twin processes of expulsion and segregation.[5] Saunt argues that geographic segregation "inscribed the Republic's racial fixation on the land," which would follow the Native groups into Indian Territory in perhaps the most consequential way just over fifty years after removal.[6]

The Dawes Act of 1887, also known as the General Allotment Act, authorized the subdivision of Native tribal landholdings, which had historically been communal, into individual allotments.[7] Through creating individual and family rather than communal Native landholdings, the act claimed to facilitate the assimilation of Native people. The process was fostered by the creation of the Dawes Rolls, overseen by the Dawes Commission, which consisted of members Henry L. Dawes, Meredith H. Kidd, and Archibald S. McKennon. The Dawes Commission registered qualifying tribal members after determining their eligibility for qualifying as "Indian" and thereby their entitlement to property ownership. The commission determined this based on strict notions of blood descent. This blood-quantum formula and enlistment on the Dawes Rolls, both used as methods for determining qualification, led to the prevalence of racialization as a mode of belonging and identity among Native people.

Blacks who were enslaved in Indian Territory were fully emancipated in 1866. Though the extent of incorporation varied between Native groups, emancipated Native Blacks received tribal membership, making them all "Freedmen," a designation modified by their tribal affiliation, such as Cherokee Freedmen and Creek Freedmen.[8] As such, the Dawes Commission enlisted them through a secondary category called the Freedmen's Rolls. Although they formed a discrete and less Native category, Freedmen's enlistment came with an allotment—also less than that of full-blooded Native people.

Following the Dawes Act, the Curtis Act in 1898 brought Indian Territory under federal control, weakening although not entirely eroding tribal sovereignty.[9] The 2020 Supreme Court ruling in *McGirt v. Oklahoma*, which determined that most of eastern Oklahoma, including Tulsa, for jurisdictional purposes remained part of a tribal reservation, after nearly a century of federal presumption otherwise, proves the resilience of that sovereignty and the haphazard quality of those acts. Nevertheless, these acts radically transformed the system and method of Native land tenure and Native sovereignty through the mechanism of private property, as limiting landownership to the heads of families reinforced Western notions and structures of kinship.

Native assimilation aside, the restructuring of Native social life enacted through allotment was most pronounced in its capacity—indeed its initial intention—to produce a surplus of available land for sale. The land surplus became available to non-Native settlers under the tenets of the 1862 Homestead Act, and unassigned lands in Indian Territory were opened to settlers through the 1889 Land Run.[10] The movement to open lands in Indian Territory resulted from the demand to accommodate White settlers who had already settled in the US-owned Oklahoma Territory, which adjoined Indian Territory to the west. These two territories would later be joined to form the state of Oklahoma.

African Americans from the South migrated to Indian Territory seeking new opportunities. Post-Reconstruction racism and its accompanying violence had made life in the South much too oppressive to endure. The plantation had cast long political and social shadows within the southern geographies, and so, if only by comparison, Indian Territory represented a veritable promised land. These "Exodusters" left the South following an emigrationist impulse that, before they arrived in Indian Territory, took them to the bordering Oklahoma Territory, Kansas, Texas, and elsewhere.[11] Encouraged by Black boosters, like W. L. Eagleson and Edwin McCabe, who sought to create a Black state in Indian Territory, many African Americans took part in the land run in 1889. As a result, all-Black towns started to develop in Indian Territory. These new Black arrivants often bought land, sometimes in partnerships with Whites, from Freedmen, who had fewer restrictions on their property than full-blooded Native people.[12]

Whites were fearful of a Black Oklahoma as soon as Blacks rushed the land of the Indian Territory. Indeed, as African Americans imagined a new Black world for themselves, many White Sooners and Boomers (respectively, those who homesteaded the territories before and after the official runs began) sought their own racial paradise. The start of the statehood movement in Oklahoma immediately following the 1889 settlement of Indian Territory was joined by efforts to rid the region of its Black inhabitants. James Smallwood of the Oklahoma Historical Society writes, "For instance, a white mob ran African Americans out of Lexington in 1892. A year later all the blacks in Blackwell left the town when threatened with violence. Poor whites 'hounded' blacks in Ponca City, and masked raiders attacked African Americans in Lincoln County. Indian Territory, too, saw much travail, with African Americans being run out of many areas."[13]

Nevertheless, access to land and reduced, though not absent, racial restrictions in Indian Territory, given that it was jurisdictionally not part of the United States, materialized a solid opportunity to pursue the Black future envisioned at emancipation. The first among the all-Black towns was Langston, established in 1890 on 320 acres of land by Edwin McCabe, a native New Yorker, trained lawyer, and "exoduster" who had moved to Kansas.[14] McCabe would be one of the earliest boosters for Black migration to Indian Territory, which he facilitated through his Black newspaper, the *Langston City Herald*, which debuted in May 1891. The *Langston City Herald* circulated throughout the South and Southeast and regularly featured articles encouraging its readers to consider homesteading in Indian Territory. The paper published maps of available plots with headings that read, "Freedom, Peace, Happiness and Prosperity, Do you want all of these? Then cast your lot with us and make your home in Langston City."[15] In developing Langston, McCabe advanced a broader goal of making Oklahoma an all-Black state. That dream never materialized, and the paper folded in 1902, followed by McCabe's departure to Chicago in 1908. However, McCabe's legacy endured through the Colored Agricultural and Normal University of Oklahoma, which he had established in 1897, now Langston University, the only historically Black college or university in the state.

McCabe's efforts, along with others', contributed to the development of more than fifty all-Black towns by 1920, with thirteen still in existence in

Oklahoma today. A prime example of the potential of the all-Black town is the town of Boley, Oklahoma, considered the largest of the twentieth century. Boley, opened for settlement in 1903 in Creek Nation, Indian Territory, was founded by John Boley, a White official of the Fort Smith and Western Railway, and Thomas Haynes, a Black Texan farmer and entrepreneur who was chosen as the townsite manager. The land was bought from Creek Freedman Abigail Barnett. Boley began as a camp of Black railroad construction hands but became an archetypal example of an "all-Negro" town's political and racial self-fulfillment, which in its founding and early years "furnished the material out of which the Negro may carve and shape his future destiny."[16]

Alaina Roberts, in *I've Been Here All the While*, argues that Black "connections to the space of Indian Territory were often more important than political rights" and situates the value of those rights as being primarily tied to the ability to maintain land claims.[17] Roberts seeks to broaden the understanding that Reconstruction "revolved predominantly around the pursuit of political rights by people of African descent."[18] For Roberts, Indian Territory was "a space where a different sort of Reconstruction project occurred, one that allowed for the successful pursuit of land," which Roberts frames as being concerned not with political freedom but rather with a sense of belonging.[19] Roberts uses belonging to "signal" that Black people in Indian Territory "did not always seek citizenship, the legal conveyance of certain rights and privileges upon a person by a state. Rather, they often clung to kinship networks and natal communities in locations where citizenship was an impossibility in order to possess land."[20] Roberts uses as evidence of her point that Chickasaw freedpeople, typically referred to as *Freedmen*, "were offered no tribal membership by the Chickasaw Nation after emancipation" but that "even without the prospect of tribal citizenship, Chickasaw freedpeople stayed within the nation, demonstrating that for them, kinship ties and generational connections to the space of Indian Territory were often more important than political rights, insofar as they allowed them to stake a claim to the land."[21]

However, according to the 1974 National Register of Historic Places nomination form for Boley, "Boley was portrayed as a haven from oppression and a place where blacks could govern themselves."[22] The commitment and success of Black politics in Indian Territory are evidenced by the resistance from Whites, such as in the story of Boley. In 1906, in an election in the seventy-ninth district for the representatives to the state constitutional convention, the Black residents of Boley swayed the vote and elected a Republican, against the wishes of the "county Whites," who backed the Democratic candidate. This display of Boley's political agency angered Whites in Ok-fuskee County, who set out to disenfranchise Boley and eliminate its emerging political and economic power. This, plus the depression in the cotton industry, Boley's primary agricultural commodity, interrupted Boley's goal to materialize the dream of racial self-fulfillment.

Further illustrating the import of politics to the Black imaginary of Indian Territory, Black migrants to Indian Territory, beginning with early Black pioneers like McCabe, pursued an all-Black state. There was a horizon of racial sovereignty that followed emancipation. It was the freedom represented in Indian Territory, rooted in land, and made material through political advancement. The all-Black towns like Boley and Langston and towns like Muskogee with a high Black population represented and forwarded this promise. Boley and other Black towns like it provided socioeconomic and political opportunities to acquire land and work, both of which were seen as necessary to achieve political and economic self-determination. And, to return to McCabe's intentions of forming an all-Black state in Indian Territory, Black arrivants wanted more than belonging; they wanted political power and, as I argue later in this book, sovereignty. Moreover, the emigrationist history of Black people before their arrival and during their tenure in Indian Territory signals that land was the means of accomplishing this sovereign future. The all-Black town, like Boley, would serve as the model for the geographic rendering of self-determination, which would be present in the founding of Greenwood only a few years later.

Greenwood

While not a Black town in the formal sense of being relatively isolated and predominantly rural, Greenwood in Tulsa would follow the same pattern of land acquisition—especially of land held by Creek Freedmen—and settlement.[23] Tulsa's origins, and specifically those of Greenwood, were rooted in the transformation of Indian Territory through allotment.[24] The Muscogee (Creek), in particular the Lochapoka (Turtle Clan), who had been removed from their original home in Alabama, had settled Tulsa by 1836. The city's name came from the original Creek settlement's name, Tulasi, meaning "old town."[25] Tulsa wouldn't become a White "settled" town until nearly fifty years later, when the St. Louis and San Francisco, or "Frisco," railroad finally arrived in 1882.[26] Still, the population of Tulsa wouldn't grow significantly until the discovery of the first oil gusher, Sue Bland No. 1, at Red Fork in 1901. But it was the second gusher well, the Ida Glenn No. 1, in the Glenn Pool Field in 1905 between Tulsa and the nearby town of Sapulpa that made Tulsa the oil capital of the world.

The promise of the oil industry drew Greenwood's early entrepreneurs to Tulsa that same year to follow the newfound and growing wealth of the city. Greenwood spanned about four square miles from the Frisco tracks north. Entrepreneurs O. W. Gurley and J. B. Stradford purchased, parceled out, and planned dozens of acres of Creek land to develop the all-Black community of Greenwood, named after Greenwood, Mississippi, with a mind toward encouraging commerce adjacent to the growing oil economy of Tulsa. The resulting development became a social hub of economic activity that would earn the main corridor, Greenwood Avenue, the nickname of Negro Wall Street.

John Baptist "J.B." Stradford was born in 1861 to a freed slave emancipated in Stratford, Ontario. J.B. was a graduate of Oberlin College and Indiana Law School. He had found some success in St. Louis and Kentucky, where he ran several businesses, including pool halls, shoeshine parlors, bathhouses, and boardinghouses. Stradford moved to Tulsa in 1899 and began to invest in real estate north of the Frisco railroad tracks, focusing on rental properties and reselling them to other arrivants. He opened the Stradford Hotel in Greenwood, which would come to prominence as one of the largest Black-owned hotels in the United States.[27]

Gurley was originally from Pine Bluff, Arkansas, and was self-educated. He became a homesteader in the Oklahoma Land Rush, joining the tens of thousands of individuals who participated in Oklahoma's fourth and most significant land run, the Cherokee Outlet Opening.[28] Gurley ended up staking claim to a piece of land that would become part of Perry, Oklahoma, a town home to a significant African American homesteading population during the first decade of the twentieth century. Gurley sold his land and his Perry store and in 1906 purchased forty acres of Creek land in Tulsa, north of the Frisco tracks, that had been initially sold to white developer Giuseppe "Joe" Piro.[29]

Gurley and Stradford shared a particular vision for what Black life could be in the Territory and in the state of Oklahoma, which would form shortly after they founded Greenwood. Greenwood's growth followed Tulsa's. A decade after statehood in 1907, Tulsa's population had quadrupled to more than seventy-two thousand, and Greenwood's had grown to almost nine thousand. Despite the Jim Crow segregation that followed statehood, Gurley, Stradford, and many other entrepreneurs developed Greenwood as a mecca for Blacks moving to Tulsa.[30] John and Loyal Williams built the Dreamland Theater, and A. J. Smitherman would start one of Greenwood's two newspapers. Simon Berry ran a transportation network of Model T cars and buses throughout Greenwood.[31] Greenwood was a comprehensive and complete town that offered leisure spaces like a roller-skating rink, pool halls, and a YMCA; everyday services and goods suppliers like auto repair shops, beauty parlors, grocers, and barbershops; and neighborhood staples like churches, schools, funeral homes, a hospital, and a US post office.[32]

The discovery of oil, statehood, and segregation would have curious consequences for Greenwood's future. Before the state's adoption of Jim Crow, interracial economic, if not social, activity was common in Tulsa and specifically in Greenwood—mainly because it abutted Tulsa's downtown.[33] When the city formally annexed Greenwood in 1910, segregation became more pronounced, having an even greater impact on Greenwood's internal economy.[34] Segregation isolated many Black towns throughout the state, as well as Black areas in multiracial cities like Tulsa and Oklahoma City. But despite, and perhaps because of, segregation, Greenwood enjoyed relatively successful community development. Segregation made Greenwood a primarily closed economy, where each dollar circulated in the community as many as thirty times before being spent outside.[35] While Greenwood's wealth circulated within its community owing to segregation, very little of that wealth was generated within the community. Tulsa historian James Hirsch writes that "while Greenwood may have been socially and physically segregated, it was closely bound economically to white Tulsa."[36] This was because segregation and overall racism restricted Black Tulsa from directly participating in the oil industry, which provided much of the general wealth of the city. Thus, Greenwood's residents found employment in the service sector in the White parts of the city. Nevertheless, the money came north to Greenwood through their labor, and Black businesses supporting the local community flourished, providing a full array of educational, commercial, health, cultural, and social resources. The growth and diversification of the Greenwood community created an overall cycle of development, which drew more and more aspirant Blacks from the South and neighboring states.

We must be careful in associating economic activity with affluence when discussing this period of Greenwood's history. The moniker of Negro Wall Street had everything to do with the former, but over the long history of what would later become Black Wall Street, the mythologizing of the latter would become more pronounced. The wealth of Greenwood's business district, referred to as Deep Greenwood, was limited in the extent to which it carried over into the surrounding residential neighborhoods. As Hirsch argues:

> "Black Wall Street" hardly suggests the poverty, squalor, and neglect that were common outside Greenwood's vibrant business district and a block or two of prime housing. . . . By 1920, only six blocks in Greenwood were paved; the rest were uneven dirt roads with ditches that drained the rainfall. Sewage connections were rare; bathrooms and indoor toilets were luxuries few could afford. The Colored Public Health Nurse of Tulsa reported in that year that a single outdoor toilet was used by one eleven-room house and seven adjoining houses. While the elite streets had brick homes and bungalows, many people lived in weather-beaten shacks with planks, sheds, two-room cottages, the remains of old barns, and even tents. Wood from packing crates was often used to build homes. Mangy cows roamed around the outhouses, chickens ran across scattered sand, and refuse fires burned in corner lots.[37]

Hirsch notes that the American Association of Social Workers had surveyed the miserable conditions in which many of Greenwood's residents lived and had drafted a report on this in 1920. However, he states that the report concluded that even though Greenwood was a rather "dismal picture," "the colored community has very outstanding assets—its people."[38] It was the people, not their capital—after all, in Tulsa, the world's oil capital, Blacks had neither oil nor capital—that held the most promise for Greenwood.

Greenwood's promise was also viewed as its greatest threat to White Tulsa. Increasing racial tension followed the increase in population. And since the "district was now larger than all but a few towns in Oklahoma . . . the growth of Greenwood frightened Tulsa's whites."[39] Some narratives portray Greenwood's economic activity and its resulting, albeit circumscribed, wealth as inducing envy among White, especially poorer, Tulsans. And while that may be true, particularly on an interpersonal level, what was most threatening about Greenwood's population was the political influence they might have been able to wield. This potential had precedent in all-Black towns' political and population dynamics, like in Boley. These towns were ready references in White Tulsa's defense against Black encroachment that emanated from Greenwood. Hirsch evidences this claim through reference to an April 12, 1912, lead story in the *Tulsa Democrat*, whose headline was "SHALL TULSA BE MUSKOGEEIZED?" Muskogee had been a notable Black town located southeast of Tulsa. The *Tulsa Democrat* argued, as Hirsch notes, that Tulsa was "in danger of losing its prestige as the whitest town in Oklahoma."[40]

So the reference to Tulsa becoming "Muskogeeized" and the already circulating nicknames of Little Africa and Niggertown given to Greenwood, as seen in the press, made clear precisely what cause for concern Greenwood represented.

At play, then, was an insistence on containment. It was more than a racial preference for segregation facilitated by Jim Crow; it was an existential racial and geographic anxiety about White space. Recall that alongside the Black homesteaders who arrived in Indian Territory, White Sooners and Boomers sought their own locus of freedom, implicitly framed as a White racial paradise. A contest of space, politics, and race was present from the start and would play out in the violence of the 1921 race riot. Long after the riot, that violence would continue to mark the life experiences and circumstances of Greenwood's descendants, now located in what was figured as North Tulsa.

Violent Utopia

Based on archival work and ethnographic fieldwork in Tulsa, Oklahoma, from 2014 to 2021, *Violent Utopia* explores the juxtaposition of violence and Black freedom and progress in a direct assessment of the paradoxical circumstances of Blackness in the United States. *Violent Utopia* examines the current condition of Black life in Tulsa as mediated by that community's history through the five analytic themes of violence, inheritance, restoration, repair, and territory. The book is concerned with understanding the qualification and condition of Blackness. The argument relies on the history of Black life in Oklahoma but is not limited to or by it. Tulsa's Black history and contemporary reality have a much more universal purchase than many of the existing discussions have allowed for, which is yet another form of exception.

More than a "cultural" phenomenon, the question of Blackness at the heart of the project maintains that histories have material consequence. This book aims to advance an understanding of Black life's core geographic constitution. It draws on the structural analyses that drive the political and economic thrust of critical human geography; the foregrounding of Blackness's qualification as an analytic and a subject is the central imperative of Black studies. Also, it meaningfully draws from anthropology's ability to think through the phenomenological systems that we humans use to understand and organize our social worlds.

With the history of Greenwood's foundation established in this intro-duction, chapter 1 investigates the boundaries of White supremacy and the modes of violence that police them through an analysis of the 1921 Tulsa Race Massacre. Those boundaries represented an intricate system of values, norms, and expectations that upheld the order materialized by social and geographic delineations codified as Jim Crow. The chapter advances a broader understanding of regimes like Jim Crow laws and their contemporary it-erations as social and legal systems undergirded by anti-Blackness and re-sponding to a threat to White social order. The chapter analyzes how the violence of the race riot reappeared in later forms of social organization like urban renewal. Both Jim Crow and urban renewal as formal policy and so-cial philosophy advance and require the racist relegation and subjugation of Black populations through isolation, control, and violence.

Nearly a century after the massacre, chapter 2 examines the afterlives of the violence of 1921 and urban renewal in contemporary North Tulsa, marked by the scars of structural impoverishment. Greenwood's past commercial ac-tivity has been replaced by austere public service and a devastating lack of commercial life. The consequence, framed as an inheritance, of the terrorist act of 1921 is social instability; a restrictive, if not arrested, local economy; and intergenerational poverty. The community's difficulties accessing neces-sary goods have led many state agencies, churches, and nonprofit organ-izations to intervene in North Tulsa's poverty. These interventions and the policies that facilitate them weaken the state's obligation to provide care and services to these communities and dampen the community's ability to pro-vide for themselves. The chapter shows how these programs, which function not as catalysts of mobility but rather as mechanisms of dependence, are tied to, arranged by, and underwritten by underdevelopment, which comple-ments the violence of community destruction in 1921.

North Tulsans recognize the devastation of their circumstances and seek to develop resources for self-determination, as they did a century ago. Chap-ter 3 focuses on community organizing around food access, specifically the lack of a grocery store in North Tulsa. What becomes clear is the centrality of restoring Black Wall Street in the community's self-narrative. The chapter traces how the community works to reconcile their circumstances with their history, framed as how they, the inheritors of a legacy of prosperity, have found themselves incapable of sustaining their community with essential services. The chapter begins to examine the racialized notion of commu-nity through the multiple ways its development has been articulated around community revitalization through commercial ethics and activity. Studying how North Tulsa pursues community based on this longed-for legacy, the chapter advances that this process yields both aspiration and frustration, which becomes mobilized in various assessments of Black Tulsan life in impoverishment.

Chapter 4 contends with the conflict inherent in North Tulsa's politics of recollection as restoration. In doing so, it examines the full scope of possible reconciliation in the face of community challenges founded on the poverty of community dispossession, beginning with the 1921 race massacre. As African Americans continue to face systemic and overt violence, they are required to continuously seek to make a world worth living in and for. The chapter illustrates how that process unfolds in the North Tulsa community, based on Greenwood's narrative, revealing a reparative framework based on restoration. The chapter traces active attempts to mobilize the narrative power of Greenwood by the local North Tulsa community, politicians, and other Black communities leading up to the 2021 centenary of the massacre. The chapter illustrates how Black Tulsans' articulations of repair extend beyond common slavery-based reparations. The destruction begun in 1921 is formally framed as a "nuisance" that has caused the systematic dispossession of the community over the past century and requires reparation.

The fifth and final chapter examines the conditions that made Greenwood possible and thus served as the basis for contemporary Black Tulsans' efforts to restore its legacy. It traces back to the decades following Reconstruction and describes how the emancipated sought to reorient their relationship to the country by migrating to Indian Territory. The chapter looks to this moment of "post" freedom to analyze and clarify the central role that geography played in that freedom's articulation. Through an analysis of this history and the popular notion of Indian Territory held by inhabiting Blacks, the chapter advances a novel but material notion of Black freedom, centered on the meaning and operation of land, sovereignty, and futurity. Examining the possibilities for freedom, organized by this notion of territory, the chapter engages the complication that is Black settler colonialism, providing a meaningful engagement in the debate on Black and Indigenous relations through placemaking. The chapter ultimately argues against the working notion that Black place is already and always contingent and determined by existing racist structures. Through Black settlement in the territory, the chapter considers racialized geography as providing the terms and conditions for a material freedom dream.

Violent Utopia concludes by recognizing that the narrative of Greenwood for Black Tulsans is a horizon that is situated in the past but that they use to navigate and overcome North Tulsa's contemporary poverty. Using the massacre as a means of seeking reparations for the history of violence, North Tulsa's residents' current activity and ambitions might provide a basis for determining what repair and reparation might be. As a reparative framework, Greenwood urges looking to moments in Black history for alternatives in articulating freedom. This process for North Tulsans was inseparable from the seeking of redress for the massacre. Thus, in North Tulsa the repair of reparations takes on a much deeper meaning than compensation. Instead, restorative justice engenders a utopic rendering of Greenwood, by which the utopian promise of Greenwood anchors North Tulsans' ideas of who they are to become. Thus, community formation becomes tied to the desire for a utopian future, which will remain complicated if the material means of its accomplishment fail to be achieved through a reparative reordering of Tulsa's racial political economy.

Riotous Massacre: A Brief Note on Limits

Throughout *Violent Utopia*, the terms *riot* and *massacre* appear interchangeably to refer to the terrorist attack on Greenwood between May 31 and June 2, 1921. In 2017 the Tulsa Race Massacre Centennial Commission was formed to develop programs, projects, and events to commemorate the loss of life and community over those two days and the community's resilience in rebuilding both. The commission was initially called the Tulsa Race *Riot* Centennial Commission. It later changed its name to use *massacre*, "based on community input" and "to shed the name given by the offenders and reclaim the narrative of our history."[41] That decision also reflects that calling the event a riot allowed insurance companies to forgo paying out on property policies that many of Greenwood's Black residents held. It's also crucial that we recognize that in the United States, any significant ethnic conflict has historically often been categorized as a race riot. The Tulsa Historical Society and Museum, on their page on "the 1921 Race Massacre," give the following definitions for the public's consideration: "RIOT: a tumultuous disturbance of the public peace by three or more persons assembled together and acting with common intent" and "MASSACRE: the act or an instance of killing a number of usually helpless or unresisting human beings under circumstances of atrocity or cruelty."[42]

In my first few years researching Tulsa, beginning in 2014, North Tulsans exclusively used the term *riot*. For many of my interlocutors today, it is still the term of choice. However, acknowledging the public use of the term *massacre*, though certainly not agreement on it, I use it in identifying Black Tulsans' experience of the event. Because while many Tulsans fought and were by no means massacred, the longer-term process of dispossession that Greenwood and North Tulsa faced was a slow massacre of their community. To that point, when I speak about the White engagement in that violence, I use the term *riot* because the White perpetrators were rioting and, as I argue in the first chapter, revolting against what they saw as a perceived threat to their power. The US Capitol riot on January 6, 2021, is a contemporary example of the belligerent violence of so-called self-defense of order perpetrated by Tulsa's White mob in 1921.

North Tulsa has endured several wakes from the violence initiated by the race massacre of 1921. This claim is the central argument of this text. As such, I have decided not to reproduce any of the images of those two violent days or their immediate aftermath. The circulation of that destruction has been wide. Moreover, during my visit to Tulsa during the massacre centennial, I had the opportunity to interview some of the descendants of the Williams family, who owned the Dreamland Theater in Greenwood. In that conversation the family shared how they struggled to reconcile with the fact that their family history, tragedy, and images were now part of the public domain. That framing was both personally and ethically impactful and gave me a newfound respect for the sanctity of their relations to each other and the memory of their families, despite the wide and decades-long circulation of their images. I do not want to contribute to the repeated cycle of harm, of dispossession of the Williams family, the same cycles that are at play and critiqued in the broader narrative of this book.

Further, I also do not show images of Greenwood before the massacre, which are widely available and now also part of that troublingly cast public domain. Instead, I share photographs taken by photographer colleague Joel Wanek and me, with additional images licensed from local Tulsa photographer Joseph Rushmore, of contemporary Greenwood/North Tulsa residents who consented to be photographed.

Last, at the heart of the current efforts toward reparations and community healing is the location and excavation of the mass graves of the victims of the 1921 race massacre. The purported sites and the bodies contained therein have been the subject of much media attention. That recovery is taking place for the first time in earnest, and too little is formally known about the recovery process yet. In this text I briefly mention the search for the mass graves and show an image of a group gathered to memorialize the victims.

However, I neither speculate nor theorize about the lives lost. Instead, I extend my respect and reverence to the families who have been in suspended mourning for a century. Indeed, those families and the Black community of Tulsa continue to struggle to demand dignity for those lost lives. I offer the descendants of those victims compassion rather than conjecture. To some, this may present as a compromised analysis, but there are limits to commitments to analysis and empirics, and we must recognize them.

While this text resists romanticizing the history of North Tulsa and Greenwood as exceptions and extensively discusses and represents some of the challenges of life in contemporary North Tulsa, its objective is to convey the resilient spirit that has long sustained this community as they work to ultimately secure their repair. For this reason, this book is only a minor contribution.

Justice for Greenwood.

ONE. VIOLENCE

Not much is known about the encounter between Dick Rowland and Sarah Page in the elevator at the Drexel Building on May 30, 1921. As the story goes, Rowland, a teenage Black shoeshine working in a White-owned shine parlor in downtown Tulsa, crossed the street to use the colored-only restroom on the top floor of the Drexel Building. In the Drexel the elevators were typically operated by White women, one of whom was the seventeen-year-old Page. What happened next is unclear but has been the subject of numerous occasions and forms of speculation. The most accepted narrative is that Rowland tripped on the threshold while entering the elevator, causing him to stumble into Page or step on her foot. What isn't speculation is that Page screamed, and Rowland ran. A building clerk then called the police and made the initial claim of Rowland's assault on Page. Rowland wasn't responsible for it, but his touching of Page would cause the razing of his community and the murder of fellow Black Tulsans that would become known as the 1921 Tulsa Race Massacre, an event that would forever alter the future and geography of Black life in Tulsa.

Little Africa on Fire

Page initially told police that Rowland had only startled her and that she did not wish to press charges—evidenced by the fact that they initially did not seek Rowland's arrest. However, the story would develop, and Rowland was arrested at his home the following day and taken to the city jail. The morning of Rowland's arrest, the *Tulsa Tribune* printed the article "Nab Negro for Attacking Girl in Elevator":[1]

Nab Negro for Attacking Girl in Elevator

A negro delivery boy who gave his name to the public as "Diamond Dick" but who has been identified as Dick Rowland, was arrested on South [sic] Greenwood Avenue this morning by Officers Carmichael and Pack, charged with attempting to assault the 17-year-old white elevator girl in the Drexel building early yesterday.

He will be tried in municipal court this afternoon on a state charge.

The girl said she noticed the negro a few minutes before the attempted assault looking up and down the hallway on the third floor of the Drexel building as if to see if there was anyone in sight but thought nothing of it at the time.

A few minutes later, he entered the elevator, she claimed, and attacked her, scratching her hands and face, and tearing her clothes. Her screams brought a clerk from Renberg's store to her assistance, and the negro fled. He was captured and identified this morning both by the girl and the clerk, police say.

Rowland denied that he tried to harm the girl, but admitted he put his hand on her arm in the elevator when she was alone.

Tenants of the Drexel building said the girl is an orphan who works as an elevator operator to pay her way through business college.[2]

With this article and another, titled "To Lynch Negro Tonight," the White population of Tulsa began to stir, agitated by the notion of this assault.[3] Threats on Rowland's life began to circulate, instigated entirely by these media accounts. As a result, the police commissioner, J. M. Adkison, considered taking Rowland out of town for his protection but settled on moving him to the county jail, which he thought to be sufficiently secure. Such consideration for Rowland's safety proved prudent. A White mob soon gathered, seeking to lynch him.

Mob violence and vigilantism had been common forms of extralegal White justice in Oklahoma; however, it was not a feature of Tulsa's history of White violence in response to its Black population. Evan Woodson explains that "due to a combination of vigilance on the part of its Black community, the integrity of its law enforcement, and good fortune, Tulsa had mostly avoided instances of racial violence throughout the first thirteen years of statehood." Woodson also notes that despite the rise of lynching in Oklahoma during the first decade of the twentieth century, "Greenwood had experienced neither an individual lynching nor the kind of large-scale White violence that displaced African Americans in nearby Henryetta (1907) and Dewey (1917)." Instead, much of the mob violence enacted by Whites "targeted Tulsa's political radicals, pacifists, and union organizers, but not African Americans."[4]

However, as Charles Henry has noted, the lynching of a White man, Roy Belton, the summer before had given Black Tulsans reason for concern. Belton had taken part in a taxi robbery, killing the driver. Belton was taken from the courthouse and hanged outside of town. The sheriff offered little resistance and took the view that Belton's hanging would deter crime.[5] Greenwood's residents would not have assumed Rowland would avoid a similar fate.

There was a habit of the White papers in Tulsa of instigating some form or another of mob vigilantism, stoking political anxiety and White anger. A few years before the assault on Greenwood, the *Tulsa World* had encouraged the lynching of Industrial Workers of the World (IWW) union members suspected of bombing the home of Carter Oil Company's vice president. According to the IWW History Project at the University of Washington, "A masked group of fifty people mobbed and abused seventeen IWW members, whipping, then tar and feathering them."[6]

The *Tribune* had done its job. Within three hours of the Rowland story hitting the newsstands, a crowd of hundreds of angry Whites had gathered at the courthouse, where the police were holding Rowland in the jail on the top floor. By the evening, the numbers had doubled, all demanding a lynching. In response to the growing crowd, Rowland and the officers watching him were ordered by Sheriff Willard McCullough to barricade themselves inside the jail. This precaution seemed sufficient to the sheriff, who had already begun turning away Whites entering the courthouse to prevent them from attempting a lynching. McCullough subsequently ordered the dispersal of the White crowd but failed to enforce it.[7] Unsurprisingly, the crowd remained. By this time, news began to circulate in Greenwood about the crowd gathered at the courthouse, with some accounts stating that they had entered the courthouse. As a result, multiple separate efforts organized a counter-gathering of Black Tulsans, many of them Freedmen and World War I veterans, to defend against the Whites and their threat to Rowland. This group, which was only around thirty to forty strong, was encouraged by the police to leave, lest *their* presence give rise to a riot. Having been given a guarantee of Rowland's safety, the gathering of Black Tulsans dispersed, but the White crowd grew to upward of two thousand, prompting the group of Black Tulsans to return doubled in size. They were still outnumbered, nevertheless. This White crowd, which could by then only be considered a mob, became a more significant threat, having attempted to steal weapons and ammunition from the National Guard armory. What happened next, one might say, was inevitable. As historian Scott Ellsworth tells it, "Purportedly, the blacks were in the process of leaving when a white man approached one of their number. . . . The white man then attempted to disarm the veteran and a shot was fired. Sheriff McCullough stated that from that moment, 'the race war was on and I was powerless to stop it.' Black and white Tulsans exchanged gunfire, and Walter White of the NAACP reported that a dozen people fell in this initial gunplay. Numerically overwhelmed by the whites, the blacks began to retreat toward Greenwood."[8] As the group of Black Tulsans returned to Greenwood, the White mob followed them. But what followed with them was not a disorganized rage or impromptu display of violence but instead a calculated assault on Greenwood. That violence began with the Whites' careful armament in preparation for what newspapers like the *New York Times* described as a siege on Tulsa's "Negro quarters."[9]

Greenwood's residents fought to protect their neighborhood. Greenwood was by no means universally affluent, as much of the residential area around Greenwood Avenue, or Black Wall Street, was severely impoverished. Still, all who called Greenwood home had enjoyed access to a public life made mainly on their terms and crafted in their image. Whether it was going to the Dreamland Theater, attending services at the well-appointed historic Vernon AME or Mt. Zion Baptist Church, being proud of the advanced curriculum at the Booker T. Washington High School, or even enjoying the more ordinary delight of just being seen walking down Greenwood Avenue, it was all worth defending.

Many were caught off guard by the attack on their community. Perhaps confusion, doubt, and even disbelief slowed their response. Some fled, presaging the refugeeism to come in the following weeks. In one way or another, White violence stalked this Black community, which had not been involved in the matter surrounding Rowland and Page on the preceding day. This period was an ominous moment of liminality for the city. It was a moment between what Tulsa was before the Rowland-Page incident and what it would become. Whatever that might be would be determined by a trial by fire.

The first flames were started by White assailants around 1:00 a.m., beginning at the intersection of Archer Street and Boston Avenue. This assault was at the very border of Greenwood. Although the fire department attempted to quell the growing blazes, a segment of the White mob—numbering about five hundred—prohibited their access. The violence of machine-gun fire added to the inferno, contributing to the assault on Greenwood. Gunshots were fired and returned by both sides, initially at the geographic boundary between Black and White Tulsa. Fighting along the Frisco railroad tracks represented a battle line where the city's soul and the very life of its residents were contested.

Black Tulsans defended Greenwood's border for several hours until its breach at 6:00 a.m., when the full invasion of Greenwood ensued. Already outnumbered—early estimates indicated that thousands of Whites had by then joined the assault—Black residents were detained by the police, which further impeded Greenwood's ability to defend itself. Regardless of whether they were armed, Black Tulsans were pulled off the streets and from their homes by the police, the National Guard, and deputized White citizens who assaulted and detained by the dozens.[10]

Black Tulsans were interned at two primary detention camps, the first at Convention Hall, now known as the Tulsa Theater, and the second at McNulty Park, the minor league ballpark at Tenth Street and Elgin Avenue. The fairgrounds were used for overflow and longer-term detention. These camps at one point held over six thousand detainees, who, given both the warlike experience and their dispossession, had effectively become refugees in their own city. To be released from the camps, detainees had to be "claimed" by White acquaintances, with most remanded into the custody of their employers.[11]

James Hirsch estimates that 60 to 80 percent of Black Tulsans were detained. He further estimates that up to four thousand left the city, at least for some time, citing the hundreds of one-way tickets bought with destinations on the Pacific and Atlantic coasts, in particular their respective epicenters, San Francisco and New York.[12] These destinations are a reminder of the vastness of the African American network and a signal of the complexity of their racial landscape. We should also assume that those traveling such distances were relatively well off, despite their losses, compared to others who were seen walking to nearby towns, remarkably captured in photograph postcards, such as one titled "Running the Negro out of Tulsa," or another, perhaps more devastating, titled "Little Africa on Fire," showing a burning section of Greenwood engulfed in large plumes of smoke.[13]

As Ellsworth argues, "All of these actions, needless to say, rendered the defense of black property impossible. In general, police actions played right into the hands of the White rioters who were looting and burning. The internment process did not occur without black opposition, but again, Black Tulsans were simply outnumbered."[14] Meanwhile, the burning and looting of

Greenwood advanced. Alongside the arson and theft was murder. The mob killed many of Greenwood's residents who were protecting their property, even after these residents had surrendered to them. In the air, and notably in the hearts of the White terrorists, was an outright lust for racial violence and hatred for Tulsa's Black community.

That hateful violence contravened even the most racist formal codes of Jim Crow and expressed itself fully in the mob's actions. In the wake of the violence, a statement from Adjutant General Charles J. Barrett, commander of the National Guard troops, emphasizes the point: "In all my experience, I have never witnessed such scenes as prevailed in this city when I arrived at the height of rioting. Twenty-five thousand whites, armed to the teeth, were raging the city in utter and ruthless defiance of every concept of law and righteousness. Motor cars, bristling with guns swept through your city, their occupants firing at will."[15]

There was neither law nor reason nor recourse to which Black Tulsans could turn for safety in this moment of "utter and ruthless defiance," which was a performance of elated and blind violence that occurred during the suspension of lawful racism. Black Tulsans endured predatory White mobs who patrolled White neighborhoods, seeking to capture any Black person they could find. Whites dragged Black Tulsans behind vehicles as a visceral warning of the consequence of being discovered and captured. If the accounts are to be believed, the sheer horror of the ground assault was exacerbated to an unimaginable degree by dynamite bombs dropped from airplanes, raining terror and devastation on the Greenwood community.[16]

Amid the violence, the sheriff took Rowland out of town for his protection. But for the first week of June, during which Tulsa city officials governed by martial law, thousands of Black Tulsans, having been interned and having lost their property and liberty, formed a new wave of refugees following those who fled during the massacre's violence. Those who remained worked to rebuild Greenwood, though it would never again be the same since the consequences of those sixteen hours of violence would reverberate for generations.

The Tulsa massacre resulted from an array of complicit acts and parties: the Renberg store clerk who made the initial claim of Page's assault; Page, who confirmed the claim and then delayed retracting it until it was too late. The *Tulsa Tribune* instigated the furor. The police failed to disperse the White mob asking for Rowland's lynching and then "deputized" White Tulsans and provided them with weapons, directly leading to the murder and expulsion of Greenwood's residents. This violence triggered the National Guard, whose members arrested and detained Black Tulsans who remained alive and in place.

Those instigated, deputized, and predatory Whites released the hatred that drove the long tradition of the White violence of death and removal. This collection of actors and their assorted actions together comprised this violence's singular thrust: destruction. The violence was simultaneously destructive as well as constructive. Over those two days, the violence facilitated the resumption of a particular order of the world. Indeed, these acts recalibrated Tulsa's racial, economic, and political relations. The recalibration did not simply return White Tulsa to the status quo but expanded the reach and impact of White control over the entire city.[17]

Specters in Structures

The control that followed the massacre would, across Tulsa's history, maintain order in different ways but yield the same effect as the massacre's violence. This control manifested as an arresting containment of Black life in a city that was directly committed to preventing Greenwood's reestablishment.

On June 4, just days after the massacre, the *Tulsa Tribune*, which had run the "Nab Negro" article that stoked the violence that led to the massacre, published an editorial, "It Must Not Be Again," imploring the city not to allow Greenwood's rebuilding, much less its revival:

> Such a district as the old "Niggertown" must never be allowed in Tulsa again. It was a cesspool of iniquity and corruption. It was the cesspool which had been pointed out specifically to the Tulsa police and to Police Commissioner Adkison, and they could see nothing in it. Yet anybody could go down there and buy all the booze they wanted. Anybody could go into the most unspeakable dance halls and base joints of prostitution. All this had been called to the attention of the police department, and all the police department could do under the Mayor of this city was to Whitewash itself. The Mayor of Tulsa is a perfectly nice, honest man, we do not doubt, but he is guileless. He could have found out himself any time in one night what just one preacher found out.
>
> In this old "Niggertown" were a lot of bad niggers and a bad nigger is about the lowest thing that walks on two feet. Give a bad nigger his booze and his dope and a gun and he thinks he can shoot up the world.

And all these four things were found in "Niggertown"—booze, dope, bad niggers and guns.

The *Tulsa Tribune* makes no apology to the Police Commissioner or to the Mayor of this city for having plead with them to clean up the cesspools of this city.

Commissioner Adkison had said that he knew of the growing agitation down in "Niggertown" some time ago and that he and the Chief of Police went down and told the negroes that if anything started, they would be responsible.

That is first class conversation but rather weak action.

Well, the bad niggers started it. The public would now like to know: why wasn't it prevented? Why were these niggers not made to feel the force of the law and made to respect the law? Why were not the violators of the law in "Niggertown" arrested? Why were they allowed to go on in many ways defying the law? Why? Mr. Adkison, why?

The columns of the *Tulsa Tribune* are open to Mr. Adkison for any explanation he may wish to make.

These bad niggers must now be held, and what is more, the dope selling, and booze and gun collection must STOP. The police commissioner, who has not the ability or the willingness to find what a preacher can find and who WON'T stop it when told of it, but merely Whitewashes himself and talks of "knocking chairwarmers" had better be asked to resign by an outraged city.[18]

There was a moment when it seemed that Tulsa would resist the vitriolic admonitions of the publication's racism. The Public Welfare Board, a group of sympathetic private citizens, moved to assist with Greenwood's rebuilding. The mayor disbanded the board in favor of the Reconstruction Committee and the Real Estate Commission, which sought to convert Greenwood into a White industrial zone.[19] This plan sought to bolster industry in Tulsa and create a commercial and geographic partition between the races. As the *Tulsa Tribune* stated days after the massacre, "The two races being divided by an industrial section [would] draw more distinctive lines between them and thereby eliminate the intermingling of the lower elements of the two races, which in our opinion is the root of the evil which should not exist."[20]

The city did what it could to obstruct Greenwood's redevelopment, at least for the benefit of its Black residents. In total, Greenwood suffered an estimated $1.8 million of property damage, equivalent to about $26 million in 2020, for which insurance companies declined compensation owing to a riot clause in many policies.[21] As noted in the introduction, this clause led to the massacre being named a riot in the first place. Additionally, claimants needed to prove negligence in protecting their property on the part of either the city or the state, which was effectively impossible. Furthermore, the city created new ordinances, ironically requiring that new buildings be constructed with fireproof materials. The requirement served as a financial deterrent to Black Tulsans' rebuilding efforts.[22] Many White developers from Tulsa and elsewhere sought to take advantage and openly preyed on struggling Greenwood residents.

Several Black lawyers, including the firm of Spears, Franklin and Chappelle, which formed in response to the riot, defended the property of many of Greenwood's residents, thwarting the racist industrialization project.[23] Having mostly overcome the commercial and legal obstructions and the predation by White developers, Greenwood's residents marshaled their long-established industriousness and mobilized their own recovery effort. Joining the lawyers, Greenwood's entrepreneurs and churches formed the foundation of Black Tulsa's revival.[24]

Churches' and business people's material resources, knowledge, and skills were matched by their will and resolve to rebuild. As Hannibal Johnson notes, "More than half of the destroyed churches began to hold worship services again. More than eighty businesses in the Greenwood District reopened. 'The Negro Wall Street' (later referred to as the 'Black Wall Street of America,' reflecting the African-American community's changing sociopolitical identification) was well on its way to reclaiming its national reputation as an African-American business center par excellence. The burned-out shells of the pre-Riot structures were, for the most part, torn down. Many of the new buildings, however, assumed the forms of their predecessors."[25]

By the 1930s, with the urging and support of civic and economic leaders who formed the Greenwood Chamber of Commerce during that decade, Greenwood had again become an active hub of Black social and economic life.[26] Black Wall Street fared better than Wall Street during the Great Depression, one might say, owing to the closed economic circuits that existed in Greenwood because of segregation. Also, eastern Oklahoma, which included Tulsa, had not been impacted by the Dust Bowl like cities in western Oklahoma and its panhandle.

Black economic development in the city continued as war manufacturing needs in the 1940s increased Tulsa's industrial profits. A similar boom first occurred in the early twentieth century, when the development of the oil industry in Tulsa began with the big oil strike at Glenpool in 1905. That increase in economic activity benefited all who lived in the city, helping to jump-start many Black businesses.[27] World War II partly suspended, or at least deprioritized, the racist and sexist norms of the day, yielding an uptick in Black employment opportunities.

When Black labor was needed for industrial productivity during the war, Tulsa's Black population was incorporated into the general economy. But once society and seemingly the world settled after World War II, Black community dispossession once again came to facilitate White development. Indeed, with the war's cessation, the full resumption of Jim Crow racism meant that even as the local military industry transformed to serve new economic purposes in Tulsa, Black job opportunity would again decline. This followed a national trend, as Daniel Patrick Moynihan asserted in his *Negro Family* report: "The fundamental, overwhelming fact is that Negro unemployment, with the exception of a few years during World War II and the Korean War, has continued at disaster levels for 35 years."[28] This resumption of barring Black Tulsans from equal economic participation was compounded by the increased migration of Mexican and White laborers from rural Oklahoma to Tulsa. With stiffer job competition added to anti-Black discriminatory employment practices in place, the Greenwood District's economic productivity fell further.[29]

As happened throughout Black areas across the United States, the mid-century, for Black Tulsa, marked a changing landscape within which racial discrimination was fully imbricated with the policies, imaginaries, and overall notions of progress of the postwar American dream. Like elsewhere across the country, the agitation for civil rights occupied the minds of Tulsa's Black community, particularly its youth. As Hannibal Johnson explains, "The youth chose their battles. They simply wanted what all the other kids in Tulsa back then wanted: to be able to play in public parks; to be able to swim in public pools; to be able to try on the latest fashions before they purchased them; to be able to eat in the hole-in-the-wall diner or the elegant restaurant of their choosing."[30]

However, the cost of fighting for this dream, one that did not seem too far off from what life was like for many in Greenwood's heyday, would be the hope—and the accomplishment—of Tulsa's Black pioneers. Although promising the end of racial discrimination through integration, the cessation of segregation in the city also meant the prohibition of the restrictions that, while limiting, had historically concentrated the Black dollar in Tulsa. With integration, White businesses began to actively solicit Greenwood's capital. Hannibal Johnson further explains, "The opening up of the Tulsa economy afforded African-Americans choice. At the same time, it eliminated self-sufficiency by forcing the smaller, often undercapitalized, sometimes marginal African-American businesses out of the market. By 1961, more than ninety percent of African-American income—some $12–$15 million—was spent outside the Greenwood District. To go 'outside' for needs was to add another hole in the dike that surrounded the closed economy of the district, whether or not anyone intended that result."[31]

While promising greater rights to its Black residents, integration sounded the death knell in many ways for the once-thriving Greenwood commercial district. Greenwood was made possible by the economic opportunities provided at the turn of the century by the burgeoning oil industry, which followed on from land availability that just preceded it. As the state of Oklahoma was formed and soon adopted segregationist codes, Tulsa's Black settlers' early wealth and general earning power provided for their community's economic prosperity. Greenwood was a stable and developing Black community that was not only self-sustaining but also increasingly productive. However, this stability and productivity were possible not only despite but also because of segregation. The isolation of segregation helped make Greenwood socially and economically productive. But a new form of isolation, through incorporation and integration, would come in the form of urban renewal, which would bring lasting damage to the neighborhood.

Disintegration

To get a firsthand account of the period of integration in North Tulsa, I spoke to Reverend Jonathan, who was a high schooler at the time. Reverend Jonathan was one of the many unaffiliated minsters, or "walking pastors," that made North Tulsa a fascinating place. "The Reverend," as he wanted me to call him (I assumed to distinguish him from the *many* pastors like him), was involved with a variety of social programs in North Tulsa. Turning down his offer to "save" me, to "get that good cleansing in the blood of the Lamb," as he put it, I asked that he help me instead with his impressive sense of Tulsa's history.

"Go back in time," Reverend Jonathan began. He had a presence that made you believe such a thing was possible. His weight and stature grounded him in a way that conveyed authority through the authenticity of his belonging. In other words, Reverend felt emplaced. Given his persona and the way he commanded his knowledge of North Tulsa's history, going back in time might as well have been possible.

"Start with around the time of the race riot in '21," he began, "and what you had in the geography of the area—my family was here then at that time—you had what's now North Tulsa." As a native Tulsan going back a few generations, Reverend's preliminary comments helped orient me to the area's complicated landscape and history.[32] Reverend's claim referenced the geographic shift that the massacre induced, where displaced residents from Greenwood began moving farther north. In truth, many who accessed the amenities and services on Greenwood Avenue already lived farther out in smaller satellite pockets of the Black community, and the massacre's population of internal refugees grew their number.

As if to inform me of this fact, and presented as a necessary, even urgent, correcting of the historical record, Reverend declared, "Not all of Greenwood was like they make it seem. *A lot* of folks were poor." And, as if offering another revelation, he continued, "And that included *the White folks* in North Tulsa who were also poor, working class at best." Indeed, Reverend's account of North Tulsa appeared as a community not often depicted in the popular media representations. But given the history and process of Black and White settlement in Indian Territory and the geographic heterogeneity that it produced, such a thing as the presence of poor White people was not surprising. Further preventing me from thinking that North Tulsa was some monolithic Black space, Reverend clarified that "you had White families—you *still* have White families—throughout North Tulsa that have lived there, that stayed the whole time." "There's a dynamic to this place," Reverend concluded in a final declaration that there is much beyond the neat racial narratives told about Greenwood and North Tulsa.

This narrativization was especially illuminating when discussing North Tulsa during the mid-century development around integration. Talking about Greenwood during his youth, Reverend shared, "You know, Greenwood was a small business area, and it was *developing*." His notion of Greenwood developing matched with the record of wartime economic progress in the district. However, Reverend also noted how limited wartime economic opportunities were for Black Tulsans overall, as there were neither formal development policies nor initiatives directed toward their communities. This denial had everything to do with the racism of segregation.

"Black folks were pretty well contained because of the segregation," said Reverend, but that would all change with the arrival of integration in the late 1960s, the transformations of which Reverend experienced firsthand. Reverend was one of those "youths" that Hannibal Johnson references above, "back when I was just Johnny," Reverend shared with a smile. He, like others in his generation, wanted what they understood as equality in their experience of American citizenship. The fulfillment of that promise was thought to have begun to arrive when, in 1967, the Tulsa public schools were forced to integrate. In fact, integration started in far North Tulsa at McLain High School, which opened in 1959.

Reverend was among one of the first classes to integrate McLain, and he recalled that his time there was a period of significant transformation for the school and neighborhood. Prior to McLain's integration, Reverend said that the school's student body was primarily White, with some Native students. To him, integration at McLain made sense because African Americans who lived close by had to travel some distance to go to their "separate but equal" school farther south. "In one decade," Reverend recounted, illustrating the effects of the gradual Black migration north of Greenwood, "you went from 90 percent White to 90 percent Black at the school. And that reflected the community around it."

Ironically, what the promise of integration offered, in the end, was segregation, but of a different sort. Reverend explained that almost as soon as the school integrated, blockbusting began. "You had realtors going through the neighborhoods telling the White residents that that they had just sold their own house—whether they had or not—to a Black family, and so they had better sell to them because their property values were going to drop. And so, a lot of the realtors made a killing off this. You know, White flight! And so you had just this big exodus over those ten years, most of it happening fast within about five years. I graduated from McLain in 1972. And my year, we had about 60 percent White, 40 percent Black. [The class of] '72 was right in the middle of that—'67 to '77. We had our first African American homecoming queen my class year. Something like that."

"The Whites," Reverend said, "went from a majority culture to a minority culture within a really fast period, and then the shock waves of that, you know, that had [hit]." He was referring to the common effects of the widespread White flight in the postwar period, which also took the form of abandonment by local White businesses in North Tulsa. "It wasn't just White flight from the people who were living here. It was actually the business flight."

While houses became available, the lack of businesses would seed the conditions for the commercial absence that is so characteristic of North Tulsa today: "The businesses just left. All the department stores, everybody began to move out, and you begin to have the abandonment of the shopping areas that we see still to this day." This business flight was compounded by what Reverend called the "abandonment" of McLain High School: "Soon as they integrated the schools, they also began to lower [McLain's] academic offerings. So, the kinds of college preparatory classes that they had when I first got there, a year later we were seeing those dropping off until it became more and more not that different from what the stereotypical kind of segregated Black school had been. And so the school in some ways was the first to abandon the area." With a hint of lingering disappointment in his tone, Reverend concluded, "And, you know, there was nothing, there was no training. There was no education. There was no help."

Reverend argued that the lack of businesses and the reduction of school training, both of which induced the structuring of poverty, became the basis for the troubles that would come to plague North Tulsa in the following decades. Thus, these were yet more of the slow violences that came to shape the circumstances of North Tulsa: "By the '80s out here, you had the introduction of crack. And the rise of the beginning of some of the gang problems that came along with that," Reverend explained. "And you had the media and how quickly the community was stereotyped by them, and it didn't take much because people were primed to, you know, to kind of see it as a place where you didn't want to go to." And so, as Reverend put it, "When you hear the words *North Tulsa*, you think *Black*. You say *South Tulsa*, you think *White*."

The result was a spatial-racial fix in which investment in the area slowed and then stopped altogether. The disinvestment was made possible through the racial overdetermination of Tulsa's northern geography. North Tulsa became a Black space through the interrelated recession of Whiteness and spread of Blackness that originated with the violent assault on Greenwood.

What's remarkable is that this was not done under the guise of overt segregation but, rather, through integration. White flight as a phenomenon of residential transformation is now understood as a quintessential form of American racism. The case of Tulsa, however, makes visible the direct correlation between North Tulsa's underdevelopment and South Tulsa's development. As Reverend would tell me, the city developed southward, which we can easily trace by the mobility of capital, value, and racialization in South Tulsa today, in a way that elucidates more than the typical urban-suburban narrative of White flight does. In other words, it was not racism alone that lured White Tulsans south but, rather, a choreographed racial capitalist direction of the population through incentives and disincentives. The choice to integrate the school in the north, the systematic decrease in business services, blockbusting, and media perceptions all combined to facilitate the development of South Tulsa at the cost of the north.

By undermining education and decimating local industry, or at least commercial life, in this way, the underdevelopment accomplished as much as the race massacre had. It devastated the material resources and the infrastructures that had facilitated Black progress. But this process, I argue, went a step farther than the massacre. Indeed, it was integration that formally ghettoized North Tulsa through a pernicious act of incorporation.

We would be remiss to think that the consequences of the disinvestment and underdevelopment were purely material. Reverend said that a sense of shame came to be associated with being from the area: "We often had an element of shame built into being from the north. We thought, Well, if I was, you know, if I was wealthy or if I was better educated, if I hadn't made this mistake or that mistake, right, I would be able to leave, you know—a lot of us internalized that." This shame had consequences, as "all that shame," Reverend continued, "acts out in isolation and triggers violence and everything else you get with those kinds of dynamics." The result was a complete degradation of the sense of sociality in the area: "You know, so part of the abandonment, you had the clubs, civic groups and whatnot began to be in decline. And then, after [Ronald] Reagan came in, you know, you started having the cutback of public support. So you had the loss of . . . I mean, it was like one layer upon one layer upon another layer; it was kind of like an archaeological dig. You can kind of see all these kinds of forces that came into play to keep isolating the community."

The transformation, the result of the shame, led Reverend to a particular revelation:

One thing about North Tulsa, comparing it [to] when I was growing up, when I grew up, there was something to being a North Sider. [It] was kind of like being a Southsider from Chicago; there was a huge thing identified with it, no matter where you were. And that was one thing that kind of connected us together, Black, White, Hispanic, whatever they were from the north side of Tulsa. You had an instant sort of kinship because you had always felt like you were kind of the stereotypical kind of stepchild of the community. Or . . . sort of the forgotten neglected ones, but over the years—partly because that whole social network has been fractured—now there's not so much of that left.

North Tulsans, it seemed, lived in the wakes of both the massacre and the notion of the golden years that followed it, and together these formed a peculiar challenge structured around both meaning and materiality. Both were the consequences of intentional racism—the blockbusting and stripping away of school funding—as well as that most pervasive form of racism, masquerading as individual choice and rational liberty: the White flight of both residents and business. As if apologizing for the state of things in North Tulsa, Reverend reflected, "All along there were people, you know, doing it, trying to remain, and trying to make the place feel a little bit better. They were trying to do things, but it's not so easy without the resources." North Tulsa would become defined by the issue of resources and what those resources—or the lack thereof—meant for and said about its community.

Blade of Progress

Despite rebuilding following the 1921 massacre and the economic peak provided by war-induced industrial opportunities in the 1940s and 1950s, Greenwood experienced a secondary destruction by government through urban renewal and the expressway's construction. Indeed, the incident of 1921 was acute and exceptional when compared with the process that got underway during the 1950s and 1960s. "The development of Tulsa, the city, never really came out north. It all kind of began and kept going south and kind of east and out west," Reverend told me. The directional choices of Tulsa's city development were an initial sign of a quieter form of violence. This process is formally called *municipal disinvestment* and is best understood as the root of urban development—or, rather, underdevelopment—policies such as the much-maligned practice of redlining.

The Home Owners' Loan Corporation (HOLC), established in 1933 as part of President Franklin D. Roosevelt's New Deal, began a City Survey Program to assess real estate and neighborhood conditions, drawing data from mortgage lenders and real estate developers. The result was a series of now-iconic "Residential Security" maps that presented a polychrome of poverty and prosperity with the four graded color categories of green, blue, yellow, and red, respectively indicating "best," "still desirable," "definitely declining," and "hazardous." As the maps served to signal lending risk, the centrality of housing and mortgage policy to the New Deal and postwar development meant that being redlined would render those communities unworthy and thereby incapable of accessing capital, generationally deepening and geographically widening the wealth gap. The HOLC would determine that 35 percent of Tulsa was "hazardous," unsurprisingly including the Black district of Greenwood and the growing Black neighborhoods that had grown north of there, which would later become the predominant Black space of

Tulsa known as North Tulsa. The vestiges of that early designation can easily be witnessed in the contemporary geographies of Black impoverishment.

Urban renewal followed redlining by building on and exploiting the narrative of ruin and blight that the red designation of neighborhood "hazard" communicated. The process was underpinned by the notion of rehabilitating blighted areas. The circular thinking that these communities were incapable of developing their neighborhoods justified local municipal and federal disinvestment in their development, from the maintenance of infrastructure to the provision of services, thus rendering the neighborhoods structurally underdeveloped. Even where these circumstances didn't fully present themselves, the power of the narrative was enough to have these neighborhoods rendered as blighted and in need of redevelopment.

Through urban renewal's tools of property condemnation, eminent domain, and various relocation policies, Greenwood's demise was cemented. Hirsch notes that "Greenwood's families and businesses were further dispersed in the 1960s through urban renewal. The federally financed effort tried to rehabilitate blighted areas by condemning property, paying occupants to move, then redeveloping the land. It achieved its first two goals, but most of the blacks who moved never returned, and the promise of redevelopment proved hollow. In time, black Tulsans would call urban renewal 'urban removal.'"[33] Urban renewal helped to clear areas of Greenwood adjacent to downtown Tulsa, specifically the northeastern corridor that the Reconstruction Committee and the Real Estate Commission had sought following the riot decades earlier. Greenwood became unexceptional in the most devastatingly banal way.

Following the 1956 Federal-Aid Highway Act signed into law by President Dwight Eisenhower, urban renewal took the form of the development of highways that bisected Greenwood, which, like redlining, served to all but cement North Tulsa's demise. Eminent domain and the condemning of property facilitated the construction of the highways, which were up to 90 percent federally subsidized. These highways, particularly Interstate 244, led to another period of displacement.[34] The sense of community and its geographic makeup were forever impacted by the creation of the highway splitting the community, which made it difficult for someone from Forty-Sixth Street North, in deep North Tulsa, to access the main thoroughfares of Pine and Peoria located at the boundary of North Tulsa.

The consequences for the structural navigation of North Tulsa and the sense of community were evident in the area's spatial imaginary of Black emplacement. This process was facilitated by demolishing established neighborhoods, and Greenwood was one of the primary ones. By the late 1970s, the Inner Dispersal Loop—a highway that encircled downtown Tulsa—cut clear across Greenwood. Hirsch notes, "By the early 1970s this initiative had claimed and demolished more than a thousand businesses and homes in Tulsa, many of them in Greenwood, and the blacks moved north, east and west—but with few exceptions not south of the railroad tracks. De facto segregation remained."[35]

The highway construction projects in Greenwood, as in Black neighborhoods across the country, did anything but provide the progress that was claimed, save for the White-run municipal government's local development ambitions and the federal vision of postwar American renewal. Urban low-income Black people and the geographies they inhabited were the literal grounds for American capitalist development and expansion. And in the process, Black people in Tulsa once again were unmoored through destruction. Greenwood, once alive and active, itself the result of another kind of renewal—that of the resilient spirit and collective capital—had largely dispersed. The abandonment left the space Greenwood had once inhabited mainly dead, cast into the shadow of the freeway.

A May 4, 1967, article in the *Tulsa Tribune* by Joe Looney lamented the loss brought about by Interstate 244:

Ed Goodwin and L. H. Williams grew up with Greenwood Avenue. They remember the early days, when the first buildings were put up in the two blocks north of Archer Street.

They saw the riot of 1921, when many of the buildings burned. They saw the street rebuilt, grow, and prosper. They saw, too, as a slum festered.

And now they are watching Greenwood Avenue die.

Its business district will be no more.

The Crosstown Expressway slices across the 100 block of North Greenwood Avenue, across those very buildings that Goodwin describes as "once a Mecca for the Negro businessman—a showplace."

There still will be a Greenwood Avenue, but it will be a lonely, forgotten lane ducking under the shadows of a big overpass. *The Oklahoma Eagle* still will be there, but every forecast is that some urban renewal project will push down the buildings that have not already been torn down by the wrecking crews clearing right-of-way for the superhighway.[36]

Thousands of Black neighborhoods shared the fate of Greenwood between the 1940s and 1970s. Slum clearance, urban renewal, and interstate highway projects became the shorthand for a particular form of intentional violence. As historian of the era N. D. B. Connolly has argued, Jim Crow–era development "required an awful lot of violence." He explains, "White authorities charged with building—and, in this instance, rebuilding—city infrastructure relied on seemingly exceptional shows of white power, such as lynching or forced conscription. Violence helped hold in place the daily racial indignities upon which American capitalism and its many forms of segregation stood. Fear of lynching and other acts of racial violence was an integral feature of economic development."[37]

The violence of urban renewal was different in form but familiar in its consequences, as lynching, a tool of spectacular violence like the massacre, "gave way to more benign tools of segregation, including racist zoning practices and promiscuous use of eminent domain."[38] Connolly expands upon this transition:

> The fact of white supremacy's evolution was not lost on black folk. Burning crosses illuminating dark lawns or hooded white men marching down the street could be frightful sights. Still, for many, one of the most terrifying sounds in the postwar, Jim Crow South was an unexpected rapping at one's front door. It might not be a lynch mob, as it easily could have been . . . [b]ut a knock on the front door could be the police coming to serve a warrant for "permit violations" or officers and city officials there to carry out an eviction with a writ of possession. White supremacy's more ancient expressions were never far away, of course. White violence often preceded and precipitated state action, and it was the foreseeable consequence of state inaction. There was nevertheless an increasing professionalism to white racism in the 1940s—an expanding infrastructure.[39]

This process formed "infrastructural power," which drafted and enforced land law that used roads, highways, government services, mortgages, slum clearance, public housing, and eminent domain as its instruments of violence.[40] Infrastructural power was just another layer of "an apartheid system reliant on layer upon layer of violence," laying atop one another "white vigilantes, excessive law enforcement, and serial acts of forced land expropriation."[41]

Perversely, the construction of highways was argued to be a means of universal progress. Indeed, urban renewal, generally, and its constituent policies, "like code enforcement, public housing, and Jim Crow itself, began as a reformist idea."[42] But as these policies worked to the advantage

of capital, Black communities, while not entirely powerless or wholly inno-
cent, were unable to impede the "blade of progress" that severed them from
their neighborhood.[43] A primary facilitator of it all was eminent domain,
by which private property is seized by the state for public use. The practice
became a principal means by which the state used geography and property
to control and contain racialized groups. But beyond, and perhaps behind,
the state, "eminent domain helped protect white homeowners, contain black
renters, and keep the racial peace."[44]

Marginal Dangers

From Jim Crow to urban renewal, the above discussion has shown that
as formal policies they reflected a social philosophy whose advancement
seemed to demand the racist relegation and subjugation of Tulsa's Black
population. Through violence and isolation, the principle of social control
that drove the massacre are evident in these processes. What needs to be understood is what stands behind the anti-Blackness of regimes like Jim Crow
laws and their contemporary iterations as social and legal systems. In other
words, in a moment when we have come to recognize the reality of "systemic" and "structural" racism, we have yet to fully understand exactly what
orders those processes.

Even if Dick Rowland had been guilty of assault, the incommensurability
of the act and the consequences of the massacre should seem nothing less
than bizarre. Sarah Page had moved to Tulsa from Kansas only months before. Therefore, one wouldn't assume she was a beloved community member
whose assault would stir a community to rise to her defense. Her defense
hardly needed qualification as Page joined a litany of White women who,
through their claim of harm, however minimal, brought the threat of actual
violence against Black men.

As Ann Stoler has argued, the need to protect White women formed part
of the "terms and tensions" of White racial order and was "repeatedly invoked
to clarify racial lines."[45] White women represent so much more than their
individual and singular personhood. White women are the devices through
which White society's racial order, harmony, and even these concepts' meaning are facilitated. Rowland's perceived harm of Page was a threat less to her
body or her person than to an entire apparatus that produces the necessary
scaffolding of White social order. This order, represented by White women,
is materialized through customs and geographic restrictions, codified in this

case as Jim Crow. To be sure, this codification has also presented as the inner logic of colonialism, in particular the settler variety, and the terms by which European notions of civility are exercised through class distinction. Upholding them all are Western principles of purity and pollution.

Anti-Black violence, while materialized as acts of death and destruction, and whether or not facilitated by the claims of White women, is fundamentally about the recovery of White social order. This process of violent ordering, today commonly represented by police murders of Black men, can be traced to long-practiced and celebrated acts of lynching. As Ida B. Wells argued in her seminal 1895 lynching study, *The Red Record*, lynching before and during the Jim Crow period was the legal and extralegal murder of Black people as a necessary form of recovering order and control in postemancipation America:

> Emancipation came, and the vested interests of the white man in the Negro's body were lost. The white man had no right to scourge the emancipated Negro, still less has he a right to kill him. But the Southern white people had been educated so long in that school of practice, in which might makes right, that they disdained to draw strict lines of action in dealing with the Negro. In slave times the Negro was kept subservient and submissive by the frequency and severity of the scourging, but, with freedom, a new system of intimidation came into vogue; the Negro was not only whipped and scourged; he was killed.[46]

Blacks' subservience and submissiveness represented order. And violence, the "school of practice" in which Whites, according to Wells, were long educated, maintained it through killing.

What determines the qualification of social order in the United States' racialized society is the maintenance of a stable and stabilizing value regime, understood in everyday terms as social hierarchy. On that basis, we see Jim Crow as a structuring of hierarchy, the codes of which were meant to maintain its order. Saidiya Hartman has contended that there is a White predilection for administering society through Black subjection and violence. After slavery, this administering became a corporeal structure of difference that formulated Jim Crow violence.[47] Jim Crow was a response to the need to reconcile social order with racial value following emancipation.

Understanding this claim requires contemplating Wells's line that "emancipation came, and the vested interests of the White man in the Negro's body were lost." In that sentence we can interpret "lost" to mean either the intentional forgoing of interest or the taking away or the sensed irretrievability of something of value. We can see emancipation as a significant loss figured in the latter sense when considering W. E. B. Du Bois's meditation on emancipation's meaning and consequences. When Du Bois wrote, "The emancipation of man is the emancipation of labor, and the emancipation of labor is the freeing of that basic majority of workers who are yellow, brown and black," he was asserting that the exploitation of "the dark proletariat" allowed the filching of the extreme surplus value that had made slavery so profitable.[48] Thus, emancipation was the freeing of Black labor and, critically, of Black labor value.

Stephen Best argues that this value and its attendant Blackness, once emancipated, became "fugitive," meaning that, in exercising their freedom, the formerly enslaved "reneged on a promise to provide [their] labor."[49] Indeed, the "promise" of labor that bound and indebted the enslaved African to the plantation was particularly odious contract.[50] As emancipated or lost labor value, one might argue that since emancipation, Black life has been socially, politically, and juridically organized around the pursuit and recuperation of this lost value. What we have seen is that this value's repossession and recovery has been pursued through the violence of order.

How does fugitive labor operate? What does it mean to be the embodiment of value that has been lost? Emancipated Black people were neither enslaved nor properly free. When they no longer held value for Whites as slaves or as a "vested interest," the function of Blackness became uncategorizable, or what Katherine McKittrick, after Sylvia Wynter, calls "demonic." To McKittrick, the demonic "cannot have a determined, or knowable, outcome"; it is a "nondeterministic schema" that is "hinged on uncertainty."[51] The postemancipation Black subject was no longer enslaved, not properly free; still, this subject, once understood as property, endeavored to become fully human.[52] Because the transition from slave to human failed, as a subject of demonic value, Blackness became liminal and thus ambiguous.

This is the problem of Blackness. I am reminded of the formative quote from Du Bois's *The Souls of Black Folk*: "Between me and the other world, there is ever an unasked question: unasked by some through feelings of delicacy; by others through the difficulty of rightly framing it. All, nevertheless, flutter round it. How does it feel to be a problem?"[53] The problem of Blackness was and is an issue of positioning and placement. One can see this in the introduction of Du Bois's seminal concept of double consciousness:

It is a peculiar sensation, this double-consciousness, this sense of always looking at oneself through the eyes of others, of measuring one's soul by the tape of a world that looks on in amused contempt and pity. One ever feels his two-ness, an American, a Negro; two souls, two thoughts, two unreconciled strivings; two warring ideals in one dark body, whose dogged strength alone keeps it from being torn asunder. The history of the American Negro is the history of this strife—this longing to attain self-conscious manhood, merge his double self into a better and truer self. In this merging, he wishes neither of the older selves to be lost.[54]

Double consciousness, to my mind, is the experience of being out of place, the precise condition of being beyond proper characterization. It is, therefore, the embodied sensation of being an anomaly.

We can discern the anomaly of Blackness and its lived consequences—those represented by the massacre and the contemporary marginalization of Tulsa's Black community—by considering the racial framework of taboo. To understand the value and function of racial taboos for this purpose, it is helpful to turn to the work of Mary Douglas in her seminal 1966 text, *Purity and Danger*, in which she examines the themes of taboo and ambiguity.[55] Taboo is a term that exists as a familiar reference to things or actions that are prohibited. However, while it is accurate that taboo signals the forbidden, the notion of taboo precisely functions as "a spontaneous device for protecting the distinctive categories of the universe [which] protects the local consensus on how the world is organised." As such, taboo "shores up wavering certainty [and] reduces intellectual and social disorder."[56]

In short, taboo is the system humans put in place to maintain order around how they make sense of the world. For Sylvia Wynter, this would qualify as the White community's "descriptive statement," or governing master code, which "command[s] obedience and necessitate[s] individual and collective behaviors" around the principles of what it means to be human, and by which the "mode of being human [is] brought into existence, produced, and stably reproduced."[57]

Taboo, then, is a response to "the cognitive discomfort caused by ambiguity" within that order and works to resolve that which doesn't fit within the description, or the system, which helps us make sense of things. We confront this kind of discomfort all the time and enforce impromptu but often established cultural taboos in response. Examples most frequently fall within the general category of what constitutes sanitary versus unsanitary behavior. Taboo thus works to correct matters that are "out of place" and that disturb the order of things, an order that grants security and stability.[58]

When we are unsure of which category a practice, an object, or even a person fits, they represent categorical ambiguity, which Douglas tells us is threatening at an epistemological level. And so, we fall back on or create systems of rationalization that confront the ambiguous and, when it can't be resolved, "[shunt] it into the category of the sacred," or that which is beyond categorization.[59] These kinds of ambiguous, uncategorizable things are what we call anomalies.

Douglas proposes various ways that communities respond to anomalies, and here is where we begin to understand the operation behind the above histories of race-based social relegation. Anomalies can be responded to negatively, through disregard or condemnation. Alternatively, in what Douglas calls a positive approach and which amounts to incorporation, she says that "we can deliberately confront the anomaly and try to create a new pattern of reality in which it has a place."[60]

Anomaly and ambiguity are addressed by standardizing their interpretation, through labeling, which demands the consequent conforming of the ambiguous subject; by eliminating them; by avoiding them, which Douglas says "affirms and strengthens the definitions to which they do not conform"; or by labeling them as dangerous.[61] In these approaches we see that act of violent dispossession—displacement in the former and harmful integration in the latter. But, critically, we see the apparatus by which a system of recognition and order is produced, which in turn strengthens and reinforces the prevailing worldview.

Specifically, taboo confronts the ambiguous by functioning as a "coding practice" through boundaries and signals that organize and establish the normative parameters for social relations. In other words, taboo creates order through classification. This practice of coding and boundary making, both of which determined that which was normative, produced the system of classification that we know as Jim Crow. Classifications like Jim Crow determine the quality, or even the nature, of things and are the rubrics by which the social world and its orders are made legible, navigable, and, critically, violable. Objects, subjects, or practices that did not fit within this classification were rendered ambiguous and their ambiguity taken as inherently dangerous, thus requiring a taboo to classify and categorize them.[62]

Sylvia Wynter helps us to directly appreciate Douglas's notion of classification with her own notion of the overrepresentation of European man as "human," which left non-Europeans to be dispossessed, "dysselected," and thus "otherly" classified.[63] Otherly and dysselected classifications are, through their marginalization, rendered functionally or *structurally* dangerous. The structure articulates the "spatial limits and [the] physical and verbal signals" to control or correct that which is dangerous because it threatens the social order. Douglas calls these threats "vulnerable relations."[64]

Contextually, we can see the vulnerability in the relations between Dick Rowland and Sarah Page. They rode together regularly in an elevator, a scenario that arguably was fraught with vulnerability. This vulnerability is also understood as the fragility of social orders, which in this case should be recognized as White existence's fragility. This fragility was proven by the minor incident of Rowland accidentally stumbling into Page. A touch by a Black man was all it took to throw Tulsa's White social order into crisis.

Jim Crow, the system of taboo, upheld order by determining what was dangerous, which actions and distances were prohibited, and what was permissible. As Douglas puts it, taboo "threatens specific dangers if the code is not respected . . . extend[ing] the danger of a broken taboo to the whole community."[65] This danger threatens the coherence and existence of a community—in our case, the White community of Tulsa. We see this notion of danger placed upon the geography of North Tulsa. Going back to Reverend, the designation of North Tulsa as a dangerous place, drug and crime ridden, was not simply a means of identification but an intentional classification. In other words, in a system of White supremacy, Black communities only make sense as dangerous and therefore subjugated places. The practices of urban renewal simply made them so.

White (Geographic) Anxieties

Commitment to upholding social taboo requires "community-wide complicity."[66] Complicity and danger undergird the process of taboo that maintains White supremacy.[67] White supremacy was the social order that Rowland threatened through his encounter with Page. This threat created an anomaly. Rowland produced a radical and threatening breach, an aberrance that disrupted, threatened, and undermined that order. As a result, Rowland was figured as out of place and out of order, the correction for which was violence. Indeed, Rowland, the anomaly, dictated and made rationalizable and reasonable the hysterical, irrational, and unreasonable violence in the service of defending against it.

Rowland represented a deeper set of anxieties held by White Tulsans, and they had a great deal to do with the actual and perceived success of Greenwood. The history of migration to Indian Territory and the subsequent early days of Oklahoma's statehood brought the weighty questions of race and labor into the refrain. In a significant way, the rapid adoption of Jim Crow policies, which began before Oklahoma was formally a state, responded to Oklahoma's Black communities' growing political and economic might and influence. While initially tolerated because of both the need for Black labor and their general isolation in all-Black towns, Black economic activity and progress soon threatened Whiteness's everyday existence and sense of future in the state.

In *Black Reconstruction*, Du Bois cogently presents the "public and psychological wage" of Whiteness, which provided Whites with a stable and secure, if not superior, categorization.[68] Du Bois writes, "It must be remembered that the white group of laborers, while they received a low wage, were compensated in part by a sort of public and psychological wage. They were given public deference and titles of courtesy because they were white."[69] This categorization of "deference" and "courtesy" went on to firm up the recognition of White geographies. This categorization is understood through what George Lipsitz calls a "possessive investment in Whiteness." Thinking through distinct White and Black spatial imaginaries, Lipsitz argues that the White spatial imaginary draws on the operation of space as exclusivity, identified most clearly through private property.

Building on Du Bois's notion of the psychological wage of Whiteness, David Roediger examines its impact through its materialization in working-class White racism.[70] Roediger deploys Du Bois's framework to effectively show how anxieties around opportunity and advantages are affectively and psychologically tied together. Specifically, these anxieties went beyond the issue of labor competition with Blacks and represented anxieties about Whiteness itself, whose value and meaning were mediated by work. This anxiety often produced the need to exercise its underlying frustration against, or rather with, Blackness. Critical to my discussion, Roediger examines this expression through race riots, saying, "The riots bespoke the anxieties—not just or mainly centering on fears of Black competition for jobs—of a working population experiencing new forms of industrial discipline."[71]

Greenwood represented the fear of Black competition in the various industries that would rapidly and unevenly develop in Tulsa and ultimately involve a multiracial, albeit unequal, labor force. It was also a foil for thinking and living with the anxieties of the limitations of working-class Whiteness. Thus, Black success in Tulsa, which earned Greenwood the moniker Negro Wall Street, would bring anxiety, uncertainty, and a troubled sense of being in the White communities that surrounded it and their residents. These are the same sentiments that underpinned Rowland's threating of Page: the anxiety over the stability of one's world, which would necessitate correction through the enforcement of taboo. Thus, whether because of Greenwood's relative, though not universal, prosperity or Rowland's breach, the violence over two days in 1921 would serve to restore that order.

Framing the violent response of the massacre as enforcing a taboo is critical in demonstrating how these systems became structural forms of inequality and bias over time. Structural processes like Jim Crow and urban renewal segregate, dominate, and police Black populations. These processes signify more than procedures and policies. Indeed, they are materializations of worldviews, which are reproduced by *becoming* structural, with that process often facilitated by means that could be read as a form of violence. Thus, abolishing structural inequalities is often arduous, exhausting, and seemingly impossible. The challenge is that these practices reproduce an underlying ethic by which Blackness is deemed aberrant and then codified as such.

Central to the establishment of the ethical order is the functioning of emplacement. As we see with the massacre, violence functioned as an overt concern with remaining in one's *place*, with urban renewal later being a violent emplacement of displaced subjects in the margins. This marginality might be best understood as the general experience of being "black in a white space." Elijah Anderson tautologically defines white spaces by "their overwhelming presence of white people and their absence of black people" and as "off limits" for Black people, even though they are required "to navigate the white space as a condition of their existence."[72] However, Anderson provides a less direct but illustratively operationalized definition of White space by describing how White spaces *respond* to Black people. He starts by stating that "when the anonymous black person enters the white space, others there immediately try to make sense of him or her—to figure out 'who that is.'" They do so as an act of emplacement or, as Anderson puts it, "to gain a sense of the nature of the person's business and whether they need to be concerned."[73] Anderson continues by saying that this anonymity leads to a stigmatization and association with "the putative danger, crime, and poverty of the iconic ghetto."[74] This stigmatization occurs because, as Anderson notes,

> In the white space, the anonymous black person's status is uncertain, and he or she can be subject to the most pejorative regard. Almost any white person present in the white space can possess and wield this enormous power. And those who feel especially exercised and

threatened by the rise of blacks may feel most compelled to wield that power. For many of them, blacks in the white space may be viewed as a spectacle of black advancement at the expense of whites. Black presence thus becomes a profound and threatening racial symbol that for many whites can personify their own travail, their own insecurity, and their own sense of inequality. When black persons lack moral authority, those who are inclined to offend them on the basis of their color may know no shame and face few sanctions.[75]

Anderson critically demonstrates the everyday experience of taboo and anomaly that leads to the structural marginality of Blackness. He writes that "without such authority, the black person moves through the larger society in a vulnerable state, which is particularly so when navigating the white space—a world in which he typically has limited social standing, and thus limited respect," poignantly concluding that "the most easily tolerated black person in the white space is often one who is 'in his place.'"[76]

What is created through this process at the structural level are the parameters for access, which amount to a racialized sense of privilege facilitated by generalized segregation.[77] This claim points to the ethics that underlie the racism and racist violence rooted in processes like Jim Crow laws and their iterations like redlining throughout contemporary social and legal systems. This is a structural anti-Blackness that shapes much of the modern experience of Black life. However, terms like *structural* and even *systemic* obscure that this experience is a product of something much harder to trace or hold accountable, namely, the very systems of thought that shape the ideas that human beings have about the world.

We see this when examining the encounter between Dick Rowland and Sarah Page and the massacre that followed. Rowland, a Black man, belonged in segregated Greenwood, a marginal space, a Black space. When Rowland left Greenwood for downtown Tulsa, he became an ambiguous figure. The shift in geography would reorder him. He was no longer what he was in Greenwood, and in the White space of downtown Tulsa it was not clear what he would become. This is the danger that ambiguous figures represent.[78] While Rowland could enter into it, he did not belong to the White world of downtown, so his very existence had to be regulated. Where he worked and where he went to the restroom were regulated; otherwise, Rowland would be out of place. Thus, he was a *tolerated* anomaly only insofar as he comported himself in accordance with the controlling regulations of Jim Crow, that most severe and intricate system of classification. Indeed, Rowland's Blackness occupied a liminal place when he was present in White Tulsa. This potential misplacement created his anomalousness.

Blackness's qualification is context dependent. The anomalousness of liminality is the very quality of marginality and is therefore dangerous. This was the dynamic of Du Bois's "color line." Sylvia Wynter writes that the color line was "projected as the new 'space of Otherness'" that "recoded" difference on "new terms."[79] From this position, the racist relegation and subjugation of Black populations through their isolation, control, and surveillance and the very notion of criminal justice have functioned to maintain White social order by managing that liminality.

Segregation determines what belongs and especially *where* it belongs. It is a primarily geographic structure—a process, a culture even, of recognition. And through that recognition, one is readily identified as belonging or not; if the latter, one is easily and appropriately "placed."

In the course of their experience since the massacre, Black Tulsans have endured multiple attempts to put them back in their place. From being detained in camps to their emplacement in impoverished communities lacking adequate resources, they have withstood more than just a symbolic return to the margins. But in the everyday context of Black spaces and their geographic iterations is the *making* marginal of Black place, with the protective order of White racialization calling that marginality into existence. As productive as Greenwood was, in the broader circuit of society, it was the margin; it was where Blacks and their Blackness were detained. Margins are full of danger and vulnerability, both of which operate in a variety of ways; margins threaten not only those who exist in them but also the very structure of normative order, always posing a possible threat, an impending breach. And so, today, we see the overpolicing of Black spaces, surveilling them for danger, and executing that danger when there is a feeling of being threatened.

Dangerous subjects or objects project anomaly and ambiguity, with their ambiguity and anomalousness rendering them vulnerable. We can trace the operation of this violent codification of marginal danger and vulnerability in contemporary acts of police violence. Police violence results when the citation—meaning the detection of an infraction—functions as a racialized method that recognizes and codifies anomalousness and executes order, too often through execution. A central example is the 2016 killing of the unarmed Black Tulsan Terence Crutcher by the White female police officer Betty Jo Shelby. Crutcher's car was inexplicably parked in the middle of a road, presumably broken down. *It didn't make sense.* As Shelby and three officers approached, Crutcher moved to place his hands on his vehicle with his hands up. But to Shelby, Crutcher looked "like a bad dude," and appeared "zombie-like."[80] Crutcher's anomalous placement of his car, the ambiguity of his presentation—like a zombie, no less—made him uncategorizable and therefore dangerous. Crutcher's movement formally brought him into the domain of a dangerous subject and caused one officer to tase him—but Shelby instead fired her weapon.[81] Terrence wasn't ambiguous. He was a family man who sang in his church choir and was studying music appreciation at Tulsa Community College.

Those in a marginal state, like Crutcher, and as Douglas has noted of marginal subjects, are "left out in the patterning of society"; they are "placeless" and their position and status are "indefinable."[82] As such, they live a perennially "transitional" existence in which danger is ever present. This particular notion of transitional placelessness evokes Saidiya Hartman's meditation on the geographic sense of "not belonging and of being an extraneous element" that she places at the heart of slavery:

> Two people meeting on the avenue will ask, "Is this where you stay?" Not, "Is this your house?" "I stayed here all my life" is the reply. Staying is living in a country without exercising any claims on its resources. It is the perilous condition of existing in a world in which you have no investments. It is having never resided in a place that you can say is yours. It is being "of the house" but not having a stake in it. Staying implies transient quarters, a makeshift domicile, a temporary shelter, but no attachment or affiliation.[83]

"Danger lies in transitional states," Douglas tells us, "simply because transition is neither one state nor the next, it is undefinable. The person who must pass from one to another is himself in danger and emanates danger to others."[84] Therefore, the ghetto as a place of staying is a most dangerous and vulnerable margin, filled with that and those deemed anomalous and ambiguous.

Marginal subjects are not only so while "in" the margins, geographically speaking. Their marginal status follows them wherever they might be, carrying with it danger and vulnerability and, with that, the *expectation* of dangerous behavior. Thus, the marginal is coded as suspicious and ripe with the potential for criminality, which must be accounted for through violence. There is no contradiction with the classificatory integrality of Blackness in this recognition. Indeed, as Mary Douglas shows, taboos are those classifications that determine order through their regulation. As we have seen from the nearly full-century that spans the 1921 Tulsa Race Massacre and the murder of George Floyd in the summer of 2020, the demonic, the anomalous, and the out of order are categories sought out by normative systems for regulation, policing, or, in other words, control.

Violent Orders

In the process of urban renewal, we can see the features of anomaly, taboo, and violence behind the recognition of Dick Rowland's crime in the elevator of the Drexel Building. His Blackness made him ambiguous. Sarah Page's scream, regardless of its reason, brought him into a mode of recognition that cast him as anomalous. This anomalousness needed correction, lest the order of Whiteness be permanently disrupted by the implication that Black men can make White women scream. A world in which that was possible, much less permissible, was a world under threat. Thus, the threat had to be contained and the anomaly corrected. Unable to lynch Rowland and thereby execute the correction, the process would be accomplished by proxy. Tulsa would burn, and others would die for Rowland's breaching of order. The world *would* be made right again.

The incident punctuated a generation of Black progress in Tulsa and forever impacted the city's Black residents' future. But it signaled something more widespread: the underlying operations of Jim Crow White supremacy, which reappeared during the era of urban renewal. The Tulsa massacre demonstrates how violence facilitated this process. The violence in Tulsa in 1921, and the anti-Black violence that preceded it and has plagued Black communities ever since, represent the corrective function that maintains the balance of social order in America. From this position, the racist subjugation of Black populations is thus the cornerstone of the very notion that upholds (White) society's balance.

And so, as Tulsa sought to expand, to develop, to progress, Blackness again was cast as anomalous to that project. Greenwood became the geographic referent, the aberrant figure once again for the out-of-placeness of Blackness in the White spatial imaginary of the city. And thus, the violated taboo of that racial geographic disorder required correction. To facilitate that process, Greenwood would have to be legitimately qualified as anomalous; its potential danger would be rendered as *hazardous*, marked by the HOLC's redlining. Its community would be deemed blighted and thus deserving of correction through demolition.

The highway placed over those demolished neighborhoods would work to secure order. As a result, Greenwood would be pushed farther back into the margins, with its marginality qualifying the boundaries that make up order. This is what segregation is: the boundaries of order. And so, as Greenwood became marginal, it would be coded as such with the moniker *North Tulsa*. Figured as North Tulsa, the Black community faces the slow consequences of what the violence of urban renewal wrought, which is denial.

This denial functions in a double manner. First, the city's planning directives choose investment routes that circumvent and outright avoid the development of the area that was home to historic Greenwood and part of the now-broader area of North Tulsa. Second, denial is perhaps most meaningfully epitomized by Daniel Patrick Moynihan's phrase *benign neglect*.[85] Connolly writes that "if laws under slavery made black people disposable," then "the institution of racial apartheid" that was Jim Crow urban renewal "made black people negligible."[86] In his prescription to Richard Nixon, suggesting that he ignore race as a point of discussion, Moynihan said, "The subject has been too much talked about. . . . We may need a period in which Negro progress continues and racial rhetoric fades."[87] While the thinking goes that Moynihan's intention was to help dampen what the administration regarded as the much-heightened and polarizing "hysterics" of racial discourse following the civil rights movement, his recommendation of discursive neglect led to the structural neglect of Black neighborhoods. Rather than being a problem that needed solving, the Black condition became a problem that could be altogether avoided. North Tulsa's underdevelopment and the willful silencing of the history of the massacre both demonstrate and facilitate such neglect and denial.

Through neglect and marginalization, dispossession and disqualification, the presence of these violent forms of order's correction shows that we must look beyond the spectacular for the ways that violence operates. Deborah Thomas argues that we should instead pay attention to the "*repertoires* of spectacular violence," which are "techniques of performance that have been developed over time" and which make violence "available in various ways."[88] Drawing on performance studies scholar Diana Taylor's notion of repertoire as "a constant state of againness," Thomas argues for how "repertoire differs from . . . archive" by functioning "as an ongoing process of building from the past to the present."[89] For her purposes of examining how the violence of slavery as repertoire helps to articulate violence in Jamaica, and for the benefit of my argument in Tulsa, Thomas shows us how "repertoire provides a way for us to imagine continuity in more complex terms, [and] how spectacular violence itself is incorporated within and reproduced through the processes of everyday life."[90] And perhaps most directly relevant to the history of the race massacre, Thomas writes that violence truly functions as "no single riot, no massacre, no extremely violent event that appeared as an aberration from everyday life, no one occurrence that resulted in a new reckoning of time . . . dividing that which happened before the event from that which happened after."[91] Thomas asserts that, instead, violence presents as "a series of events that provoke ever increasing levels of shock and disbelief but that nevertheless are quickly enfolded into the realm of imaginable possibilities."[92]

Thomas writes that "spectacular violence cannot just disappear from the repertoires of rule" but continues to "exist as potential resources" for the display of power.[93] What we see is the repertoire of violence as it exists in North Tulsa. It exists through how both the spectacular and the ordinary violence of the state are continuously exercised against the Black community there. Mob violence, lynching, and the insidious destruction of urban renewal each have the performative quality of "againness" that is demonstrated by the continued marginalization of Black North Tulsans. Their poverty serves as the peculiar archive of violence.

A century after the massacre, this againness is present in the ethical and material afterlives of violence that make up the condition of contemporary Black life in North Tulsa. The scars of structural impoverishment mark its geography. These scars are due to the city's and the state's historical reluctance to aid in rebuilding Greenwood in the wake of the massacre and the area's intentional depreciation and exploitation through a regime of underdevelopment. What has replaced the mostly self-determined and self-reliant past of Tulsa's Black community today is austere public services and a devastating lack of commercial life.

The community faces chronic difficulties in accessing necessary goods. There is an absence of grocery stores and services; public transportation, when available, is irregular. Overall, opportunities are mainly provided by a matrix of state agencies, churches, and nonprofit organizations. These programs typically fail to be catalysts of mobility and instead unwittingly sustain the effects of community underdevelopment, which was induced by the destructive violence of 1921 but reproduced through the more mundane violence of urban renewal and the poverty that it brought. These interventions and the policies that facilitate them in many ways complement the weakening of the state's obligation to provide care and services to the community and dampen the community's ability to provide for themselves.

The Tulsa Race Massacre violently interrupted the development of Greenwood's prosperity. By the time of the massacre, Greenwood had existed for only about fifteen or so years. To be so severely impacted so early was devastating materially but also narratively. As Greenwood rebuilt its buildings and businesses, its reputation underwent its own recovery. Nevertheless, that early assault may have produced a structural vulnerability, as the costs of the recovery in terms of monetary and human capital would otherwise have been invested in the community. As urban renewal and, later, integration opened the local economy to White capitalists, North Tulsa found itself part of a narrative history of underdevelopment marked by a dearth of resources. Over time, that narrative became seen as a form of inheritance, signaled by a toponymic slippage by which Greenwood became North Tulsa.

The geographic boundaries of these places overlap, some might say neatly, but the meanings of these places, and their attendant value, are discordant with regard to the memories, attachments, and investments they evoke. The coordinates of each place signal and symbolize frictions that add a semiotic complication to an already structurally challenging life. If one looks at a Home Owners' Loan Corporation map of Tulsa, the "hazardous" red zone of Greenwood is today precisely the same area that has the highest concentration of poor Black residents in the city.[94] The disparities in Tulsa residents' social and economic circumstances overdetermine their existence in the city. Indeed, the designation of North Tulsa as poor is another example of what Claudio Saunt termed *geographic segregation*, by which the United States' racial fixation is inscribed into the land.[95]

Thus, if the two days of the race massacre razed the Black city, then the slow process of dispossession that followed was the salting of the earth. As I discuss in the following chapter, its inheritance is seen in the social and economic instability, restriction, and arrest of the North Tulsa community. Thus, we can read the pervasive poverty in Black communities as a cascading of violence, perhaps not as exceptional in its narrative as the Tulsa massacre but no less impactful. The consequences and complications of this violence play out over various socioeconomic challenges. Whether the result of overt racism or the everyday encounter of racialized poverty, such challenges produce trauma and stress that are socially, psychically, and even genetically carried across generations. Those experiences form the precariousness and vulnerability of intergenerational poverty, a more damning form of violence than any massacre.

The cardinal directions of north and south are often the main reference points for thinking about Tulsa, with Interstate 244 being the most significant border between them. Zip codes even more finely designate the relationship between place and the quality of life. As I talked to Darrell, it became clear how much residents identified by and with their zip codes: "So actually, growing up in Tulsa, we didn't grow up wealthy at all. My parents worked multiple jobs, and they never went to college. Of course, that wasn't an option for us—we had to go. Although it wasn't the mindset for a lot of kids. It was only later that I could really appreciate that because, when you think about it, in our zip code, 74106, which has the highest African American population, they say that the average life expectancy for us is fourteen years less than for folks who live in 74133! We're two miles north!"[1] These two zip codes effectively lay on either side of 244 and indicated the division and disparity of the outcomes that the highway represented and initiated.

The disparity in life expectancy that Darrell struggled to make sense of is only one of many that stalk the territory of North Tulsa. Deep impoverishment afflicts nearly 35 percent of North Tulsa's residents, while in South Tulsa—glossed as mostly White and comparatively more affluent, despite pockets of poor communities of multiple races—that number is just over 13 percent. The suspension rates of Black students and the high percentage of segregated schools are products of a crisis of school underfunding across the state. Infant mortality rates for Black Tulsans are triple those of Whites.

Critical to it all is that Black unemployment is nearly three times that of Whites across the city, which partly explains why the median income for North Tulsans is half that of South Tulsa.[2] The vestiges of past injustices—the race massacre of 1921 and even more so the more recent violence of urban renewal—impact the lives of Tulsa's Black people in the present. The absence or deterioration of essential infrastructure produces a peculiar map of inequality whose contours represent points of unequal value and uneven relations to the economic and social circumstances of "average" life in Tulsa.

The lived experience of this inequality is evidenced in accounts shared with me by several women I met through the Center for Family Resilience. Their stories of intergenerational complications are deeply imbricated with the history and geography of North Tulsa. The stress, for some, is inescapable, as was the case for Keisha, a twenty-eight-year-old single mother of two girls. When she was twenty-one, Keisha, whose daughters were toddlers at the time, took custody of her two younger half-sisters, who were eleven and eight. Their mother had been absent for some time owing to a jail sentence for drug use, and their father had recently been sentenced for dealing. Faced with raising four children without the means to do so effectively, Keisha suffered a mental breakdown, which she described for me:

> KEISHA: I had a mental break when my oldest daughter was like four or five. I had my two little sisters—my stepdad's kids—and my daughters. So I had an eleven-year-old, an eight-year-old, a three- and a two-year-old. I was twenty-one and went looking for my grandma at her old house in Catoosa—this is after she's passed [away], and I went in the house, and I told the lady [current resident], "What are you doing here?!" I had Burger King, I had the kids, the door was open.

> JOVAN: Why do you think you did that?

> KEISHA: I don't know, something told me to go home. I guess I missed her, or maybe it really hit me. Because I had my little sisters for a year, and foster care told me I either need to adopt them or put them in the system, and I didn't have anybody to call, and I was like, "I don't know what to do!" I was doing it because my mom was in jail in Arkansas, and my stepdad went to prison for dealing drugs.

> JOVAN: Your mom was in Arkansas?

> KEISHA: Yeah, she was always a wanderer. That's why I looked to my stepdad because even though he would do what he did [deal drugs],

he had his kids. He had just got an apartment, had two cars, getting his SSI [social security—he was already retirement age], so when the caseworker told me that they weren't gonna give them back to him [when he got out of prison], I think it just triggered something. I went to all our old houses looking for my grandma that day and ended up in Catoosa [a town just outside Tulsa's border]. So it was crazy because the screen door was open, and I walked in and was like, "What are you doing in my grandma's house?" Then I blacked out. Whatever happened, the police were coming; I don't know. Anyway, I was in a mental home for eighteen months.

JOVAN: Really?

KEISHA: Yeah, I thought I worked there [*chuckles*] when I came to. I had no idea. I was like, where's my car? So, the incident happened in Catoosa, which is very racist; it's all White people. I had never been in trouble, they could verify that I used to live there, and they tried to send me to prison. First offense, never been in trouble.

JOVAN: For what, going into this house?

KEISHA: Yeah, they gave me a first-degree burglary, even though I didn't break in, no forced entry. I did push the lady, but she dropped the charges, but the state picked them back up. They said I also assaulted an officer, but all I remember is the police slamming me on the ground, so if I did, it was a natural reflex. So I had all that on my record.

JOVAN: Were there any consequences?

KEISHA: Uh-huh. That's how I lost my job at Capital One doing customer service. So it sucks; you know you're doing good [working at Capital One], then all of that happens. I mean, how do you go from Capital One to Sonic? I mean, that really bothers me. And that's how I ended up working at the Mexican restaurant [thinking it was an improvement from Sonic].

JOVAN: And then what happened to your kids?

KEISHA: My god-mom took my daughters, but my sisters went into foster care. They're still in foster care, but they're with a great family.

JOVAN: Oh, so they're together?

KEISHA: Uh-huh, they're with the [foster family name], a White couple. They [the sisters] look great. I haven't gotten to talk to them. I talked to my little sister right after I had my mental break. She knew my mom was staying at the homeless shelter, and she told me to tell her to visit, and they went, and it traumatized the younger daughter, so they just cut all communication.

JOVAN: So how old are they now?

KEISHA: Seventeen and fifteen. But I'm so glad because it was bad. I used to pick them up to do their hair and to wash their clothes . . . that's why I felt like I needed to get them.

JOVAN: They were staying with whom at this time?

KEISHA: My stepdad and my mom. But he tried, but he was still doing his own thing as well. So I would pick them up every week to make sure their hair was combed . . . I think like my grandma did, I'm like the one who's holding everything together. Like, when she passed, everybody went crazy, and they looked at me, and I'm like, "I don't know what I'm doing!" I guess I'm gonna be the "big mama" in a few years . . . [laughs]. You know that's what it feels like because that's how it is; they're like, "Keisha," you know, always calling me, but I don't know, I'm just making it up as I go along. I don't have nobody to mimic, nobody to mirror; I'm just making it up; there's no female role model. You know, when I went to counseling, they were like, "Who do you look up to?" and I was like, "Nobody! God?" They were, like, they wanted to know a physical person, but I don't look up to nobody because there's nobody.

JOVAN: There's no one?

KEISHA: Well, like my pretend cousin, she was like, "I think you're afraid you're gonna be like your mom but need to know you are already better than her because you went through all this, but you still pick up your kids, and you don't have to; you could've ran like she did." I didn't even think of it like that, and she said, "Quit thinking you're gonna turn out like your mom; just because it's your mom, you're not gonna be her." She just told me that a year ago. But you know, I've been told, "You're just like your mother" from my grandpa. And I think that just stuck with me, and every time I see her, I just look at her, and I'm like I see a reflection, and I don't want to feel like that. I know what it feels like to wonder, "Why doesn't she want us?" but not really understanding. Now I'm afraid my kids felt like that when I was gone [owing to the mental break].

From my exchange with Keisha, we see that her parents' challenges led her to become entirely responsible, much too young, for her sisters alongside her daughters. Desperate for assistance, with no living person to whom she thought she could turn, Keisha went to the former home of her deceased grandmother, because her mental crisis led her to believe somehow that she was still alive. Returning to the answers Keisha gave when I asked her why she thought she went to her grandmother's house is critical. She replied, "It really hit me. Because I had my little sisters for over a year, and foster care told me I either need to adopt them or put them in the system, the pressure was on, and I didn't have anybody to call, and I was like 'I don't know what to do!'" The demands of her life were too much to bear. She sought help beyond this world because this world provided insufficient care; all it did was demand, add pressure, *break* her.

The current owner of her grandmother's home called the police on Keisha but later dropped the charges. Nevertheless, the state charged Keisha with burglary. I suppose their recognition of the psychosis at the heart of the event meant that she should serve time in a mental facility rather than a jail, but that recognition was insufficient to drop the charge of assault on an officer.

Keisha unfortunately was part of a trend in which people in need of mental care have become overrepresented in police encounters, a statistic that indicates the general failure of Tulsa's health-care and social-support systems.[3] In 2018, Joshua Harvey, a twenty-five-year-old Black man diagnosed with bipolar and paranoid schizophrenia disorder, was killed by the Tulsa police. Clearly in crisis—Joshua was found taking his clothes off and screaming in the middle of the street—the police responded by tasing him twenty-seven times. Joshua died three days later.

Keisha didn't lose her life, but the assault on her record impacted the quality of that life. She could not get another "good" job like working in customer service at Capital One. Losing her job and nearly losing her daughters, on top of losing her sisters to foster care, was a staggering amount of loss for Keisha. The mental breakdown resulted from her poverty and the inequalities and adversities that caused it, whether owing to the extreme stress of her circumstances or a lack of medical care that might have diagnosed any underlying psychological concerns. Living with the financial repercussions of losing her job, the enduring heartbreak caused by the loss of her sisters, and the remaining anxiety about a future incident possibly leading to her losing her daughters to the system left Keisha vulnerable to another stress-induced breakdown. Keisha's lack of capital and the limits of her community meant that she and her family lacked adequate care.

Community Disorder

In both its meaning and its teleological outcome, it was evident that Keisha found it hard to reconcile with the circumstances of her geography. Greenwood, a landscape that was once considered an active economic hub, is now North Tulsa. While not emptied of the Black life behind Greenwood's thriving, North Tulsa was made, through repeated waves of structural assault, into a space pockmarked with payday lenders and dollar stores. While this problem might be irreconcilable for Keisha, that she would face them in Tulsa is not surprising considering the city's budgetary commitments. In 2019 the city directed only 10 percent of its budget toward public transportation and other public works and 4 percent to social and economic development. Meanwhile, it earmarked over a third of its budget for policing.[4]

This mix of fiscal priorities is common in underserved minority neighborhoods and constitutes the now common practice of municipal disinvestment, discussed in the last chapter, that structured North Tulsa's historical experience of receding state support in key service areas. Unsurprisingly, the combination of financial commitments in 2019 had changed little from the 1980s, when North Tulsa is thought to have found itself in the midst of a drug and crime crisis.

By the mid- to late 1980s, as Reverend recounted, a drug epidemic was seen to have taken over Tulsa, with North Tulsa as its epicenter. Throughout the decade North Tulsa experienced higher crime rates than the remainder of the city, with Tulsa Police Department (TPD) statistics in 1988 showing that the community represented 48 percent of drug arrests and overall violent crimes, which included homicide, rape, robbery, and assault.[5] Like elsewhere in the national "war on crime," public housing in North Tulsa was seen as the principal site of the problem. North Tulsa public housing complexes like Comanche Park, Morning Star, Osage Hills, Seminole Hills, and Vernon Manor were targets for police surveillance and arrest.

In 1984, the TPD initiated a five-year "Plan of Excellence" that reoriented the department's policing philosophy away from "reactive patrol to community-based, proactive policing," as an attempt to improve service to the community.[6] Four years later, in the summer of 1988, TPD set out to formally study the drug problem in North Tulsa, with a focus on illicit activity in the public housing developments mentioned as well as in others. They had received funding from the Bureau of Justice Assistance (BJA) to join in a five-city project to bring problem-solving strategies to the drug control problem. Taking part in this "Problem-Oriented Approach to Drug Enforcement Project," TPD assigned ten officers to address "the underlying conditions" behind the drug related criminal activity.[7]

The notion of underlying conditions is critical because TPD was required to use "the problem-oriented policing approach." Problem-oriented policing was considered an innovative means of addressing "persistent community problems that require a police response."[8] The thinking went that in traditional policing, real-time identification of criminal problems was seldom accompanied by analysis of their causes. In an example given by the BJA, they note that "on a call for service at a notorious drug trouble spot, a traditional police officer might make an immediate arrest with little effort to measure long-term results. On a similar call, a problem-oriented officer might also make the same short-term response, but include an effort to determine why the scene was an almost constant trouble spot. This officer might determine that poor lighting encouraged drug activity on the corner. Getting the lighting upgraded might accomplish more lasting results."[9]

As indicated by the BJA example, problem-oriented policing was a community policing approach closely related to the "Broken Windows" theory advanced by Wilson and Kelling in 1982.[10] As "place-based, problem-oriented interventions," both methods focused on proactive responsiveness to crime that paid attention to the environmental conditions of so-called troubled areas.[11] Problem-oriented policing, with its focus on community, has typically framed their geographies of interest using delimiting language like "hotspots."[12] Place-based crime-prevention strategies moved the focus of criminological analysis from individuals and groups to the places that they inhabited. This environmental perspective asked that crime policy and police practice "consider a wider collection of characteristics of opportunity and physical space" than had been previously.[13]

Underlying both approaches was the sense that these poor conditions, which exacerbated crime, represented a sense of disorder. In this model, disorder "is not directly linked to serious crime; instead, disorder leads to increased fear and withdrawal from residents, which then allows more serious crime to move in because of decreased levels of informal social control."[14] As noted by the BJA, the criminal activity of the project's selected sites, which ranged from active drug markets to violent crime, all stemmed from "poor environmental conditions that indicated community disorder."[15] The resulting principle of this form of policing has been identified as "order maintenance policing."[16] When TPD undertook its study and engaged with the community of North Tulsa while keeping these problem-oriented and place-based principles in mind, they set out, in sum, to police geographic disorder.

It has been argued that in the implementation of the disorder framework, going back to James Wilson and George Kelling's first use of the term, there has been little to distinguish what determines the designation of disorderly environments, whether it is the presence or absence of markers, such as graffiti or litter, or "the presence of a delinquent versus rule-abiding citizen."[17] In answering the question of this distinction, the history of North Tulsa shows us that this form of policing joins the procession of the violent ordering of geography administered in the processes of urban renewal, eminent domain, and, of course, the massacre, discussed in chapter 1. Indeed, the transformation from Greenwood to North Tulsa through the determination of disorder has been the direct result of this ordering.

Dick Rowland was used to both claim and cause disorder. The rendering of Greenwood as blighted was the recognition of disorder that ushered in urban renewal. And again, TPD in 1988 had used crime to locate disorder in the community, maintaining the same racial geographic principles of control and containment that had long ordered North Tulsa's Black community. It is obvious to assume that their determination of disorder wrought overpolicing, which of course it did and which I will discuss. However, there is another consequence that is perhaps less expected and seen as being less problematic than overpolicing.

When TPD issued its report in 1989, *Drug Problem Inventory: Problem-Oriented Approach to Drug Enforcement*, it wrote in the section titled "Important Findings" that "even though the extent of the drug abuse problem in Tulsa is not entirely known, there are some important findings that have surfaced as a result of the drug inventory analysis." One of the summarized findings was subtitled "Residents in public housing are isolated from the community at large." From its study, TPD determined that

> less than 30% of the complex residents have a telephone to access services.
> Less than 20% of the complex residents have their own transportation.
> Social service agencies are not located near north-side public housing.
> Interstate Highway 244 serves as a geograph[ical] barrier, separating north Tulsa from south Tulsa.[18]

TPD, in its problem-oriented and place-based approach, found that North Tulsa suffered from a lack of social services and transportation and communication access, and that the highway was a barrier that caused geographic isolation. In this abbreviated list of four items, TPD illustrated the consequences of urban renewal and the disinvestment of North Tulsa over the previous five decades: isolation. Here, North Tulsa was officially found to be at the margins of the broader society. While the highway was identified, the solution that TPD put forward was a foregone conclusion since the implementation of their "Plan of Excellence" strategy was to remedy North Tulsa's lack of services.

In TPD's "Summary of Potential Responses" the first suggestion was, perhaps unsurprisingly, to "Eliminate overt street dealing from target complexes through stepped-up police enforcement." However, interestingly, the majority of the recommendations across the board for areas of concern was an increase in agency and nonprofit engagement such as "assess and help coordinate the need for social service agencies to bring programs to residents in public housing"; "encourage service agencies to locate closer to the clients they serve through relocation, satellite offices, or provide mobile service centers"; "assist with the Brokered Transportation Program to provide residents transportation to shop, visit the doctor, wash laundry, and obtain other needed services;" and "encourage low-cost and no-cost substance abuse treatment agencies to target low-income public housing residents for extended services."[19]

In facilitating part of what it called "The Future Plan," TPD identified that "several social service agencies are now establishing satellite offices in North Tulsa [and] 'self-help' groups have agreed to do outreach in public housing."[20] Just before TPD began its study, the Oklahoma Center for Nonprofits (OKCNP), an organization founded in 1981 by Pat and Ray Potts in Oklahoma City, with the mission to support nonprofit development, opened its first Tulsa office in 1986.[21] The OKCNP would help catalyze the development of nonprofits in Tulsa. And with TPD's assessment, there was a clear target population to which it could provide services.

This is the other consequence of the problem that the police identified as disorder in North Tulsa: they designated the area as blighted, suffering from the decay of isolation, problems in which Tulsa's history would tell you the police had a direct hand. However, here was TPD recognizing that those issues required remediation and that the solution was agencies and "self-help" groups. The result is that Greenwood became the geographic and semiotic site known as North Tulsa and a quintessentially underdeveloped space.

As Walter Rodney has defined it, an underdeveloped society or, in this case, community is one that loses control over its destiny and thus falls victim to external dependency for core services like health and education.[22]

Underdevelopment thus thrives on creating local dependence on external sources, which can then profit from a community's poverty through the guise of supporting it. Thinking with Rodney, we see how Greenwood underwent a process of underdevelopment in its transition to North Tulsa via the rapid and wide proliferation of nonprofits in the community.

The Foundation

It is for these reasons that the nonprofit scene in North Tulsa is unlike any other that I have encountered in the United States. In fact, it reminded me of the myriad nongovernmental organizations and missionary groups that commonly provide health and other services in developing nations. Similarly, dozens of organizations seek to intervene in the multiple disparities that afflict the underprivileged community in North Tulsa. Many, if not most, are concerned with early education and the related development of parenting. Others are concerned with addressing essential health and nutritional concerns among the most vulnerable, which would include the elderly, children, those living in abject poverty, or those suffering from debilitating disease or disability.

Critically, these organizations rely on funding from private philanthropies. Philanthropy has increasingly become aligned with capitalist frameworks within these funding relationships.[23] As a consequence, capitalism—functioning as a way of thinking, structuring time and place, and a means of imagining society and its future—orients foundations around the belief that they can avoid the seemingly inefficient state funding practices. In turn, their presence in the provisioning of necessary community resources means that the state can more clearly align its revenue and expenditure models with the values of the market. Neither of these outcomes is beneficial to society; however, the "giving" element of philanthropy obscures this reality. These shifts signal an alignment between neoliberal governance and charity, which ultimately places the state's and the foundations' interests above those of the people they are literally in the business of serving.

Moreover, because foundations are privately administered, they are not required to represent the public interest or protect the rights of poor or marginalized people, Indigenous communities, or other groups in society they claim to serve. Philanthropy is thus structured to base its decisions on market fundamentals and not considerations of distributive justice. In that sense, philanthrocapitalism and strategic funding are ultimately tools and ideologies that allow funders to impose a market logic on philanthropy in the same way that the state's belief in free markets often trumps concerns about the distribution of wealth.

In Tulsa no philanthropy had a deeper impact and broader reach than the George Kaiser Family Foundation. The Kaiser family's wealth originated in the oil industry. That wealth later grew through banking, as in the 1990s they acquired the Bank of Oklahoma, a bank that also got its start with oil. The Kaiser Family Foundation (KFF), much like other large foundations, such as that of Bill and Melinda Gates, seeks to invest in social issues. However, the KFF focuses squarely on interrupting poverty's intergenerational cycle by concentrating on its inputs. Through conversations with Erica, a program operator at the KFF, I learned that these issues are matters of deep and personal concern for George Kaiser. According to Erica, the poverty in Tulsa "kind of upsets him, it makes him very incensed because he really . . . his phrase is that he really hates that the fate of someone is left up to the genetic lottery; that bothers him. It is very hard for him." My thoughts lingered on this notion of a "genetic lottery." It willfully ignores the effort it takes to produce systemic poverty and the way that poverty then secures the "lottery" for the wealthy.

Nevertheless, that was the ethic behind the KFF. Its mission includes providing equal opportunity to all children born in Tulsa, with a serious commitment to the city's geographic boundary. This aim to secure equal opportunity for every person in Tulsa is a seemingly impossible challenge, given that 80 percent of all children under the age of nine in Tulsa live in poverty or near the poverty line.[24] Further, the state of Oklahoma incarcerates more women per capita than any other state.[25] To make matters worse, Oklahoma schools have the forty-ninth lowest funding rate in the country. A common joke is "At least we're not Mississippi," which ranks last. The KFF sees a need to address these complex and interconnected intergenerational problems and contemporary circumstances, all of which require a comprehensive solution.

To enact these changes, the KFF runs a suite of programs. It draws on, supports, and even creates various institutional partners that can provide the leadership necessary to champion its causes. However, the foundation is very much the personal project of George Kaiser. Erica said to me, "He's not a Bill Gates where he wants to be in public a whole lot. He doesn't love to meet with policy officials that don't agree with him. That's just not his favorite. He's a very smart, educated, brilliant guy and hires program staff to execute what he wants to get done." The foundation invests heavily in all its areas of concern, working with several industry partners, leaders, and community advocates. However, North Tulsa continues to pose a specific challenge:

> So there's a lot that we're trying to accomplish there. But with North Tulsa, something really has to be done, but we don't really know what will work. It's going to be a suite of a whole lot of options. So we're trying to develop optionality for those residents, which is extraordinarily important. They don't have an opportunity for jobs and don't have an option for schools, even though that's getting way better through our education programs, or they don't have the option for where they shop from. Like they don't go to the hospital that is up there—we built that for them.

Part of the challenge is the shifting demographics of North Tulsa. Specifically, significant Black flight of moderate-income earners to places like Broken Arrow, a suburb twenty minutes southeast of Tulsa, which has slightly less affordable housing but perceivably better schools, has only deepened the poverty in North Tulsa.[26] Thus, neighborhoods like Springdale, which has long been thought one of the most impoverished and dangerous, are becoming increasingly poor. These communities face ongoing and increasing challenges in their circumstances. The increase in policing has caused these poor and racialized neighborhoods to suffer disproportionate rates of incarceration. As stated, in Oklahoma, many of those incarcerated are women. The challenge is exacerbated by the state's private prison industry, which has grown owing to lobbying efforts.

The KFF seeks to intervene in incarceration rates, primarily because of the impact on the children of the incarcerated. The foundation created a program called Women in Recovery (WIR), which is "an intensive outpatient alternative for eligible women facing long prison sentences for nonviolent drug-related offenses." It works with the criminal justice system and community partners to provide program participants with services such as "supervision, substance abuse and mental health treatment, education, workforce readiness training and family reunification." The program aims to "help women conquer their drug addiction, recover from trauma and acquire the essential economic, emotional and social tools to build successful and productive lives" by reducing recidivism, strengthening families, and breaking the cycle of intergenerational incarceration.[27]

With regard to WIR, Erica said that the foundation "didn't want to work with those, you know, who stole something from a candy store. We wanted the worst ones, the ones whose kids are put in foster care." And from Erica's and

WIR's account, these women are now often gainfully employed and reunited with their families. Programs like WIR are funded through novel schemes like Pay for Success, which is "an innovative financing mechanism that shifts financial risk from a traditional funder—usually government—to a new investor, who provides up-front capital to scale an evidence-based social program to improve outcomes for a vulnerable population. If an independent evaluation shows that the program achieved agreed-upon outcomes, then the investment is repaid by the traditional funder. If not, the investor takes the loss."[28] Erica explained that with WIR, "For every woman that's successful, the government will then compensate us. Up to that point, we're assuming all of the risk." Instruments like Pay for Success allow the foundation to expand its suite of offerings and increase its expenditure on each.

Women in Recovery isn't the only reentry service that the foundation funds. One, called the Center for Employment Opportunities (CEO). The center provides employment training services to help provide individuals with a job. As Erica explained, "You've just committed a second felony or whatever, and you're needing some help. You're being monitored by GPS. You can walk into CEO's door, and they're gonna take care of you and make it happen. They're gonna try and reunify you with your family, they're going to get you employment and get you back on your feet." Another program, called Tulsa Reentry One-Stop, "works with tougher folks," according to Erica, who explained it like this: "You've just left prison. Life is rough for you. You just walked out the door of the prison. They give you that one free bus ticket that they give you here, and you take that ride, to Tulsa Reentry One-Stop. And if they haven't reached the five hundredth [case] that year, you can walk in with nothing and they will find you housing. They will literally buy you suits."

The matter of early childhood education is at the core of the foundation's concerns and, in its estimation, stands at the heart of Tulsa's social and economic ills. "Yeah, our first real major focus is early childhood, and it still is that that's what we care about most of all because that is where most of our money has gone. Billions and billions of dollars," said Erica. As a result, the foundation started the local Educare Tulsa program. Educare was founded in 2000 by the Ounce of Prevention Fund, a nonprofit founded by businessman and philanthropist Irving Harris. The nonprofit opened Educare Chicago, the first Educare school. These schools provide full-day, year-round early childhood education with an added focus on family support services. In Tulsa the first Educare opened in 2006 in the Kendall-Whittier neighborhood and included an on-site health clinic. The second school opened in 2010 in North Tulsa, and the third Educare opened in 2012 in East Tulsa. Tulsa is the only city in the country with three Educare schools, and Educare I and III serve primarily Hispanic families. "Our three Educares, they're located in some of our most challenged communities. And we use the Educares as kind of a point around which we develop those communities through providing initial capital for a grocery store development, the reduction of food deserts and food swamps, kicking out criminals, the rehabilitation for criminals, you name it, all those efforts are centered around that Educare," Erica explained. "For example, in reaching more into the community in Kendall-Whittier, which has a massive Hispanic community, we've done a massive amount of mixed-income housing work there."

Educare's objective is to intervene in the lives of underprivileged children as early as possible. Erica told me, "We want to start as early as possible, right after a child is born. Six weeks after, we want to have your child in our system if they are high risk." She explained that Kaiser developed this interest in early education based on a study that demonstrated the impact of "the word gap."[29] Effectively, the theory, the reliability of which had already begun to face criticism by my time in Tulsa, states that preschool-age children from lower socioeconomic backgrounds have half as many words in their vocabulary as their counterparts from middle-class and higher-income backgrounds.[30]

The understanding that Kaiser took from this was that the word gap serves as an adequate proxy for the achievement gap seen in schools. "That child is not ready to learn how to read. They don't have the words. So the learning curve that that child steps into is massive. So we started to think about it. Like, we need to figure out a way of reducing the word gap and not for everywhere in the world, at least for Tulsa," explained Erica. In partnership with the Clinton Foundation, George Kaiser launched the initiative "Too Small to Fail," for which Tulsa was the initial launch site. The program seeks to promote early brain and language development by using tools like talking, reading, and singing with young children starting from birth. With that program and parent integration into the Educares, "the essential message we're trying to convey is, as a parent, you're your baby's first teacher, your baby's best toy, baby's first advocate, and best advocate. You don't need to be very wealthy to have a conversation with the babbling child. And that conversation will have massive impacts on your child's brain development going forward." Beyond the Educare and early learning initiatives, the foundation also funds and creates partnerships with the state government agencies working toward the same goals, such as contributing funding to Head Start programs across the state and the various Community Action Project Tulsa (CAP TULSA) initiatives.

Erica shared that across all its programming, the foundation serves about two thousand kids at roughly a cost of $50 million per year, which she breaks down and qualifies for me: "It's $25,000 per kid per year—they're getting amazing services; those kids make tremendous gains. But what, two thousand kids, and we're spending all this money nonstop, there's no way; it's just a drop in the bucket in terms of the size of the problem. We have three thousand on the waiting list, and these are the people who know enough to say that I want this for my child. We have countless others that aren't even on the waiting list that might not be aware." Given all the programs the foundation supports, I asked Erica about their long-term feasibility; she replied, "That's a very significant problem that we have with the foundation because it's unsustainable for us alone to take care of all of this. We fund 224 different organizations completely outside of our health-care spending or education spending. We give a ridiculous amount to Tulsa public schools. So these programs are primarily funded by us."

The KFF funded 97 percent of WIR but received some partnership support from the federal government, such as Head Start and Early Head Start initiatives. However, according to Erica, the foundation spent about $200 to $300 million a year to support 224 organizations. "Tulsa is very program rich. We have nonprofits for days. Nonprofits here are everywhere. Everyone works in the nonprofit sector. It's massive. It's absolutely massive with us, really." The number of nonprofits was one effect of a lack of direct government resourcing, which marked the long-examined impact of nonprofits on local economies and communities.[31]

In conversation with Reverend Jonathan, he shared, in frustration, "You know, our government doesn't resource the things that really make a difference?" He was explaining to me the presence of so many nonprofits, which had come in to make up the difference, and why they weren't terribly effective. "What happens is that so many small nonprofits . . . have such a hard time really doing what they want—[what] their vision is—because they're not getting the kind of resources to do it, or those that have it are getting more." Reverend pointed to a secondary circuit of the poverty cycle, in which the institutions meant to serve the underserved also struggle for resources. "So that just filters everything. So the money kind of goes, you know, into established systems. And so it makes it real hard to sustain, for local folks to organize for on-the-ground kind of issues." Several years later, Shameca explained that the local enterprise ecosystem had become so overrun by nonprofits that she admitted to beginning the paperwork for a 501(c)(3) for her health business because it was easier to fundraise startup capital for a nonprofit compared to a private company.

In a curious approach to providing social resources to poor communities through property development, the foundation has been investing heavily in the Thirty-Sixth Street North development in North Tulsa. The City of Tulsa has identified Thirty-Sixth Street North as a prime site for significant economic development and has discussed the possibility for several years. Through property acquisition, the foundation hopes to bring employment to the area and provide training for North Tulsa residents. In the foundation's thinking, its aim of over a thousand jobs would improve the livelihoods of North Tulsa residents, which in turn would improve the life chances of their children and, ultimately, their communities.

Despite their ambitions and even accomplishments—after all, the Educares and other outreach programs were bringing resources to the community—critically, or maybe just cynically, the KFF's and other nonprofits' model troubled me. But in fact, we can readily identify the frameworks often applied to urban development as applicable in the cases of subject development through such initiatives. Malini Ranganathan, writing on liberalism and urban planning, makes the point when she writes, "Urban improvement fundamentally entails enhancing the value of urban space through the mobilization of corrective behaviors. In so doing, urban improvement subjectifies target populations, while eliding the structural causes of inequality." When we scale this point up to the context of North Tulsa, the point holds; Ranganathan explains that "in this process, improvement grafts race, class, caste, and other forms of social difference onto urban space, which in turn provides the justification for more improvement. Improvement thus entails rule by difference."[32] This point is evidenced by how the agencies orient their services around the values of the (White) middle class, many of whom serve as the workers in these initiatives. These programs facilitate and reinforce the neoliberal scaling down of the state's commitment to providing social services, or what James Ferguson seminally called the "anti-politics machine" of development.[33] For these reasons, after my conversation with Erica, I needed to know what members of the North Tulsa community thought about the prevalence and the function of the nonprofits.

Who Is That White Organization Telling Me How to Raise My Child?

I met up with Dr. Anthony Marshall, who told me to call him Tony, to discuss the subject. Tony is a former Booker T. High School teacher, and he founded Men of Power, a mentorship program at the high school to support young Black men preparing for college. He also worked on getting the B. C. Franklin Park funded and built in North Tulsa and had an intimate sense of the community's issues. Tony asserted, "In Tulsa there are avenues to help. But it goes back to who has access to those resources? Do they really know they're there? Because *I* know that there are resources out there. So, some like that guy you talked to may say that we don't have resources in Tulsa. I wouldn't necessarily say that; the question is, do people know about certain resources?"

An example that Tony provided was CAP Tulsa, a community "action agency" "focused on interrupting the cycle of poverty."[34] It offers early education services for children and support services designed to help their parents' economic development. "Right now," Tony began, "CAP Tulsa is literally begging people to bring their kids for pre-early childhood development. And we all know that effective early childhood development can have long-lasting effects on individuals' learning ability. So why don't some of these women who are still carrying their babies around with them all day not take their babies?" he concluded somewhat rhetorically. "Why aren't they going to CAP Tulsa?" I asked. "I can answer that," Tony replied confidently. His answer was as surprising as it was illuminating. Tony started, "Who is that White organization telling me how to raise my child?" He went on, "You know, when CAP Tulsa had their recruitment thing set up at Booker T., I found it very interesting that all I saw were White females there [doing the recruiting]. And, you know, some of the mothers maybe don't trust that what *they* are saying, but that's who is there, and maybe they don't know how to reach into the community."

I had spoken to Kiara, one of the moms I met through the Center for Family Resilience, who had two children enrolled in CAP. She talked about her experiences of getting her children enrolled, which supported Tony's assertions. "You got to enroll them early, because there's a long waiting list," Kiara began to explain when we discussed the program a couple of weeks before my conversation with Tony. "And people say, if you don't have any money, you should just try. My daughter got in quick, and my son, I signed him up from [when] he was four months, and he's just now starting." And while Kiara didn't have trouble enrolling her children, through what seemed like good timing in the case of her daughter and good planning for her son, there were some points Kiara didn't take to fondly. "Even while you wait, they send out these people, they're [from] 'Parents as Teachers,' who come and show you stuff to do with them, like to help them learn. But it wasn't helping me, because I'm with kids all day; how can you teach me things?"

I could confirm what Kiara said because, at the Center for Family Resilience, I spoke with Hispanic and Black mothers who worked there as lay advisers, like Shameca. Like the "parent educators" in the Parents as Teachers program that Kiara mentioned, in these roles women conduct personal visits to provide child development and parenting information and other support to Hispanic and Black mothers, respectively. They noted how even they were treated with suspicion. Shameca told me that "often these moms felt like we're there to 'teach' them how to raise their kids. Honestly, these moms don't want us to come around." The lay advisers were part of the project Minding the Gap in Early Childhood Education: A Lay Advisor Approach, which ran from 2013 to 2016 and was sponsored by the KFF with a $358,981 grant. The project managers based the program on the Parents as Teachers model of early childhood parent education. The home-visiting model was intended to foster family support, well-being, and school readiness for families in Tulsa who could not afford the costs of pre-K early education and could not gain entrance into any of the available early-intervention programs, such as Head Start or Educare.

The project and its funders saw the families as being in the "achievement gap." The Parents as Teachers model involved the participation of "parent educators" trained and certified to work with families using the Parents as Teachers curriculum. The curriculum sought to "strengthen protective factors and ensure that young children are healthy, safe, and ready to learn."[35] In exchange for taking part, the participants received twenty-five dollars for completing a survey at the program's start and then again at its completion. Beyond this, compensation primarily came through the program's assistance with finding necessary state and nonprofit resources and helping the parents meet their basic needs.[36] Shameca demonstrated an example of this support when I accompanied her to one of her ten case visits. Shameca noticed the mother's broken car window and, after inquiring, learned that the air-conditioning wasn't working. "So, where your children sit, the windows can't go down?" Shameca asked. The answer was no. Shameca replied to the mom that she knew of a program "where they'll actually fix your car for you because of the fact that it impacts your children." Even with this kind of assistance, Shameca explained that although she was a Black mother, the parents were suspicious. This suspicion came from the insulting form of civilizing that these programs demanded. It also came from a more profound institutional distrust that is common among African Americans.[37] The program was also housed at Oklahoma State University–Tulsa (OSU-Tulsa), which warranted suspicion despite being a university. As a large institution, it seemed effectively distant from the community, as is the case with so many universities that border Black neighborhoods. Also, OSU-Tulsa suffered stigma because it's located on the grounds of historic Greenwood.

Tony saw similar implications for this kind of suspicion: "I mean, look at what we saw in Ferguson. I mean, it's a very tense relationship with the Black community and various institutions, especially state institutions. Right? And so, therefore, I think there is a natural kind of suspicion [of] someone who's going to take my kid for eight hours a day, six hours a day. What are you gonna do with them? How are [they] going to come back to me?" However, Tony was more concerned with what would come from not taking advantage of these programs. "Some of these parents don't understand that if they go to CAP, if their child goes to CAP, then that child would probably pass the third-grade reading score and then the eighth-grade OCCT [Oklahoma Core Curriculum Tests], and then they'll be able to go to Booker T. But when their child can't get into Booker T., they'll forget that ten years ago they refused to put their child in a program because they can't conceptualize a benefit because they didn't think ten years down the line."

While insightful, Tony's response contradicted the idea that there weren't sufficient resources, which required foundations' intervention. To Tony, there were resources, but because of their structure, the community was unable or unwilling to access them or even seek them out thoroughly. I shared my confusion over this with Tony, who responded, "So you are asking, do people have access here in Tulsa?" Replying in the affirmative, he continued, "Let me make it simple. Why is it that in South Tulsa if I go up and down Seventy-First Street, I can find 'twenty hundred million' restaurants, CVSs, etc., but if I come north, I don't have any of that?" Perhaps anticipating my lack of an answer or demonstrating his mastery of the suspended rhetorical question, developed over his decades as a teacher, Tony replied, "Brother, you can't access what you don't have!" Admittedly, Tony's conflation of social services and commercial choice was confusing, until I realized that this was because I was narrowly focusing on the services. For Tony, the lack of commercial choice and social services were related by the absence of adequate capital in the community, which if present would have provided both.

Lacking "restaurants, CVSs, etc.," North Tulsa was bereft of the required economic foundation that would shift the responses and even the very presence of these services. But the circumstances of the community entirely determined the choices of its meager resources. The community had no choice but to rely on the limited forms of community support. When this support wasn't sufficient, they reluctantly sought help from agencies and nonprofits, as engaging in outright refusal would only exacerbate the need for these options. It was a powerful cycle of need and support that undermined the community's capacity for self-reliance. There were, of course, exceptions to this binary in which an organization of means could provide support on the terms that the community could appreciate. The local chapter of the Omega Psi Phi Black fraternity provided scholarships to and through a partnership with Langston University, a historically Black university based in Langston, Oklahoma, with a satellite campus in Tulsa. But these programs were not meant to serve the structural needs of the community. They were exceptions based on exceptional circumstances. What was required was a standard form of support.

Tony brought another program to my attention. It's called the ADvantage Program, and it's part of the Home-and Community-Based Services division of the Oklahoma Human Services agency, which provides Medicaid services to help people stay at home instead of going to a nursing home.[37] "Many Black folk I know in this city would qualify for it. But it is not a well-known program," Tony began to explain. "So you're sitting at home struggling, having aunty and them come over to see about you when the ADvantage program is there, and aunty and them could even get paid to come see about you? But most of our people don't know that." I asked Tony what the reason for that was, especially since he seemed to be gesturing toward some other issue than institutional suspicion. His answer: "I mean, I guess they are living day to day. How am I getting to work tomorrow? How am I going to get through? It's hard to look at the future when you're struggling from day to day. I guess that's a difficult idea to conceptualize, like changing from the everyday struggle." The question, or more so, his answer, seemed to have hit him hard. "I don't know. I don't have the answer, but I think that's the problem." Even though he didn't have "the answer," I thought that his response was revelatory, and so I asked him to ponder it a bit further. "Yeah, well, I will try. OK. So, I think the idea is that because the environment is so depreciated, you know, time after time there is failure. Time after time there were failed promises, time after time. You know, there is a loss of faith, or a lack of faith about if something will work, or whether it's even worth it to try."

In North Tulsa all these organizations—whether nonprofit or government run—form a landscape of social-service provision akin to the practice of third-world aid and development. The Black community in North Tulsa, the descendants of the famed Black Wall Street, is incredibly proud of its history. However, they are faced with a choice, which is either struggle to produce community development on their terms, to limited or inconsistent effect, or make use of programs initiated by state agencies and nonprofit organizations aimed at reducing the inherent inequalities of poverty. The decision is complicated because the practices organizations use and the discourses they often employ, such as training, empowerment, and capacity building, seem ostensibly good, regarding their assumed effectiveness and the moralities they imply. However, perhaps unsurprisingly, the values and practices of self-reliance can often be at odds with development projects, particularly at the community level. Despite their best intentions, they consistently relay a message of ineptitude or deficiency to those they seek to help. Philanthropic and nonprofit organizations often focus on remedying the circumstances of the poor through their behavior, instead of directly trying to resolve the root causes of structural inequality, such as disparities in power relations and capital. As argued by Erica Kohl-Arenas, development initiatives are rife with ambivalence and contradiction but are consistent in their notions of "improvement."[39]

One point of evidence is the experience of North Tulsan mothers who enroll their children in early childhood intervention school programs like Educare. Through partnerships between philanthropists and the local Tulsa government, these programs seek to narrow the achievement gap for children in their communities through a curriculum that develops school readiness. The hope is for their students to learn on par with their middle-class peers when they start kindergarten. While providing necessary educational opportunity, these programs further perpetuate the ideology of bringing the poor "up" to the middle class in terms of access and values. In Tulsa, as in many other places, this is construed as being almost explicitly White. Additionally, this "civilizing" is hard to reconcile with how often it comes through increased disciplining. Schools have become sites of increased policing and punishment for Black students, who are disciplined at greater rates and for more trivial reasons than their White peers. This practice often effectively starts at kindergarten.

Given the demands on and limited resources of poor parents, educational opportunities like these early childhood intervention schools do much to secure as great a chance as any for the eventual mobility of their students. However, despite those demands and limited resources, these programs often insist on what is called *intense family engagement*. This is where a disconnect occurred for the moms I worked with. One of the requirements that falls under this family-engagement regime is the Parents as Teachers program. In this program parents are given teaching tools and are encouraged to model "appropriate" behaviors. Staff usually goes over these behaviors with parents in visitation sessions. Kiara shared that some of the lessons included parenting suggestions like "labeling your own feelings in difficult situations," illustrated by telling the child, "I feel so mad. I am going to go take some deep breaths in the other room to get myself under control." She gave another example, which I received with disbelief, that she was told when standing in store lines, parents should be sure not to cut in line, to teach the child how they would want them to respond in a similar situation.

For Kiara, and other mothers, many of these prescriptions were laughable at best and outright offensive at worst. It is essential to note the early role of caregiver that many women played, as children, to younger siblings. One of the moms I worked with had helped raise her five younger siblings, and let's not discount the stripes earned by Keisha, who sustained her responsibilities as a caregiver despite dire circumstances. The parents with children at these schools saw many of the practices required of them as condescending and too like something they would perhaps encounter with the Department of Children and Family Services.

Perhaps these contradictions and incongruences are a problem of cultural relativity. But work needs to be done in revealing the complex ethical-moral terrains in which such programs and policies play out. Hopefully, doing so will get at how such programs are so at odds with historically and culturally produced ethics of the raced poor by understanding their agency, their rationalities, and the moral orders of the factors that keep them poor. When working within the poverty context, such programs should go beyond received notions of what is good for the communities they serve. Programs need to alter their logic from the abstract goal of ending poverty, which grants an unending capacity to reproduce such programs to meet the ever-increasing needs and dimensions of poverty's nonresolution.[40] Instead, they need to incorporate broader networks of support on terms that sync with those communities' ideals and expectations. Doing so requires that these groups take race seriously. I don't mean as just another adjective in a long list of criteria that locate and plot inequality, as in Poor. Single. Black. Mother. The liberal urge to overlook the experience of race has shaped the ways that organizations and agencies have ignored Black ways of being through recasting poverty's conceptualization at both the points of inception and application.

The nonprofits were getting it wrong. It's fair to say that this is not a revelation. Then, to my mind, there must be local groups that could respond accordingly to the needs of the North Tulsa community. Community centers have done that work for generations, such as the Boys and Girls Clubs. For the North Tulsa community, it was the much-beloved North Mabee Center. There, Kiara said, was "a place where people could congregate and where [her] kids could do things and have fun and see folk." Moreover, North Mabee was a place that formed a sense of community. "Look," Kiara said, "I mean if you're Black, you went to North Mabee." Another is the Tulsa Dream Center, whose motto is "See a need, meet it. See a hurt, heal it." These recreational centers are part of the local network of community-based care, comprising individuals who effectively provide their communities with core social services. These are the coaches on local junior sports teams who encourage better participation in school. And then there are people who provide informal or formal childcare through their social networks. In this regard, Tulsa and North Tulsa specifically are not distinct from many poor and working-class African American communities across the United States, where most neighborhoods have "that" coach, "that" neighbor. However, what makes North Tulsa distinct is that these communities and these informal forms of social support are insufficient, if not deficient, and they signal the community as being in perpetual need.

Erica from the KFF noted the strengths but also the limits of these community networks:

> The folks provide social services, but just not as they're conventionally understood. The problem, though, is that they're not going to be like a social worker who's had years of working on the behavioral issues. Your support comes from an overweight coach who's doing that kind of work as he's telling you how to shoot baskets; essentially becomes a father figure when you don't have a father at home. However, while that's the kind of high-touch intervention that you'll receive, it's not organizational, formal, and evaluative. And even though [that's the case], you know, those informal services are where a lot of people go.

Erica accepted that these kinds of networks worked to the extent that they did because, as she put it, "They're highly trusted." For that reason, the KFF often ended up supporting them. "We're unable to accommodate everything and everyone. So, like, if you're coming from a single-parent home where your

mom works two jobs, or your dad is nowhere to be found . . ."—the hypothetical was both obnoxious and personally irritating but spoke volumes about
how the KFF framed their target demographic—". . . you'll probably go to
the YMCA. You're going to be better off there than at home watching televi-
sion; but it's just [at the YMCA] the variability [in outcome] is much higher."

   The organization, then, was promising "outcomes." They were selling a
productive, prosperous future for Tulsa's poor Black and Brown children. To
do so, it sought greater ability to predict and determine the social outcomes
for these communities, especially their children. "For North Tulsans there's a
real desire for their child to be better than them," Erica said. "But, you know,
places like the YMCA are great, but the truth is that you go there for their services because you're broke. You've got the facilities at North Mabee, and you
pay what you can when you can." I asked why that was such a problem. Erica
explained that the lack or inconsistency of income led to an irregularity of
services and the insecurity of those that were available. For that reason, the
foundation worked to support the Tulsa Dream Center, which, over the past
year, had helped "about five to six hundred new families coming [in]. Food,
clothing, job stuff, we're partners with them, and especially on early childhood stuff." For all its ambition and promises, there was a limit to what the
foundation could do, or, rather, a limit to what they would do. As Erica mentioned, the foundation found that supporting all its programs and organizations—well over two hundred—was unsustainable. That expenditure was
not even inclusive of its spending on health and education programming.
For that reason and the others mentioned—the condescension toward and
returned suspicion by Black Tulsans—nonprofits were failing many North
Tulsans. I would learn that those North Tulsans turned to a long-serving
source of support: the church. However, I would also learn that in North
Tulsa turning to the church was also complicated by the circuits of poverty
and history that made up the experience of life there.

Jesus, Take the Wheel

Ashley was a "hustler . . . but the good kind," she assured me. Ashley, a recently divorced single mom, worked three jobs. This included her primary
occupation in childcare, where she looked after up to ten toddlers and in-
fants from her home, and many nights when she also worked as a home
health worker, caring for an elderly woman. Additionally, while she cared for
the kids during the day, she ran a "store house" from her apartment, selling

snacks and a few essentials to her neighbors in her apartment complex. I asked Ashley if her work as a home health worker was enough to make ends meet. She responded, "There are always more ends," which was her way of saying no. She also didn't have the proper certification for legit home health work and didn't have the time to get it. Doing so would mean giving up her daycare service while she took courses, and that would make things impossibly difficult. So, instead, she hustled.

All she had was her church, Gates of Refuge. It was a nondenominational church that promised "Life Changing Prophetic Ministry." Gates of Refuge offered something that the more conventional churches could not. It provided her with the necessary *how* that many of us seek in trying to navigate life, especially when that life is riddled with hardship.

At the time Ashley was going through her divorce she had struggled with how she was going to manage the process but more so the consequences. "How am I going to do this?" she shared. "I was working, and it's like I got two kids, and then. . . ." I watched Ashley's expression signal the distress of the remainder of her sentence.

The church ultimately ended up being a source of support as Ashley found a congregant willing to take her in. However, it didn't turn out exactly as she had expected. "The lady from church, she would buy food, but not for me. And plus, I lost my job, and my car broke down, so I would have to buy food when I could. I remember buying bologna and cutting it in half, so I could have something to eat. But at least I had a roof over my head." Ultimately, the "church lady" decided she was ready to leave North Tulsa. "She really wanted to leave and move somewhere else out of town," Ashley shared. When the day came, Ashley was again back on her own.

Despite the inconsistency of its support, the church was there for Ashley. What was evident was that Ashley needed the church, however reliable it was. Hearing of Ashley's experience, I wanted to learn more about the church in North Tulsa to see how it was structurally positioned within the landscape of poverty that Ashley looked to it to help her navigate. Thankfully, I had a contact, my friend Tony, who was a member at North Tulsa's Metropolitan Baptist, a deep North Tulsa institution founded in 1917. It can count Cornel West's grandfather, Rev. Clifton L. West Sr., as a former pastor.[41]

"The churches?!" "Ha! Man, we should be the holiest place in America!" I had only asked Tony a generic question about the church's role in North Tulsa, but it still seemed to trigger an outsize response. "Look, I'm a *Christian*, OK?" Tony emphasized his affiliation to make clear where he stood before going into his characteristic forthrightness. "But we have way too many churches, way too many preachers, in my opinion. There are so many preachers, so many reverends." To make his point, Tony told me a story. "I went to this event the other night, and this lady came in and she said, well, you know, 'I'm from a small church. It's the church of just me, myself, and I.' And I was like, OK, that's your problem *right there*. 'You the preacher, you the member, and then what? What, you take yourself home and look at yourself in the mirror and say, "You sure did preach today!"?'" Gleefully reliving the moment, he asked, "Why she out there by herself on Peoria [preaching]?" He finished with a cackle of sheer sardonic pleasure. It was evident that, as a Christian, Tony delighted in the contradictions of his faith in a way that only made his faith stronger, more resolute. In a more straightforward tone, and now actually responding to my question, he replied, "But seriously, the church is still that place, institutionally, where people can receive some type of relief."

This has historically been the case in North Tulsa. In the aftermath of the 1921 massacre, churches like Mt. Zion Baptist, Vernon AME, and First Baptist Church of North Tulsa were central to rebuilding.[42] The on-the-ground context meaningfully mirrored the circumstances that many North Tulsans faced today. In the wake of the massacre, many were struggling financially, were concerned with housing and employment, and were reckoning with the trauma of surviving severe violence. These matters all show up in the contemporary lived experience, though now more chronically than in the acute circumstances of the massacre. The lack of revenue and organizational structure that prevented the North Tulsa community from receiving its required services, combined with the disconnect with nonprofits, meant the local churches took a vital role in attempting to fight North Tulsa's poverty.

Tony acknowledged that the churches provided relief, so I asked how they were helping. "Like, what part of the issues are the churches invested in?" he queried, returning the question to me as he had become accustomed to doing. I started to reply, "Well, yeah, that's right, because . . ." but before I could finish my sentence, Tony cut me off, saying, "Well, here's the thing, the business of North Tulsa *is* churches. We don't have much of most things, I mean, how many of anything else can you count?" he asked me, I thought rhetorically. He went on to give an account of the few other institutions in the area, like grocery stores, pharmacies, restaurants, and even schools, conveniently disqualifying the Educares. He returned to the question of churches, saying, "Ironically, it depends on which part of North Tulsa you're talking about. But either way, we've got a lot." With a mischievous sparkle in his eye, he finished, "Especially if you count my friend from the 'Church of Me, Myself, and I,'" again laughing.

It was true; Tulsa seemed to have so many churches that it easily warranted the joke that it was "the buckle on the Bible Belt." Just from the number of them alone, it was clear that the issue of churches was as complicated as that of nonprofits. I still wanted to better understand these churches' role, given that they appeared to be both the most present and the most capable to respond to North Tulsans' needs at the community level. Luckily, it was late summer, and school was around the corner. As a result, there were several back-to-school giveaways that I could attend to see the church in action. I attended one hosted by Harvest Time Outreach Ministries in deep North Tulsa but organized by a well-known community organizer and preacher, Reverend Casey.

I introduced myself to Reverend Casey and explained that I was interested in learning the role the church plays in the everyday lives of North Tulsa's residents. He said the best way was to see it up close. So he gave me a job to do that day, which was writing down the names and addresses of all the families who came that morning to collect the goods. These included brand-new backpacks, school supplies, clothes, sneakers, and grocery items. It was quintessential, if not cliché, ethnographic participant observation, and I reveled in the opportunity. I looked at the queue of people and knew that Reverend Casey had gotten the better end of the deal. I would learn throughout my time in Tulsa that Reverend Casey had a knack for such deft negotiations.

At least one hundred families came through that day. When I would later tell Tony that, he sardonically laughed, "Those families probably went to Metropolitan [Church] last week too! Trust me, and they got another book bag too, I see those people in *every* line. They were probably saying to they friends, 'You know, I'm going to go to this church, you going too? Yes, child, Reverend Casey is gonna get me some book bags!' Because they knew they wouldn't have to go to Walmart and buy nothing for school." Tony's cynicism would be shared by others whom I asked about these events. Some went so far as to imply that the families in line were gaming the system and took those items to local stores like Walmart to get store credit. But even that, if true, I saw as symptomatic of the structural issues at hand.

I pushed back, perhaps because I had spent the day at Harvest and heard the stories of some of the people there, saw their circumstances in their and their children's faces. I told Tony that at the school giveaway, I had spoken to several parents who would say, "Well, me and my family, we don't talk," and I would ask, "You need help. Well, who's helping you?" The answer was simply that they were just not getting help. "What are those people to do?" I asked Tony, continuing, "The woman or man who maybe has a few kids, and, you know, the bus isn't running frequently enough to make it to work on time or to their appointments, who are they to rely on?" I told him about Shantel, who was twenty-eight years old, a single mother of two, and was working two low-earning jobs. I told him how she fretted over the demands of work and parenting. That brought about reflections on her own single mother's struggle to take care of her and her siblings and the resulting instability of moving between family members and friends. I told him how Shantel thought about how her grandmother did the same, and so she feared that she might be consumed by this pattern herself, disrupting her daughters' upbringing. These anxieties of intergenerational poverty were shared by many people standing in that line waiting for backpacks, sneakers, gift cards, and books.

Sensing my frustration, Tony turned serious again and explained, "What I'm saying is that the school giveaways are a specific *kind* of thing, my brother. It's not really about the church or kind of, you know, love and caring and what have you." What Tony was trying to get across was that there was something exceptional about events like the school giveaway; they weren't really about the *church* and were not effectively translating the morality of their community. As such, they weren't good examples of how the church helps North Tulsa residents. "It's not about the churches," he added; "it's about the individuals in the church." He explained further:

> You have to get them to be a part of the vision that you are community minded, that you volunteer. This is the point. As an individual, you do have a responsibility. You understand? The pastor, his job is to get them saved and praise the Lord, and I'm with that 100 percent. But then what is your responsibility as a congregant? Not just to come on Sunday, you have to add your voice to the community. You are a participant of this local community as a believer. You have hundreds of believers sitting there saying, "What can I do? Can I do something? Can I break bread with people?" Oh, yes, you can. And if you show that you are really about something, then the pastors would get involved too.

Tony was, in his way, showing me that these exceptional moments couldn't tell me much about how the church worked. I understood, but I had visited a couple of churches during my visits to Tulsa, and I wanted to assess the sense of church beyond the service. I wanted to understand what the churches did and meant within the broader notion of community, that is, the geographic zones of residence and general, perhaps secular, sociality.

There was plenty of overlap with what I was after and what Tony was talking about, through what Todne Thomas brilliantly identifies as *kincraft*. Kincraft is the "the collective relational ethos and community fashioning that undergirds black evangelical religiosity."[43] Kincraft for Thomas encompasses the "the mobilities, intersubjectivities, and sacred imaginaries that have shaped modes of collective black Christian social life."[44] Thomas's framework is applicable in a place like North Tulsa because of the heterogeneity of church offerings. It would be pointless, as Thomas makes clear, to try to approach something amounting to the "Black Church," which Thomas notes is nothing more than an unwieldly monolith. There was certainly what could amount to a notion of spiritual kinship, which according to Thomas commonly happens "between a rock and a hard place," as we saw with Ashley's "church lady."[45] Despite Tony's insistence that the school drive was not representative of how the church worked, the regularity with which many North Tulsans "sampled" different churches, as well as the appearance of churches and the commonplace itinerant preachers—including the preacher of the "Church of Me, Myself, and I"—that circulated in North Tulsa, meant that the secular space of the community was the most appropriate space to analyze the "place" of the church. Moreover, as I would learn, and as I discuss below, the church was deeply involved with the nonprofit industry that encompassed North Tulsa's social services network.

Still, the tension in Tony's comment pointed to the underlying ethics of the church and the way it did or did not correlate with the idea of community. As it turned out, the giveaway had little to do with this idea of community after all. I thought back to the day I had spent at Harvest. I recalled how many people were there, and I don't mean residents seeking the supplies. It turned out that on that day, over five different nonprofit organizations took part in the giveaway. I was disappointed that I hadn't picked up on it right away—there were groups of people each wearing a different colored T-shirt. The volunteers appeared surprisingly multiracial and not representative of a North Tulsan congregation. Additionally, several people at the end of the day had come up to me asking permission to make photocopies of the sign-in lists.

I told the story of the day to Erica, whom I asked to help me understand the relationship between nonprofits and the church. As with Tony, I explained that my job had been to take the names, addresses, and phone numbers. I shared that I figured this was done to maintain contact with families but that I was curious why the families were required to state how many members lived at home. "Oh yeah, those were definitely nonprofit folks," Erica replied. She explained that the sign-in sheets had nothing to do with parishioner follow-up or recruitment for the church but were equivalent to a sales-lead list for a telemarketing company. They wanted to know how many people lived in the household to determine how many children were there, as the higher the child count, the greater the "impact," which I did my best not to read entirely cynically.

One of the groups there was TACSI, the Tulsa Area Community Schools Initiative, which seeks to "help schools and communities develop, align and integrate resources and partnerships between schools, families and neighborhoods to create networks of support that lead to student success."[46] "Yup," said Erica, "that's how these events go. The church has inroads to the community, or at least it's like a place they trust; so, the orgs [organizations] go to them to help host events. For the churches it's good publicity, meets their missions and so forth." After thinking for a moment, she continued, "Well, if you think about it, it's good publicity for the orgs too." I wondered why these groups felt the need to reach the community in this way.

The state and its related institutions and organizations are often viewed as a secular phenomenon that seeks to exert influence outside of, if not in opposition to, the church and not through it. "So, I mean, the Black community here in North Tulsa, I would say, is *very* insulated," Erica emphasized. "It's go home; stay home; don't come out." I asked Erica if she thought that introducing the various highways running through the communities had contributed to this lack of public activity in the community: "Yeah, the highways did a lot of that." As a result, going to church was one of the few occasions that brought North Tulsans together. Shameca's early advice rang in my mind: she had suggested attending church and Booker T. football games if I wanted to meet North Tulsans. "So, really, it's the church; I mean, everybody is going to be in church, *everybody*. Not a soul will miss it," Erica continued. I asked what that meant for community outreach, and Erica explained that the churches had access to the community but couldn't always help them. So nonprofits sought churches out to gain access to and establish credibility with the community. Erica went further, "Because everybody is in church on Sunday, and that's not an exaggeration, and people believe what the pastor says—skepticism is not paramount, and they believe what he says—it's an effective way to reach the community."

Erica's words recalled Tony's assertion about the pastors' influence over the congregation for engaging in community advocacy. For this reason, organizations sought to partner with churches. Erica helped explain why: "Churches have extensive reach into low-income communities." She continued, "I mean, I go to services to see what's going on. I mean [it's] just drastic, abject poverty. I mean, in the clearest sense, our demographic is up in North Tulsa. So if we are already capitalizing on these things and they have [access], why don't we work with these churches?"

Church and State

Organizations like the KFF wanted to work with churches in low-income communities, especially those already involved in synergistic activities—what Erica referred to as "the sort of things that we want them to be involved in." For example, churches took "a strength-based approach to these organizations," such as encouraging talking through prayer, reading through scripture, and singing through church choir. These existing strengths worked neatly and conveniently with one of the foundation's initiatives, "Talk. Read. Sing." Erica gave other examples of how her organization worked with local churches, supporting after-school programs and family nights that fostered intense educational development. The point is that the churches they selected had significant reach into the local communities, sought after precisely because they were poor. The intention to partner with smaller churches resulted from their proximity to and contact with the target demographics that the foundation sought to serve.

Not every nonprofit is as financially independent as the KFF. Many nonprofits sit on the other side of the power equation with churches and become reliant on access and resources. I returned to Reverend Jonathan, who still insisted I call him Reverend, despite the dozens of reverends I met, to ask about this relationship and wondered what he thought, given his efforts in organizing food resources for local North Tulsans. His organization was a grassroots effort that resisted the call to work within the parameters of the nonprofit-church dynamic. The partnerships between nonprofits and churches also took the form of many churches functioning as nonprofit organizations. With their tax-exempt status, they could facilitate social programs that would make them eligible for the same state and federal grants as formal nonprofits. Reverend had plenty to say about the way the whole system worked.

"When you ask who's got the power in Tulsa, there's usually a big silence. When you press people, they start thinking, well, the Chamber of Commerce and, you know, the *Tulsa World* and then folks like the Kaisers." The hypothetical choices he listed all sounded like entirely feasible, if not likely, answers. "But what you realize is that attached to all of those, when you really start thinking, they're all attached to major churches in Tulsa." Admittedly, there was something conspiratorial about the suggestion. It took a trip to Oklahoma City, the state capital, for Reverend to fully appreciate how power operated in Tulsa.

"It became really clear to me, Oklahoma City, it's just a different dynamic. It's the state capital, so the megachurches there . . . are just *a* part of the power structure of the city itself, because they got politicians who *are* the power. When you have politicians, who are the power structure, they're the ones you go after." This presumption of state functioning made me find the collaboration with the churches in Tulsa so odd. In Tulsa a different power arrangement existed that was located directly where the wealth was, and much of that wealth was in the megachurches. "It's where the wealthiest people in Tulsa are," said Reverend. "You know, in them pews, with the kind of folks who have a lot of the power sitting in them." Erica also viewed the megachurch as a site of significant power in Tulsa. In further explaining her rationale for targeting smaller churches, she illustrated the power of the megachurch: "We have plenty of megachurches, OK? You have one that has like fifteen thousand people there on a Sunday, which is in Broken Arrow, just east of [Tulsa]. And I thought to myself, you know, they're not really the population we're looking for because they're fifteen thousand White upper-middle-class individuals who donate massive amounts. That church literally owns a part of the city of Broken Arrow, and they are the largest landowners in Broken Arrow aside from the government." Erica was referring to Church on the Move, a two-campus nondenominational church based in Tulsa and Broken Arrow, with a membership of over twelve thousand.[17]

In North Tulsa, we weren't talking about millionaire megachurches with tens of thousands of congregants like in South Tulsa or out west in Broken Arrow. That said, churches still wielded significant power, even if they were poor, Black, and in the north. With or without the wealth, that power to decide what kinds of programs got access to community residents had real consequences for how organizations ran social programs in Tulsa. Reverend argued that those churches, because of the views of their congregations, "don't want to see a lot of grassroots community-based work pushing the envelope." The envelope could be anything that the church was against, and what could be addressed were largely conservative issues. "You know, they'll focus on education, and education, *and education*." What Reverend was saying made sense once I began to evaluate the programs that existed, at least in the majority.

Many organizations focused on education, as the KFF's suite of programs demonstrates. None of the organizations that I encountered during my time in Tulsa focused on many other issues. I was surprised by the lack of focus on economic improvement. "You know, first thing they say we're not going to touch social issues," which to Reverend was shorthand for topics like gender equity and overt race issues, "because if you want to touch social issues, it leads you to morality and such. And on that, you can't get any consensus. No, they're very content to focus on the, you know, the other stuff." The irony was revelatory. Here was an entire system focused on serving the poor, alleviating poverty, but none wanted to solve the core intersectional issues contributing to poverty. Instead, identifying the various symptoms of poverty, namely, poor health, education, and sometimes incarceration, was satisfactory. And somehow alleviating those symptoms was supposed to miraculously cure the disease that caused them. Such, I suppose, is how money works in the resolution of social problems.

In trying to understand the trouble of "consensus," as Reverend called it, during my visit to Harvest, I asked one of the local Black pastors, who was also on-site that day, about consensus among pastors within the Black community. Curiously, the pastor asked if our conversation was "off the record." I laughed and said that I would make sure to keep him anonymous. Agreeing, the pastor very bluntly said that Black pastors "hardly cooperate, much less come to consensus." Sensing my shock, he quickly clarified that his reason was that "there's a lot of egos involved, a lot of egos." Dissatisfied with the explanation of "egos," I asked for further clarification. The pastor explained the issues behind what he called egos: "You know, it's just scarcity. When you feel like if somebody else is getting attention, getting funds, then, you know, you're going to have a tendency to hold grudges and not want to cooperate or just do your thing to build yourself up so you could be on equal standing with others. But I can clearly say that I know that it's, you know, that narrative is alive in our Black community, all around us. And there's certainly a lot of evidence, you know, that people give, you know, you can see to kind of back that up." The pastor had a sharper criticism: "And of course, you know, you have those few that got that ideology of prosperity and everything else. So that kind of kicks in, and it feeds into that difficulty to work together. In some ways cooperation is a luxury." The idea of cooperation as luxury was peculiar and fascinating. In many of the discussions that I had in North Tulsa, cooperation, solidarity, or unity was a prerequisite for the Black community's identity and composition.

Before jumping to any conclusions about the implications of the claim, I asked the pastor to explain precisely why he felt cooperation was a luxury. He explained that it was "the hammer of inequality" that reduced available resources. "And so people blame each other. And take it out on each other. It's the hammer." He went on to explain that churches, because of this inequality, were necessarily competitive. "You know, it's not like the Catholics or even AME or maybe some of the Baptist churches where you have some real organization. Some hierarchy. You have some that have a management structure. Most of us [small churches] don't have that because anybody can just be a preacher and they can have a church and they can say whatever doctrine they want." In illustrating how this "structure" of church organization impacted actual cooperation, he explained why there were so many churches in Tulsa. "And the reason we have so many is because this preacher didn't like that preacher, so he broke away. Now we got the First United, you know, but we've got Creek District because they didn't like the leadership in Creek District. So they formed First United, and then they didn't like the leadership. So First United broke up and formed Five Star." The pastor suggested I look into ministers' experience in mostly White South Tulsa for comparison.

I brought this suggestion back to Reverend, whose own experiences brought me the clarity I sought. "On the south side of town—and I have a little bit of experience over there, where I served in a church for one year; anyway, it's all cooperation because all of those ministers have full-time ministry jobs." I was unfamiliar with the notion of a minister not being full-time. "You know, when you're bivocational or trivocational, like most of our Black ministers are," Reverend explained, revealing a significant distinction in class among church leadership. The challenges of multiple employment meant that pastors were doing their best to hustle. But it also meant that they were keen to develop partnerships with local organizations and nonprofits, who were happy to "serve" their congregations. Which institution was leading the other in these arrangements became hard to determine.

Going back to my visit to Harvest, I initially thought the church was providing the supplies for the day. In truth, the provisions were mainly the doing of the various organizations present. While the consumable and wearable goods might seem apolitical enough, to be sure, a significant amount of "educational" material, by which I mean pamphlets and other organizational resource information, accompanied the school supplies and vouchers. The church benefited from the publicity, as very few of the people in line for supplies were members of the congregation. I had my suspicions that other, more direct benefits had been arranged; however, my attempt at speaking to the pastor or even his son proved fruitless. Furthermore, I could tell the matter was a sensitive one, which perhaps provides some support for my suspicion, however speculative.

The church had played a major role in the postmassacre reconstruction of Greenwood, and I wondered how much I could or should read into what I could only call a diminished situation. It's unclear if it's fair to compare the structural circumstances of Greenwood to contemporary North Tulsa in this instance. The church during the days of Greenwood was a central institution in every way, and it was more of the monolithic "Black Church" that Thomas tries to trouble through kincraft. But the truth is that the church provided more than spiritual and personal refuge in the context of segregation and Jim Crow. It was the cornerstone of every aspect of social life, a source and site of power unlike any other. It was the place where Black potential and capability could most express itself. The church was a humanizing institution in that it provided Black people space and forms to be fully human, to pursue its perfection, and to acknowledge their shortcomings and seek redemption. It allowed for those movements to play out in a domain that was secure, or at least as secure as possible. To be sure, the church has always demanded much posturing, which has limited, and too often continues to limit, the degree to which one can exercise one's "full" humanity. For instance, queer humanity is still a threat to and in turn is threatened by many churches, especially in Oklahoma, and in Tulsa, again the so-called buckle on the Bible Belt.

Nevertheless, the authority that the church held in Greenwood was now diffused. A church's influence depends on its congregation, and its success depends on the wherewithal of that congregation. With the decades of community dispossession in North Tulsa, it is understandable for the church to have changed as an institution. There are, of course, exceptions. Metropolitan Baptist in North Tulsa is immensely popular, especially with Black professional-class Christians across Tulsa. The pastor there, Dr. Ray A. Owens, holds theological degrees from Princeton and leads a church whose motto is "The Church That Cares is WHO we are. Love Beyond Walls is WHAT we do," promising a church environment of acceptance. The foundational churches of Vernon AME and Mt. Zion continue to wield immense influence owing to the value and import of their history.

This was the case especially for Vernon AME, which in 2017 received a new young pastor in Reverend Robert Turner. He had arrived from Alabama and thought that he would "simply" pastor in such a small city. Instead, Turner worked to revive the church, where membership had fallen to below one hundred congregants. The significance of Vernon's location on Greenwood Avenue was not lost on Turner, who could see how the massacre and urban renewal had impacted the community around the church, although they occurred many years and decades before his arrival.

As part of his ministry, Turner took up the cause of reparations for that history. In 2018 he began a weekly march to City Hall to protest and demand reparations, with only his Bible, his bullhorn, and his belief in the cause. Over time the crowd that marched with him grew, as did Vernon AME's congregation. Turner became a regular advocate in North Tulsa and helped influence the relaunch of the search for race massacre victims' mass graves, joining the Public Oversight Mass Graves Excavation Committee.

Turner became a spokesperson for Greenwood with a growing national reputation that saw several 2020 presidential candidates visit Vernon during the election. He put this publicity to work, and through grants and donations from several philanthropies that included Schusterman Foundation, George Kaiser Family Foundation, and the Zarrow Foundation, Turner obtained funding of over a million dollars for church renovation, outreach programs, and a Prayer Wall for Racial Healing, officially opened during the 2021 centenary. Turner had truly become North Tulsa's pastor.

While reaching a healthy proportion of the Black community in Tulsa, these churches still exist among a seemingly never-ending offering of alternatives. This competitiveness created choice, which local Tulsans fully exploited. I recalled from our conversation how Ashley said that she had changed churches several times over the past few years. This practice departs from Black communities' historical association with their church and pastor, which commanded a lifelong and intergenerational devotion.

Perhaps the issue was not with the church but with the sense or structure of the community. Without the safeguarding that allows community residents to remain in their neighborhoods, as well as the much-mentioned lack of class diversity in those communities, the community itself lacks the kind of coherence or stability that provides for the long-term sustainability of any given church. On the other side of the equation, these churches with relatively poor congregants can't deliver the kinds of nonspiritual services that these communities need. Thus, they are at the mercy of the interests of the nonprofits and other organizations, which saw them solely as conduits for community access. Churches that were once sources of support for their communities are now mere intermediaries between the communities and nonprofits.

Though less robust a form of social security than in the immediate wake of the race massacre, the church in North Tulsa still serves as one of the only hubs of community formation. The deep religiosity of most, if not all, North Tulsans means that even though there is a broader choice of churches, many of which lie outside of North Tulsa, the church's place could not be displaced, especially not by nonprofits. Therefore, the hybridized function of the church-nonprofit would have to do. While this is perhaps a compromised arrangement of support, in which the interests of both the churches and the nonprofits often overshadow the precise needs of the community, they were necessary resources given the generations of disinvestment that fell upon North Tulsa.

Social instability, economic precariousness, and emotional vulnerability have shown up in the life experiences of North Tulsa's residents in variable but persistent ways. They show the absence of support in their networks and community. Poverty and its impact on school access, home environments, and access to health care all prevented community members, like Shantel and Keisha, from overcoming structural impediments and taking advantage of opportunities that did arise. It also reduced the ability for community members to be there for each other. Such is the life of poverty in general. But understanding this hardship within the context of North Tulsa demands looking past an individual's circumstances alone to measure their difficulties. It requires looking at the living complex of social inequality rendered through racial and gender disparities at the community level and at the way the community as a troubled form is mediated through this narrative. As it were, Ashley's need to hustle highlights the idea that through the development of varied skills, products, and services, a simultaneous growth of opportunity and autonomy can be created. The fear of reproducing the injury of intergenerational and intersectional poverty and the devastation of living through it speaks to the diminishing of support from kin relations and the security and development those relations typically provide.

These women are testaments to surviving social, economic, and racial inequality. Their survival, as a strategy of flexibility, is an act of everyday resistance, with that flexibility representing a series of techniques employed to secure economic and social mobility. However, access to the means of advancement has fallen to the control of nonprofits and philanthropies. These organizations have come to increasingly mediate the relationships and the experiences between poor African Americans in Tulsa and their economic and social circumstances and opportunities. This capacity grants these organizations the power to influence the North Tulsan community not only in the critical minutiae of everyday family and community life but as a totalizing metanarrative of their identity.

North Tulsa's community is framed as devoid of wealth and movement. As a historical and cultural narrative, these ideas contribute to the aberrant qualification of Blackness, history, and the products of that history. And so, without community resources and individual wherewithal, however imagined, the residents of North Tulsa must rely on the interventions of churches, state agencies, and other programs. For this reason, if North Tulsa is ever going to recover the legacy of Greenwood, it would need to address the root issue, which for them was the problem of community formation and functionality.

THREE. RESTORATION

Over the past century, the area that encompasses historic Greenwood and contemporary North Tulsa underwent both material and metaphoric changes. The aftermath of the 1921 race massacre and several other forces overdetermined the transformation. Greenwood transformed as it moved north, which helped to create a generalized and racialized sense of North Tulsa. "[Greenwood] was a central kind of business district. So you had kind of a purely business district that was developing up from that time," Reverend told me. "You had the development up at the time of Greenwood, you know, Negro Wall Street, which was really close to downtown, which was also a thriving White business area." He continued, "And then with the race riot in '21, you had that exodus, you know, lots of refugees from Greenwood settled even further north, and some kept going north, outta the state!" He paused to reflect. "Yeah. The riot really devastated the kind of growing Black community," Reverend said with a pensive sadness.

The race massacre in 1921 did not destroy Greenwood. Greenwood rebuilt itself through deeply sourced willpower, resources, and skill and a similarly deep well of resilience—entirely bolstered by both the capacity for and institutions of faith. I am not romanticizing the conditions of Greenwood—the Greenwood of Black Wall Street was very much a class-based society with elites, the working class, and the working poor. Nevertheless, Greenwood was self-reliant, mainly owing to Jim Crow.

The massacre had a major consequence: the capacity to produce incapacity. While the massacre did not destroy Greenwood outright and did not inhibit its ability to rebuild, it did stop the area from developing further. As the surrounding city continued to progress, Greenwood, by comparison, regressed materially and economically. This dynamic turned Greenwood into an unremarkable Black space, vulnerable to exploitation, if not wholly primed for it.

Economic hardship defines the life of North Tulsa's community, and it is the consequence of the compounding effects of the 1921 massacre, Jim Crow racism, and the systematic dispossession that followed in their wake. Leadership is a challenge, but to the folks of North Tulsa, they must employ a collective notion, or ethic, of cooperation, which was at the heart of Greenwood's historical success. This collective ideal successfully countered, or perhaps merely resisted, the overwhelming impact of Jim Crow. It is therefore a viable means for alleviating poverty and the various disparities involved in its maintenance for the community of North Tulsa.

While several issues complicate the revival of Greenwood's legacy in North Tulsa, one in particular stands out. The issue of grocery stores speaks most to the confluence of current hardship and the quality of Greenwood's past achievement. In Tulsa's District 1, which comprises most of North Tulsa, 93 percent of the population lacks access to affordable fresh food within a mile of where they live.[1] This comes out to nearly forty-two thousand people. This dearth of resources led to a furor in North Tulsa when the only grocery store in the area closed in 2014.

The store, Gateway Market, was located at Pine and Peoria. Antonio Perez, the owner, also owns several Latin American supermarkets around the city. Perez admitted that the store closed because it wasn't turning a profit.[2] I first arrived in Tulsa for fieldwork just two weeks after the closure, so the matter was still hotly debated and contested. Perez had received $2.2 million in Community Block Development Grant Small Business Loan funds from the Tulsa City Council to open the store in 2010. At the time, North Tulsa was effectively a food desert. The area had been without a grocery store since national chain supermarket Albertsons had closed in that exact location in 2007. Gateway Market had opened after North Tulsa had endured three years without a grocery store, and it was the only supermarket for miles. Its closing, then, once again left North Tulsans without accessible food options. Moreover, many of the community's members had trouble accessing the next nearest store.

North Tulsa residents shared their frustrations about Gateway Market's closure with local media. One shopper interviewed after the closure, Terri, complained that she would have to "catch a bus, then transfer and catch another bus to go, [and] it's going to be really hard because of the heat." But Terri was determined to find a way. "Gotta feed my kids somehow," she said. "I can't let them say, 'I'm hungry,' and not get them nothing."[3] Those who owned or had access to cars drove south to Midtown Tulsa or southeast, where many Walmarts and other grocery stores like Reasor's and Trader Joe's dotted the commercial landscape. To many local nonprofits working in the community, the low quality of the available options earned North Tulsa the designation of being both a food desert and a food swamp.

The memory of the Albertsons closure was still fresh enough for local shoppers to appreciate the consequences of Gateway Market's closure. Another shopper, David, declared when interviewed, "Everybody's frustrated, the whole neighborhood. You know, I mean, they ain't got no cars, no way of getting their groceries. What they going to do now?"[4] "When we say we want a grocery store, we're not talking about Family Dollar or Dollar General; we're talking about someplace to get apples and oranges for me," said Jomekia Marks in a separate interview. Another North Tulsa resident, Sheila Fuselier, agreed but framed the issue within a broader analysis of the commercial landscape in North Tulsa: "We also need shopping centers in this area. Because the majority of the time [when] we have to go out and buy clothes and materials, we have to go out south or to the east or wherever instead of spending our money in our community."[5]

"So, you know, I was driving around looking, and I hardly saw any grocery stores, none really," I explained to Marlon, a local Black Tulsan who ran a community garden project in North Tulsa. "Yeah, the food thing," Marlon said, replying in a way that made it clear that my observation was in no way a revelation. Picking up on this, I responded, "So where do they go?" He responded, "Fast food, tons of fast food—Taco Bell, Church's, Popeye's. It's basically a food desert, food swamp scenario." Reflecting further, Marlon, recognizing the intractability of the matter, acknowledged, "Yeah, that food thing *is* an issue." Clarifying, he continued, "When folks shop for food, they're going to go to like a Dollar General." Pausing for a moment to reflect, he continued, "Well, there's Warehouse Market on Sixty-First and Peoria, which is weird because the name would make you think that it's, like, bulk or cheaper, right? But Warehouse Market doesn't charge less; they actually charge more! But they're there, and because they're there, people will go. So it's the weirdest thing, because they charge outrageous prices, for crap food." I checked out Warehouse Market and confirmed what Marlon claimed. While the food cost was an obvious point of frustration, the lack of food access was nearly devastating and had become a regular talking point in the local media, especially after Safeway shuttered all its grocery stores in the state, but in North Tulsa it was the closure of the Albertsons that had portended the coming crisis in access.[6]

Over a series of discussions with North Tulsa residents, I would find that many of them did a significant amount of their weekly shopping at QuikTrip gas stations. When I asked Marlon about it, he explained, "Look, especially in some of the rough neighborhoods, they are sometimes one of the few, like, cheap options for groceries but also just for hot food. It's a gas station, sure, but the thing is gas is like only about 10 to 15 percent of their profit—it's all food. It can be quality sometimes for a lot of people, but for most, it's their *one* option." I saw the QuikTrip had QT Kitchens, which offered cooked food like pizzas, sandwiches, chicken, and hot dogs. Poor Tulsans regularly utilized QT Kitchens for breakfast. Still, Marlon assured me that that was the case for "many Tulsans, rich or poor."

Although Gateway Market's owner had argued that he closed the store because residents didn't shop there enough to maintain a viable business, he decided to reopen the store two months later. There were murmurs of government pressure among members of the community, given the millions provided to open the original store. "We have everything; we have the produce; we have the 5 for \$25 in meats," Perez said in an interview. "We have the deli, we have the dairy . . . and we'll have the bakery open too." The first version of Gateway Market had been large, comparable in size to any chain grocery store, but it reopened at a much smaller scale. "Since it's been closed already—why don't you try a smaller version and see what happens," Perez said. "Give it a last try, and if it doesn't work then say goodbye, but hopefully it's going to work. I'm going to run the store, this time if it doesn't work out then something is wrong—because I'm going to be here," he said.[7] I visited after the reopening, and it was strange to see only one-quarter of the store open. The rest of the store remained partially hidden by an aisle of refrigerated goods and stood hauntingly empty, dark and cavernous. Nevertheless, the stocked items seemed fresh and adequate to serve the community.

I was back in Tulsa two years later, just before Gateway Market would close for good. The store, while still operating within the same footprint, was markedly different. The abandoned square footage of the original store seemed even more ominous. Bare shelves dotted the store, and the ceiling leaked into at least half a dozen buckets scattered around. Despite the shop's dire shape, locals still depended on it and again lamented the closure to local media. "Now we'll have to walk further down that way," said Lindsey, who was interviewed while shopping with her husband and her baby. "There's that Dollar Store down that way," she said, contemplating her options, referring to the likely recourse of most North Tulsans. "I don't know what people would do if this store shut down," another shopper, Joel, said. "More grocery stores and less QuikTrips and liquor stores," he said in an assessment of what the North Tulsa grocery landscape needed.[8]

For Antonio Perez, the closure was due to a lack of "community support." The choice of words was bold. In the first closure, he had noted a lack of profitability. This time around, Perez framed profitability as support: "Every business is there to make money and needs the community support, and when you don't get it, you have to quit at some time," Perez explained. Oddly, Perez interpreted "support" as demand: "[The shoppers] were hoping to get very low prices, which we couldn't do because our overhead and our volume not being the same as the big chains."[9] However, the shoppers I talked to countered that the store did not cater to their needs and often sold food near expiration. Regardless of the cause, the store officially closed in November 2017. It would be another three years until a new store broke ground to serve the North Tulsa community. Until then, the residents did whatever shopping they could at convenience stores, QuikTrip gas stations, or local dollar stores, as they had done in the years between Albertsons' closure and Gateway Market's initial opening. It was, it seemed, a return to normalcy and a deserted landscape that was indeed a food desert.

The Great Gathering

The multiple grocery store closures caused North Tulsa's residents to reflect on the precarity of their food access. The instability that Gateway Market's initial closure, reopening, and ultimate closure represented meant that the only solution to secure access was for North Tulsans to open their "own" grocery store. They needed and deserved a Black-owned store and thought they shouldn't be beholden to the whims of a business owner who wasn't a part of the community. Moreover, a non-Black owner's disconnect from the community could easily mean putting profit over people. I witnessed this sentiment in action at an "all call for all people" community meeting/brainstorming session on opening and operating a grocery store. The event, superlatively titled "The Great Gathering," called on all (primarily respectable) community sectors to come together and work out what it would take. The event featured presentations by speakers who represented various Black organizations and churches in the community and video screenings of successful community-owned and -operated grocery stores around the United States.

"Greetings, friends and neighbors and fellow Tulsans! Welcome to an 'all call for all people.' A great gathering of collaboration for grocery stores in Tulsa's north community. We are very glad that you are here!" went the introductory welcome by Clifton Durante III. Clifton was a local Tulsa K–12 teacher and a community organizer through his ESTEEM Community Development Organization. According to Clifton, ESTEEM "is in the business of saving and changing the lives of disadvantaged children, their families, and individuals." Clifton was also a committed Christian with master's degrees in divinity and school administration from Oral Roberts University, a Christian university in Tulsa. On his LinkedIn page, Clifton expressed a personal mission "to help individuals reach their full potential through edification, exhortation, education, motivation, goal setting, dreaming big, and working hard."[10]

Clifton had trouble with the presentation technology at the start of the meeting. Using it as a teaching moment and the first glimpse of his manifesto, he said, "I have my tech guy because I'm not the best at technology, so when you can't do something, then you find someone who can do it better. And you bring them on board with you. And that's how you have success. You don't have to be the best at everything you do. Just find other people to put around you that's great at what you do." The "yesses," "mm-hmms," and head nodding were an immediate and telling sign that Clifton was already at work.

Clifton had called the meeting to get the community to debate North Tulsa's lack of a grocery store and imagine and decide on an alternative. Though he was adamant that this was a community decision, Clifton had already considered various models for the grocery store. The first was a community-owned and -run grocery store, something akin to a co-op. The second was for the community to buy shares in an independent, profit-seeking grocery store. The third was to open a grocery store that was a nonprofit, to which the community could make tax-deductible donations to cover part of its operational funding. The fourth option was that several individuals might open their own, albeit smaller, grocery stores.

The fifth model was a broadening of the mobile grocery store run by R&G Family Grocers. Owing to the lack of access, R&G Family Grocers' Real Good Food Truck circulated throughout underserved areas of Tulsa and dedicated half of their stops to North Tulsa. Clifton shared that a representative was supposed to be at the meeting but couldn't make it. I would later learn that R&G was run by the Healthy Community Store Initiative. This nonprofit's mission is "to enhance the health of Oklahomans by providing access to quality, fresh food through healthy community stores, nutrition education, economic opportunities and community revitalization."[11] R&G Family Grocers started with a $50,000 grant from the Helmerich Foundation and $20,000 from the Kaiser Family Foundation, as well as funding from the Zarrow Family Foundation. It was no wonder that Clifton spent extra time discussing the success of the Real Good Food Truck. While he didn't seem keen on a mobile grocery store, he was undoubtedly very taken by their ability to get it funded through grants.

Whether we decided to work toward a single community-owned grocery store, a set of community-owned grocery stores, or any of the other options Clifton put forward, he invited us to "bring new ideas to the table." "And if we want new ideas," Clifton said, "we need people to come in with different ways of thinking. We don't want to just be stuck with the old stuff. We need new thinking." We were broken into several groups to do just that. I was in group number 3 with an eclectic bunch of Tulsans; to my luck, one of them was local journalist Roberta Clardy, owner of the local *North Tulsa Magazine*.

Our discussion started with a reflection on the incident that had prompted the meeting: the closure of Gateway Market. "Before Gateway closed . . . do you remember the stock? The shelves were *very* thin. Those people [the owners] never really invested in Gateway or put stock in it. So we need to find a way to build the spirit up, the spirit of unity, and then we can move forward with that, because everybody's eating. So what's the problem?" These were the comments of Valerie, a retired Department of Motor Vehicles (DMV) employee. A talkative older gentleman named Paul insisted the problem had a straightforward solution. As we all turned to him, curious about his idea and intrigued by his claim that it was straightforward, he proceeded to sing, "You got to give the people, give the people what they want!" "Y'all remember that song?! The O'Jays, boy, I tell you!" A couple of us busted out laughing, but Paul was serious. He interrupted the laughter: "No! They said that the people want better education, *better food to eat*," emphasizing the latter to make sure we got the connection, before he continued, "better housing, and equality!" Seeing how quickly the novelty of the song reference faded, Paul followed with a more profound analysis and prescription. "There are billions of dollars in this community that is going outside to the other grocery stores, and if we can keep the same money here in the community, it'll make a big difference." Picking up on the community-centered capitalism, Paul shared, "That's right, because if we don't do it, then some company can come in and just build a business into North Tulsa, and it's their business.

And sure, they'll hire some folks, but it's not like they'll build something for the value of the community."

At this point, Valerie reminded us to get back to the questions that Clifton wanted us to address. "What were they again?" asked Paul. Stephanie, a local teacher who had arrived in Tulsa through Teach for America, answered, "We're supposed to create a vision of what kind of store that we want; think about how we want the store to look, how we want it to feel, how can we raise the funds to develop community-owned grocery stores, and how can we get others involved in developing the grocery store." Tiffany, a teacher's aide at the North Tulsa Educare, recommended food choices that went back to Valerie's comment about Gateway's thin shelves. Tiffany argued, "The grocery store is not gonna be helpful to your house, no matter how big it is or how small, if it doesn't have the things that most people use daily, like seasoned salt!" she said half-jokingly. "For instance, some of these stores don't have seasoning salt, and I like seasoning salt in my food. So, if I go to a grocery and they don't have it . . ." The answer was indicated by her facial expression. "I mean, you have to have the things that most people use *and want*, right, Paul?!" Tiffany joked, referencing Paul's O'Jays invocation.

Stephanie then suggested that we start with just a description of the qualities we wanted. "So, Tiffany is saying a store should be responsive, like they should have what customers want?" "Yeah, responsive," Tiffany replied. "You know, like what do the people like actually want to be on the shelves?" Stephanie thought for a second, then responded carefully, challenging the question of responsiveness and Tiffany's predilection for seasoned salt, saying, "You want them to be responsive, but at the same time, you don't want them to be too responsive, right? Because, you know, seasoned salt isn't the best thing for you. And so there's giving a community what it wants, . . . but you also need to give the people what they need." Paul's O'Jays reference had lasting power after all. "But," Stephanie continued, "I think we need to educate them [shoppers] about what other options there might be. And I know that might be the challenge because you don't want to simply bring in, you know, sodium facts or the harmful effects of hydrogenated oil and corn syrup." "You know," Valerie stated, "if you get to the schools and each school has a community garden, and the store has a community garden, then you're opening up the minds because the children will influence their parents, who are not likely to change."

While supportive of the general notion of a community garden, the group mainly looked perplexed because they couldn't see the connection to the grocery store. Valerie, observing this, sought to clarify: "If we start with the children, you know, and have the store have its own garden that the kids and families can access, you know, they can literally pick their own vegetable, then the whole family starts eating healthier. And then the children branch out from the seasoned salt. Right? And that kind of thing. So we really need to deal with that with the schools and the community garden."

Valerie began to develop on a proper tangent, discussing how we could use raised beds in the garden because "the older folks in the garden, with the bending over and getting down and the knee conditions, and all that, kind of makes it hard for them." Stephanie, supporting Valerie, said, "The grocery store should actually create a connection with food, right?" "Right!" Valerie began to reply before Paul interjected, "Well, not everything in those stores, of course, is grown; they had to purchase something, and finances will have to be raised to purchase certain things." It appeared that two sides had emerged, Valerie and Stephanie on one and Paul and Tiffany on the other. Valerie tried to salvage her point, retorting, "Remember, the rule of thumb is when you go in the grocery store, don't go through the middle aisles. Stay on the perimeter! That's where you get your healthy food. When you start getting into the middle, then you're getting into the processed stuff, like season salt."

"Yeah, that's right," Paul said, accommodating Valerie. "But you still have a community that wants those convenience foods, and you must appeal to that community, too. I mean, I know that I, I love healthy food—hell, I had a banana this morning!—but I still like convenience food." "So do you think maybe it's like a mixture?" asked Tiffany. Paul jumped back in, adding, "You can't forget about the food stamps! I was at a Family Dollar yesterday, and they had a sign up for one of the NOS energy drinks, and it said you couldn't use EBT for this. Make sure that whatever we're selling, you can buy on the food stamps."

For all his joking and frenetic energy, Paul, with his references to the O'Jays and EBT, was the only one in the group who seemed keen to center the current needs, or at least preferences, as he saw them, of North Tulsans. The rest of the group appeared to have interpreted Clifton's instructions as a request to not just think differently about a grocery store but also rethink the shopping population. Their recommendations were as much an assessment of North Tulsans' habits as they were about the expectations for a store. I found this particularly fascinating as the framing seemed to replicate the nonprofit model that identified the problem plaguing the community as the community. It was the community itself that needed retooling and not their circumstances. The grocery store would thus function as a civilizing device.[12] They would become better people, literally in their bodies, through better consumption. Moreover, this approach deemed the community incapable of deciding what they wanted, which was the price for being granted access to necessary services in the community. The dependency logic was profound. It had become a point of self-identification. This point was made evident by the discourse of education that came up in the discussion.

"OK, so we're going to have like an educational component, right?" asked Stephanie. "Teaching things like what ways and items can you substitute? In what ways can you, like, begin to learn how to combine different foods to make a healthy meal?" Stephanie's recommendation stemmed from personal experience, she explained. "I teach at McLain, and I would bring homemade things that students would say, 'That looks gross,'" she said. Tiffany and Valerie slyly gave a mocking look at each other in response to Stephanie's statement. Still, Stephanie continued, "They would say, 'I'm not going to eat that,' and I would say, 'You know, why don't you come over here and try it?'" Valerie's and Tiffany's looks became more obvious as Stephanie continued, "So they would try it and say, 'Oh, it's not so bad!'" Tiffany couldn't let the moment pass without asking Stephanie where she was from. "Minnesota," Stephanie answered. "Oh, OK!" replied Tiffany, transparently. Stephanie's point was about the importance of exposure. "They tried something that they weren't used to and were curious and interested. It takes talking through it, allowing them to be open." The group agreed. Our final idea was the desire for a store that sold healthy foods and convenient foods and educated shoppers on the difference and how to choose the former. It also had to guarantee that all products, no matter their health value, would be available through SNAP. It would also possibly have a community garden. "Giving the people what they want" was going to be a challenge, at least for the people in my group.

"So how we are we gonna pay for it?" asked Paul. "Because that's a biggie," he emphasized. We all bandied about a variety of suggestions. Paul suggested sending a proposal to the mother of Kevin Durant, who played for the Oklahoma City Thunder (OKC) basketball team at the time, as well as to other athletes. Felix Jones and Robert Meacham, two Tulsa natives who played in the National Football League (NFL), were obvious choices. "But anyway, I know it's just a long shot," Paul quickly conceded, "but that's my fantasy, my personal fantasy."

Next up was the idea of donations from the community. "Or, you know, like Clifton was talking about, the stock, about putting stock in or something, I don't know, but basically bringing the people into it. How do you do that?" Valerie asked.

Roberta, who had joined the conversation late, suggested memberships like at Costco. "What should the membership be? Because there needs to be funds for these stores," Valerie said, indicating skepticism that such a model would be able to support a store. Stephanie agreed, insinuating that poverty meant that North Tulsa might not be able to sustain a membership model: "I think it also depends geographically because, you know, some parts of North Tulsa are more disenfranchised than others." She continued, "We have to think about how the funds and community involvement can be connected. Specifically, how do we match stakeholders to a specific part of the vision?"

After further discussion, we had come to a plan, which Stephanie presented. As each group took their turn presenting, something of a unified vision for the grocery store emerged—or at least a consistent sense of what it needed to do. Groups wanted a larger grocery store rather than several smaller stores. Many groups suggested that a large store would produce trust and prevent competition in the community. "You know, just to decrease the sense of competition between stores and solidify a place where a grocery store can bring everyone together, get to know each other, and build trust," said the representative for group 4. All groups wanted fresh produce, and one group wanted to prioritize assisting elderly shoppers: "You know, assist them with their groceries and take them to the car, like it used to be."

Group 2 emphasized in-store education for people, "to introduce them to fresh produce, because fresh produce is not familiar to some people who are not used to eating in or, you know, to teach people what is a good choice, healthy choice, and how to cook with it." Every group identified schools and churches as crucial sources of support. "Schools and churches have the most agency currently in the area," a member of group 3 added, "[so] we would need to get people in both churches and schools involved to help elevate and get those institutions to buy in to this, which will give us the chance to make that happen." Speakers directly linked schools and churches with learning how to cook healthier. "That's important if we think about how people north of Pine die fourteen years earlier than people from the south," another group's presenter added. That statistic troubled community members, many of whom bowed and shook their heads at the thought.

That statistic also points to what Hanna Garth and Ashanté M. Reese argue "in the study of Black food and justice" is an epistemic shift in food studies—a shift that they are helping to lead—that recognizes what forces are at play in the food crises in Black communities. Black communities, like

North Tulsa, face "the same anti-Black climate that produces and reinforces the carceral state that extends beyond prisons and jails and into our homes." This relationship explains the connection between food access and the mortality of those who live north of Pine. For these scholars and the attendees at the meeting, the stakes are much higher than "simply adding grocery stores to Black neighborhoods." To fully appreciate this fact, the authors point to Christina Sharpe's notion of "wake work" to "grapple with how the 'past' shows up continuously in the present."[13]

As Garth points out, the challenge comes from how "the need to improve, reform, intervene, or change Black and Brown communities" is at the center of food studies. Even seemingly more progressive alternative and justice-oriented food studies, Garth argues, are "often steeped in a logic of white supremacy and an implication that Black and Brown people should conform to white standards and ways of being."[14] This impulse was present throughout the grocery store meeting. It flowed through the involvement of nonprofits and the city incentive that led to the opening of Gateway Market by a noncommunity member, as well as his decision to close it. And, perhaps most damningly, it informed the insistence that North Tulsans needed to learn nutrition and what good food is. Only Paul with his NOS energy drinks and Tiffany with her seasoned salt mounted a resistance. Within this complex, Garth identifies a "tension as it relates to how culturally valued foods intersect with others' notions of 'justice' and 'healthy.'"[15]

In studying the moral economies of food access in Detroit, Andrew Newman and Yuson Jung point to other tensions: "a tension within food movements between social enterprise and social justice" and "the tension between 'individual agency' and 'structural racism' in proposing an alternative."[16] With the former, there is a concern with the morality of economic exchange. In the latter, the tensions around agency become central for the food-access debates in impoverished urban communities. The moral question that pervades both issues has two parts. It's about how the community in Detroit determines the "quality" of food choices and access and how that determination is indicative of the very quality of the community itself. Thus, activists and food providers signal the quality of the community writ large.[17] This runs the gamut from mainstream chain offerings like Walmart, Reasor's, or Albertsons to the upscale Whole Foods Market. It also includes the no-frills down-market stores, which Newman and Yuson identify as "unscrupulous small merchants"; North Tulsa's Gateway Market would have qualified for this designation.[18]

Newman and Yuson's analysis reinforces what I observed in the Great Gathering meeting, especially read alongside the views of shoppers like Lindsey and Joel who reflected on Gateway's closing. That is, the grocery store debate revealed not just what was at stake for North Tulsans regarding food access but also how North Tulsans expected the grocery store to re-create community. Anti-Blackness, as identified by Garth and Reese, was absolutely at work in the food disparities North Tulsans face, but there was also a strong sense that community failure was the issue. The "wake" was real, to be sure. North Tulsa's disparities exist in the wake of decades of underdevelopment following urban renewal. However, North Tulsa's history disrupts the stability of a narrative of living in the wake of anti-Black violence. Greenwood had been self-sufficient as a result of the complicated working of Jim Crow segregation, which, while limiting opportunity, helped to keep most available capital in the community. And while overlooking this fact, contemporary North Tulsans believed they could be self-sufficient too. What they needed to build was community. The difficulty stemmed from what Clifton, and many North Tulsans, for that matter, identified as a crisis of collaboration.

All Call for All People

It seemed as if Clifton had understood this point about community all along and had already identified community as *the* problem facing North Tulsa:

> Stronger *and* better *together*, we *are stronger and better together* than we are individually. And it's so important that we can come together as one group to do great things, to make this community a better place. There are great people here [in Tulsa]. In the last year, I've been meeting so many wonderful people and so many smart people that it blows my mind. I think that's some of the problems that we have is that people are so smart and so intelligent; everybody is a leader and a great leader independently. But we need to look up to harness all that energy, all that power together, and then we'll see some great things take place. And I'm expecting some success. We're gonna have success as we join together and work together, collaborate together. So welcome to the Great Gathering, an "all call for all people" for collaboration.

To be sure, Clifton's delivery did not have the swagger or gravitas of a Baptist preacher. Still, it was evident that this was how the audience of primarily Black North Tulsa residents received him. Moreover, he rooted his message in the Christian spirit of communion. More to the point, Clifton shared that he was there and had gathered us together as a direct calling from God:

"I'm just gonna be candid: as I was reading in Matthew chapter 14, verse 16, about the disciples said to [Jesus], they said, 'Lord, obviously you been ministering to us and we're in a desert place and they don't have anything to eat. And he turned to them, and he said, you feed them.' And when I read that, it just jumped out at me, and the Lord told me, He said, 'Go and tell the pastors to feed the people; they can do it.' So my assignment is to tell them and get them together to work on this initiative." Following the declaration of his calling, Clifton asked local preacher Minister Thompson to formally open the meeting with a prayer:

> Dear God, our heavenly Father, we pray that your will, plan, and purpose be revealed in the Earth. And dear God, we believe in this mission that you put in our dear brother's heart. That it can be manifested that the whole world can see the light of your spirit through this work that you placed in the hearts of this young man, as well as to extend out through others, even to this community. Dear God, we thank you for your blessing, [for it] to be upon us as a manifestation of your presence, even as those choose to come under this banner, under this mantle, under this endeavor that we pray your will be done on Earth as it is in heaven, even through this endeavor. In Christ's name we pray. In *Jesus*'s name, we pray. Amen.

And with the responsive collective "amen" from the audience, Clifton's mission was part of *His* mission.

I observed the same overtly Christian orientation at many, if not all, the events that I attended in Tulsa. Indeed, many of the gatherings started with a benediction, and many individuals who organized these events felt similarly "called" to do good works in their communities. North Tulsa was a predominantly Christian community, and I often heard a joke that went, "You can't throw a rock in Tulsa and not hit a reverend." In North Tulsa the understanding was that spiritual intervention was the solution for social and economic problems. There was a recognizable, almost Pentecostal sense in North Tulsa that commercial revitalization needed divine revelation. I detailed in the previous chapter how, in North Tulsa, community is organized around and by nonprofits and church organizations. There was both partnership and competition between the two, and many functioned as both, with church members formally filling the ranks of a nonprofit's paid and volunteer staff. If you couldn't throw a stone in Tulsa and not hit a reverend, the same stone would hit a nonprofit as well.

Consider, for example, NorthTulsa100, founded in 2013. The organization aimed to support the opening of one hundred "new and viable" businesses in North Tulsa by the centenary of the Tulsa Race Massacre. NorthTulsa100 seeks to "advocate for business enterprises, but we promote, encourage, support and assist for the betterment of our community and its citizens."[19] The organization did not emerge out of a mandate for capitalist development, however. The founder, Donna Jackson, states that NorthTulsa100 was founded "as a result of prayer."[20] With the confluence of religion and commercial activism, North Tulsa's leaders sought to create a particular version of the "Beloved Community." *The Beloved Community* was coined by the theologian Josiah Royce, founder of the Fellowship of Reconciliation. Dr. Martin Luther King Jr., who belonged to the fellowship, promoted the term as core to his organizing work and philosophy of nonviolence in the pursuit of ending poverty, hunger, and racial inequality and discrimination. The Beloved Community would be facilitated by reconciliation and cooperation. These two themes, or praxes, would be the primary means by which North Tulsans would see the restoration of their community.

And so it was for these reasons that Clifton declared:

We need pastors. We need *that* unit. We need you to talk to your pastors and ask them to come and join and help us out. I've talked to a few pastors, and they are on board. Reverend Casey, Reverend M. C. Potter, and Bishop Gary Mackintosh are three pastors I've talked to that are on board with what we're doing. But we need more; we need more pastors. We need them to come together and work together and help lead this because, you know, they have followers, they have lots of people that they minister to every Sunday and every Wednesday. So they are a big part of the community. We need *your* pastors.

To be sure, Clifton clarified that more than pastors were needed, particularly to enable the collaboration that would make the Beloved Community. "We also need business owners, educators, and teachers," he said. "We need the doctors and the lawyers." To have success, he made it clear that "we need *all* the individuals."

Clifton loved Tulsa. He loved the place and wanted to see it united: north, south, east, and west. For all of Tulsa to do well, he told the audience, every area, meaning every community, needed to be strengthened. North Tulsa only needed collaboration to solve its problems. Clifton shared information with us about his ESTEEM organization and its model for collaboration, which he called CEED. This stood for "community development, economic empowerment, education innovation, and development of families." The principles of CEED would "help people live with purpose, break the cycle of poverty, and live productive, purposeful, and prosperous lives!"[21] The collaborative principles of CEED would facilitate cooperation among various organizations, which would share information among themselves and the public. "We'll bring leaders together. We will begin working with local pastors on this issue. And that way we will get other people involved," Clifton explained, again showing the centrality of the church in community development.

In the middle of the presentation, an audience member interrupted, "Can you tell me how you would do this?" as if reading everyone's minds. This put the very first challenge to Clifton, who up to that point had the audience in complete agreement. The gentleman continued, "All this about getting people to work together as a group? One of our most split areas in this district *is* our churches, because, you know, they have a tough time working together. And don't get me started on our politicians!" Clifton responded, "It's not what *I* would do. It's what can *we* do? That's the problem; the solution is community collaboration, which is working together. And that's why I'm here, to help and [to get us to] work together with other organizations." I thought back to Clifton's opening about being called by the Lord. He was clearly on a prophetic mission. Clifton continued, "And with anyone who is interested in making this community stronger. What does collaboration look like? It looks like this group of people working together, joining together, reaching out, pulling others in. It's brainstorming, working together, coming up with ideas on how to change things."

To help make his point, Clifton invited ESTEEM colleague James to back him up and provide a material example. James was a regular attendee at the North Tulsa District Forum. This was where local and state representatives, led by State Representative Kevin Matthews, State Senator Jabar Shumate, and City Councilman Jack Henderson, met to discuss matters affecting the community:

> Look, I was once one of those complainers. I looked at what they [politicians] do, and I got tired of coming together, "hurrah-ing," talking about what they're going to do, and everybody gets up to speak, and then a week later, nothing is going on. So I stopped going to those meetings because I was tired of seeing that. But what they're doing at the forum, for example, you know, is coming together; it's what [Clifton's] trying to do. And this is important: we're not interested in creating

another committee but instead trying to focus the multiple committees, multiple groups already out there, to aim in one direction. And right now, [Clifton's] trying to aim that at the grocery store.

Clifton tapped back in, adding, "The one thing we know we cannot do is we can't do anything separate. And that's why what we're trying to do is simply come together." As an example of how ineffective working separately was, Clifton brought up how the United States Department of Housing and Urban Development (HUD) gives out $5 million grants. Clifton asked, "How many people think $5 million is a lot of money?" To which an elderly woman quickly replied, "It is for me!" The laughter in the room was cut by Clifton, who clarified, "We're talking about for a district. We're talking about several districts. Who thinks $5 million is a lot of money, then?" And the same woman then replied that no, it wasn't a lot, then. "No, it's not," began Clifton. "It can't even touch this district. They've been giving this money out every year for the last ten years. Have you all seen any difference?" he asked as a rhetorical challenge. Answering his own question, he said, "No. No, you don't. And they're going to be giving it out again for the next five years, and you still won't see any difference then either." "Five million [dollars]." He paused a moment to let the gravity of the number sink in, only to undermine its value, finishing, "in a district like this is a drop in the bucket." Furthering his point, he added, "And then when you just split the money, tons of groups come in. Come in for fifty thousand, eighty thousand, and a hundred thousand, or even a million. What you've got is nothing that's going nowhere. It goes to multiple ideas, to multiple groups, which ends up giving you nothing!" James offered more perspective, saying, "So what Clifton's doing and what he's talking about is very important, because if we can begin to get people to work together, when HUD comes up with this money, we can aim it at one project. And you'd do it for the next five years, and instead of $5 million split up, you now have $25 million that you can spend. And $25 million *is something*."

At that point, Clifton moved to the next segment of the event, which was a shortened screening of the video "Who Moved My Cheese?" based on the self-help book of the same title. The crowd began grumbling, with perplexed faces coming up across the audience. Clifton, sensing the lack of interest, moved to persuade us: "Now we are talking about collaborating and solving the problem. And this video is about what would you do if you weren't afraid? If you didn't have fear, what would you do? And I want us to watch it, because I want us to know how can we affect our community if fear didn't exist? If we weren't afraid!" He had the room vote on whether to watch the whole sixteen-minute video or just the eight-minute clip he thought most relevant; despite his encouragement and endorsement of the video's import, we voted for the latter.

After we watched the clip, Clifton began again, "So the problem is that the cheese has been moved." The "cheese" in this context was the grocery store that was closed but also represented the broader circumstance of a lack of community resources. "Our problem is that our only community grocery store closed recently. So right now we have a food desert, but we don't have to stay there. What are we going to do about it? Are we going to just sit around and wait?" With the rhetorical questions hanging in the air for a moment, Clifton continued, "Are we going to be proactive and do something about it? We have a choice. We can accept things the way they are, or we can make a difference. And I suggest that we make a difference. I suggest that we collaborate and make a change and make a difference in this community. But to solve the problem, it will take collaboration."

By this point in the meeting, I was puzzled by Clifton's prescription that collaboration was key to North Tulsa's capacity to overcome its socioeconomic disadvantage. There was little mention of the history of structural disparities, the impact of urban renewal, or even the consequences of the race massacre. All their problems, it seemed, were due to a lack of cooperative will. Collaboration would solve all problems. To make his point about how easily collaboration accomplishes things, he again turned to inspirational videos. This time it was a series of YouTube clips about other communities who successfully developed their grocery stores:

I've done the research, and I've been looking at the different places across America that have grown community. In Kansas, not that far from here; in Chester, Pennsylvania; and in Portland, Oregon; all of these have their community-owned grocery stores, not just them. But as I was looking at some more this morning, there are a lot of areas that had food deserts. And they came together, collaborated, and made this thing happen. They didn't bring in Walmart or these other places. They did it *themselves*. Suppose we can duplicate what they're doing and what other places, people, and organizations are doing across the United States. We could duplicate it. And they gave people jobs to help people learn about agriculture and planting and farming, those kinds of things. And we could even develop a model that others can follow. I know we can. I know we can. If we could collaborate and do this thing, it's possible. It's going to take collaborating, and it's going to take planning, and it's going to take some time to get it done. But we need all of you. And we need others to come in and join us, as we join with our leaders to make this happen.

Clifton's pitch was over. He had made his case that anything is possible if we all come together, especially this grocery store. He had done his job. Or at least he thought so. Just as he finished, a member of the audience asked, "So what kind of grocery store are you going to build, and where are you going to put it?" It was hard to tell if the questions caught Clifton off guard because he had never considered them or because the woman had so obviously missed his only point, about collaboration. Clifton's response was shocking: "I have no idea." After a few seconds of reflection, probably seeing the audience's look of disbelief over that response, he continued, "Ma'am, *we* have to decide where it's going to go. *We're* going to come together and make those decisions. I'm not making any decision. I just wanted to introduce this, get everyone together so we can make plans and decisions together. Because if I said do this, this, and that, other people may not like that. But you come together and say, 'Hey, this is what we want to do,' and we can agree on it, that makes it easier and more successful."

The audience member still seemed dubious, replying, "Let me just make sure what you're saying. You want 'us' to work on this?" using air quotes to emphasize the "us." "Yes," replied Clifton, "and other organizations in the area. All of us working toward the same goal, everybody coming together." I thought the exchange would end there, but the woman queried further, seemingly even more confused, "You're not making any plans for anybody? You're just saying, let's come together somewhere, like at this library?" Clifton, impressively unperturbed, replied, "Yes, that's exactly right, ma'am. I'm just the catalyst, a catalyst, that is trying to pull all of these different organizations and the community together." The woman asked Clifton if she should consider him the "driving force" behind getting everybody together, "to find some way to come together so that we can put all our resources together?" Clifton responded, "I wouldn't even say that. Because the organizations are already working, they are the center for me, in my view. And I'm just connecting with them and working with them, everybody, all the organizations, and any individuals interested, and they can bring their expertise toward opening a store." "So you're not planning anything for anybody; you're just trying to get all of us together?" the woman asked finally, to which Clifton, remarkably patiently, simply replied, "Yes." The message was as simple as it was repetitive: collaboration was vital. And thanks to that audience member, it was as clear as it could be. It was the key to being successful, and Clifton warned against having any "big Is" and "little yous."

An accompanying ethic of forgiveness would lead to cooperation. It was a tautological obligation and consequence that both produced and required collaboration. "Another thing we need to do, we need to forgive people, to be forgiven, and to give forgiveness to others. We need to mend some of those relationships, those broken relationships. And just get stronger; and it takes a lot of strength, sometimes, to tell somebody that I forgive you, but that's the only way that you can get past that." What Clifton was referring to was unclear. With the repeated references to forgiveness, one might believe some deep community rift existed. Given one audience member's statement calling the churches one of the "most split areas," perhaps the volume of churches had created competition in the community, inhibiting cooperation. The heads nodded in agreement, as the audience very obviously recognized what Clifton was getting at. It seemed like cooperation could accomplish all these things, especially the reconciliation of the Beloved Community.

Community Trouble

At the end of the meeting, a woman across the room stood up and said, "Excuse me, I'd like to say something." The woman sitting next to me muttered, "Lord," which to me portended some excitement. "My name is Billie Parker, and I was at Gateway Market for over five years; I had a business there. I'm telling my story." I was intrigued by the force of Billie's proclamation:

> I'm telling you where we started because when the store was closing, people would come in and say, oh, they were hurt. Why are they closing? Why does it happen to *us* and all that? So I started a movement to save our community—we started *that* work, having meetings about the grocery store. And we decided that this is going to be community run. Community gonna run this; we're not getting any grants. We are just going to be a community, and I think it's going to work. And the new name is Afrika Hotep Market. *Hotep* is the African name for peace. Y'all learn something today, right? The market is going to be indoor and outdoor. And it's going to be a flea market, a grocery store, and a farmer's market.

Billie was a serial entrepreneur, even from her school days, when she sold popcorn balls to her classmates. Billie recalls "being called" to open a store in the fourth grade after going to the Ben Franklin store with her mom and seeing that none of the items for sale catered to Black people. Inheriting what she called the "entrepreneurship gene," Billie opened her first store, Pine Street Mart, in 2006; moved to Gateway Market in 2010; and changed the name to Afrika Hotep Market in 2012. Interestingly, because of the community's difficulty in pronouncing *hotep*, Parker wanted to call the store Black Wall Street Market. She chose not to, claiming that she was discouraged by community elders. The rent at Gateway increased beyond what Billie could afford, so she closed the shop. She found a new location on Osage Drive and finally named the store Black Wall Street Market. She sells traditional African clothes, fabric, small veggies, soaps, oils, and jewelry. As part of the store, Parker also runs the Community Pride Farmers Market.

The group barely responded to Billie, besides an audience member asking, "How you say it again? It's African?" Clifton thanked Billie and then proceeded to wrap up the meeting. But I found Billie thrilling and radical, embodying the spirit that I thought should have been driving the discussion that afternoon. Even so, her story raised more questions for me. With the proclamations of community and collaboration, why was her store allowed to close? And critically, with community members like her, why wasn't there already a successful grocery store?

I spoke to Marlon, who had started a community garden in North Tulsa, and I was interested in the direction the conversation was going around the grocery store in the community. Community gardens had become popular solutions to the issue of food in community development discourses. They had also come up repeatedly in the presentations during the grocery store brainstorming, so it seemed appropriate to speak to him. Moreover, running a community garden took a great deal of negotiating with the community and seemed like a perfect example of collaboration.

The topic of community collaboration was a point of significant frustration for Marlon. The frustration was not just about the challenges of uniting people but also about the need for unity:

Let's say you got a problem in your neighborhood, like food access, which, of course, we do with all the cutbacks, cutbacks, and more cutbacks. The county or the city is not able to do much really to address that problem. These problems get out of control. So, you say, OK, let's have a group. So you organize a local group to try to take care of that problem. Right? But how do you go from getting that local group to (1) trust each other and (2) to keep from having fights among themselves so they can carry their mission forward? How can you build and resource them to where they can make that difference? You know, in their area, building it up, you know, really empowering them, you know? You see, we don't have a system for how to do that. People try things and fail, and then people go into that despair cycle, and that cynicism says, well, that's it, I'm not going to go to that meeting.

Marlon had sat in on his fair share of meetings to answer these questions and find solutions for their sources. "I spent hundreds of hours in meetings," he told me. "Every kind of community and association meeting you can think of, brother!" He considered his commitment to be somewhat exceptional for today. But interestingly, he thought that in the past that commitment was much more universal. "Twenty, thirty, forty years ago, people went to them!" "Call it a generational change," he suggested. To Marlon, there had been a sense of institutional ownership in the North Tulsa community in previous decades. "There was *community*," he insisted. "And they had, or at least they thought they had, power." With that sense of power, Marlon speculated, these previous generations thought they could effect difference. "Now it's really hard. Now what you usually get are not people who are showing up. By and large, I mean, a lot of people who show up are not showing up really to be a part of building a community, a collaborative community response. They're showing up [about a] particular issue that they're mad about. All they want is a place to vent and rant." According to Marlon, that was the reason the Great Gathering had such a good turnout "for a community meeting today," he clarified. "But really, nobody wants to show up because they don't want to sit there and hear what people are venting and going on about, right? Who wants to listen to somebody vent and rant?" Marlon explained that communities had to overcome this resistance to coming together.

"Brother, you can't claim White supremacy when people treat you bad and we treat ourselves bad!" I had asked Tony his views about community, and I hit a nerve. From his firsthand experiences working with young Black men in Tulsa who faced significant trouble to the struggles involved in building the B. C. Franklin Park, there were too many "obvious issues, with obvious solutions," that just couldn't get resolved. For Tony, as a member at Metropolitan Baptist, the problem was even more puzzling. There he would sit every Sunday amid hundreds of Black Tulsans who could mobilize their capital anytime the pastor requested it. "Listen, we gave away 573 backpacks for our back-to-school event. And for us, it was nothing. The pastor said I need $17,000. He got it." Cynical, Tony continued, "So they'll do stuff like that, but at the same time, are they really connected to the community? Because, you know, a lot of them do that kind of stuff because they can write it off their taxes." Tony sat with that claim for a minute and then continued, "[Are] you really writing that check because you want to help this kid?" Tony was beginning to unpack the politics of community. He added, "Maybe it's not that you get a tax write-off, but because you're cooperating *in church with our pastor* on things that benefit the community. But sometimes I wonder what would motivate them to cooperate *with the community*?" "What motivates them?" Tony pondered. "Do they have a passion for giving back?" The question was rhetorical, apparently. "We have a lot of people who feel like they have arrived, and they don't realize that they are being looked at too even though they're driving, you know [fancy cars]. One day the pastor preached a long time about stratification, about how we have allowed White folk to tell us if you're dark skin, you're not right, and all that. He went in! I tell you, I sat there, and I watched," Tony said while making a binocular hand gesture over his eyes. "I mean, it's sort of a disconnect for them, basically, because I expected them to be up on their feet! But nothing." "Jovan," he continued, "the bad part about it is that I know most of them. And they just one generation removed from the hood themselves! You know, they think, 'Yeah, I've made it,' and so for them, I don't think they could get emotionally . . ." Tony's words trailed off but then returned with, "I work with young Black men; they have me in tears."

"Now, the real question is," Tony said, with some urgency, "is this something that's systemic within our culture?" I assumed I knew what Tony meant, but I needed to be sure, and so I asked him to elaborate. "What I mean is, is it something within us as a people? This lack of organization?" To Tony, Black culture generally, or at least specifically in North Tulsa, was framed by a built-in expectation for cooperation, which became codified into the idea of community. Tony's willingness to ask this question, then, was remarkable and even radical. "You and me look alike, but do we need to think alike? And so, what it looks like is that success and our challenges, whichever one it is, comes back to this, this kind of Black thing. So we're doing good because we're Black and we're brothers, you know, but when we're doing badly and we can't get along, it's also because we're Black, you know?" I was surprised but also encouraged by the observation. The narrative of racial commonality in the community had glossed over a host of tensions in Tulsa. Here, thanks mainly to Tony, it was evident that the political process and the economic circumstances revealed community limitations. Tony expanded on his thought:

I'm saying that we always look, and we're all guilty of looking at the old Black folk who, like, they always worked together, which makes us look at each other different. You don't *need* everybody. But we fixate on it. We got to get *everybody* together. We gotta get everybody to unify. But you don't need that. You just need people who think like you; you just need the people who say they down to be down, right? You just need that core group and get to work. But we wait and say, "Well, we can't move until we get everybody here on one accord." But it doesn't even happen in any community or any group of people, not really. No one is on one accord. What is it about us that makes us feel like because we're Black we're all supposed to be in one accord, we're all supposed to think the same way? I don't believe all Black folk need to think the same way, but we can work together. Unfortunately, many of us feel like, "I didn't agree with him on this or that issue; I can't work with him at all."

I asked Tony why he thought this need for community-level accord existed, to which he replied:

I don't know why. Let me see. These expectations are because this kind of idea about the community, you know, probably comes from pre-1921. You had by necessity, right, to be a community. I would say that cooperation revolves around the issues of the time, so you had segregation, and that was what you had in common, you know. They were all niggers in the eyes of those folk, right? That was like the issue of the time. And it was clear since we're segregated, even if we wanted to disband, we got no choice but to work together. But now? Now there are so many issues within the Black community that I would say the leaders don't know which one to tackle first: incarceration or education? Economic development? The list goes on and on. So, until I think there's at least one major issue that we can tackle, there won't be a majority of cooperation. I don't think.

From the conversations I had, it is evident that there was a challenging relationship between the perceived well-being of the community and that community's leadership. In many ways, this concern was entirely unexceptional. Many, if not all, communities and societies have the same struggle. What made that struggle exceptional in the North Tulsa context, given the discussion with Tony, was the issue of the relationship between Blackness and community, which the lack of resources in the community strained considerably. The need for resources underlay Clifton's insistence on collaboration and cooperation. The core messaging behind both the churches' and the nonprofits' attempts to provide services to North Tulsa, and the through line for their narratives, was Black Wall Street and the legacy of Greenwood.

Moreover, for the community that saw itself as the inheritors of Black Wall Street, that legacy increased their expectations and heightened their anticipation of prosperity. Greenwood's reputation for prosperity was a burden to the community. It formed part of the idealized notion of community grounded in the "theological expectancy" of the Beloved Community. Everyone anticipated North Tulsa's restoration as a modern-day Greenwood. They were awaiting the Pentecost, the descent of the Holy Spirit of prosperity's fulfillment. In other words, Greenwood's restoration was a matter of race and faith.

Leadership Trouble

I spoke with Roberta Clardy, the owner of *North Tulsa Magazine* and a decades-long organizer and committed member of the North Tulsa community. I asked Roberta what she thought would come from the meeting, and her reply supported much of what Marlon had told me:

Twenty years ago, that room would not have been big enough to fit all the people who would want to be there to talk about something like this. Fifteen years ago, it would have been maybe half that amount of people; ten years ago, perhaps you could have filled the room we were in. Two years ago, about half of that room would've been filled because no matter what, people wanted to have a say in whatever and all of that. But what's happened is that this community's done that over and over and over. We've come to the table. We've had a say. We've given our ideas. We've done that. And this is not me saying this; this is moms and dads. McLain High School called a meeting for all the parents to show up. Nobody showed up.

According to Roberta, the North Tulsa community was ready for somebody "who's just interested in this community twenty-four hours a day, seven days a week, every day. And people will gather around that." Roberta said, "The community has made a billion mission statements, and as it always happens, everyone comes away [from a meeting] feeling like you just don't want to do this anymore, you know you get burned out. So, if somebody can do something, get it done, that is a firestarter. Yeah. That would be awesome." Roberta contextualized the possible dynamic between the audience member and Clifton. Clifton's reluctance to lead and the audience member's difficulty in accepting this revealed a core vulnerability, or at least point of contention, in the hope for collaboration, and it posed consequences for the recovery of the North Tulsa community. This issue was one of leadership. The audience member had just wanted Clifton to do it, get the grocery store built. She must have been tired of these meetings, for which, in North Tulsa, there were always plenty of reasons. "But," Roberta concluded, perhaps now clarifying Clifton's response, "we don't have leaders."

I broached the same topic with Tony. I asked him to reflect on leadership to explain why getting a grocery store was challenging. "You know, when you're talking about the issue of a grocery store in the community, there's only so much that a representative can do. I mean, they can try to do some things legislatively, maybe to get some tax credits, something like that. But you've got to keep in mind that they are minorities within a superminority. Meaning they are Black in an all-White political space, and Democrats in a mostly Republican space." The point was poignant given that of Tulsa's nine city council districts, only District 1, which was North Tulsa, typically ever had a Black representative. "So, you know, they're contained a little bit by what they can do. Sometimes we don't understand all the different constraints available or all the different roles that people can play. And a lot of the time, if you don't understand that, then you get there, and you made all these promises [you can't keep] because you don't understand the politics of things. Right? And so it just doesn't work out."

"Still," Tony continued, "people tired, man; you get tired of waiting, you know? But there's an expectation that *someone* has to take the lead." I asked for clarification. "Well, look, I don't like when people say there's no leaders because people are leading in the way that they can best lead, within their skill set." As an example, he mentioned a longtime pharmacist, Bobby Woodard, who owns Westview Pharmacy. Bobby, by reputation, was a quiet, reserved man. "He doesn't want anyone to know he owns Westview," Tony said, illustrating Bobby's humility. Bobby had won accolades and awards for his service to the community and his success as a businessman for thirty years. Through paid internships he had trained numerous Black students who aspired to go to pharmacy school. He also ran a medical clinic with a dentist, a pediatrician, and a family doctor. In reflecting on Bobby as an example, even a model, of leadership, Tony mused:

He's bringing all that type of leadership from that level. The problem is, like you said, how do we emulate that? In other areas. Yeah. And we have to multiply that. I mean, my pastor talked about that last week. In our community we don't need just one more pharmacist; we need ten more. We don't need just one more good teacher. We need a hundred more. And how do we emulate that? And I think part of it is identifying those who show leadership in areas that we need and then gravitate toward them and not try to elevate people to be the leader. And so I think we need to identify what people are good at and say, OK, let's empower them to do what they are naturally inclined to do. Not saying that someone can't step outside and grow a little bit, but why are you keeping people in a role they shouldn't be in? And that is the issue that we have a lot of the time with our elected leaders. So basically, you know, you don't want to send people to school for leadership. You want people to kind of organically become leaders.

I brought this question about leadership to Jacob, who had worked on several local and state political campaigns, mainly on behalf of Black candidates. His assessment of North Tulsa's leaders confirmed Roberta's judgment. He also had a significantly more critical view. "They're very emotional, nonprogressive. A lot of North Tulsans can't stand them, but they don't have many better options," was his opening salvo against North Tulsa's leadership. "Those folks are *just* there. And many of them are aging. The question is, what's going to happen when they're gone? Because at least they are there, they're showing up, and they have been informally trained from the school of hard knocks. So we have to create a pipeline."

According to Jacob, one solution was an organization called the North Tulsa Development Council (NTDC). "It sounds like some sort of housing authority, but it's not," Jacob joked. Created by then mayor Kathy Taylor and sponsored by the Bank of Oklahoma, ONEOK Inc., and Williams Cos., the NTDC started as a pilot leadership program in 2007. "The problem, though," Jacob continued, "is that it's a leadership development program that didn't do a very good job of developing leaders. They didn't market. They didn't recruit at all. There's no way you would have known about it." As a result, the George Kaiser Family Foundation acquired the NTDC and created LEAD North, which then functioned as a subsidiary of another program called Leadership Tulsa. On its website, LEAD North states that it "was designed to equip current and future leaders in Tulsa with the skills, knowledge, and network needed to make meaningful change in North Tulsa."[22]

"What North Tulsa needs," Jacob continued, is "a very rigorous program that helps people who have a demonstrated interest or passion in North Tulsa to take leadership positions in North Tulsa." Going back to his earlier description of existing Black leaders, I asked Jacob to explain his contention further. "Take Jack Henderson." Henderson was first elected to the city council, representing North Tulsa District 1, in 2004 and had served continually for twelve years. "I mean, people complain about Jack, but he keeps getting elected. You know, anybody that comes to town can look and say, 'What the hell is going on? Why does he keep getting elected?!' I'm not saying as a city councilman Jack Henderson has the power to, for example, say, 'There must be a grocery store'—I understand that in their elected positions they have certain parameters, but . . ." Jacob paused to think for a moment, ". . . are you galvanizing the people to meet their needs? You know, there's a small minority that elects them, folks like Jack, that elected them because of who they are. But have they ever shown the ability to be a galvanizing force?"

As it turned out, Henderson was up for reelection a couple of months after this conversation. He beat out Vanessa Hall-Harper, who lost to him in a three-way race. She received just 33.1 percent of the vote, thus proving Jacob's point. However, two years later, Henderson would end his twelve-year streak. He would wind up losing to Hall-Harper, who had worked for the Healthy Living Program at Tulsa Health Department for twenty years and led an effort to upgrade the facilities at B. C. Franklin Park.

After Henderson's loss, voters in North Tulsa echoed Jacob's sentiment about Henderson in the local independent media outlet *The Frontier*. They reflected on the limits of leadership overall as well. "Let's let someone else in there for a change. Give someone else a chance. I think he's been in so long, and there's not really been change. I'm not saying he hasn't done anything, [but] where's the progress?" said a North Tulsan, Sidney. Sheila added, "Jack has been in there for a number of years, but there hasn't been a whole lot of progress. So we need some new blood. We need some new ideas. We need some new things done within our district." Another, Jomekia, didn't see "Jack doing what's necessary," and therefore, she commented, "Maybe with a younger person, maybe she'll be more forward-thinking to the needs of North Tulsa." Given Henderson's tenure on the council, voter Annie Bell "was really surprised that he lost" but said, "I just don't think he's been doing his job over here in North Tulsa. Our streets have not been swept this year. . . . I think that is one of the simplest things."[23]

Hall-Harper mused on her win: "People have eyes; the community continues to deteriorate. I think people saw that, and they got sick of that, and they saw an alternative with me. I think people just saw that we were working diligently to be a voice for the community. And people were just ready for a change." Hall-Harper finally said, "We just need someone to do the work." She sounded like someone who represented what Roberta Clardy meant when she said, "This community is ready for somebody who's just interested in this community twenty-four hours a day, seven days a week, every day."[24]

Nearly six years after the Great Gathering, Hall-Harper would seem to make good on that promise, as North Tulsa finally broke ground on a new grocery store on June 26, 2020, at North Peoria Avenue and Seminole Street. Tulsa mayor G. T. Bynum, City Councilor Vanessa Hall-Harper, executive director of the Tulsa Economic Development Corporation, Rose Washington, and other local and state leaders were in attendance. Oasis Fresh Market materialized the aspiration for a North Tulsa grocery store. Hall-Harper noted, "Having a quality grocery store in District 1 has been a four-year journey."[25] However, for residents of her district, it has been a decades-long struggle.

Oasis Fresh Market opened in 2021 a mere couple of weeks before the events commemorating the centenary of the 1921 race massacre. It was located literally across the parking lot from the closed Gateway Market, which to my mind was a haunting reminder of the community's struggle for access. However, when I visited, the store was bright, fresh, and full of promise. The store is operated by EcoAlliance Group and offers standard grocery fare, including meat, produce, and dairy departments. The store has a demonstration kitchen and a multipurpose room to provide a space to educate customers on cooking affordable, healthy meals. It seemed to tick many of the boxes proposed at Clifton's meeting.

The store is part of Project Oasis, which seeks to provide improved access to affordable fresh food in areas defined as a food desert by the US Department of Agriculture. "Just imagine a desert. In a desert it's hot. In a desert there's a lack of water. In a desert there's a lack of opportunity. And that's what this community once was. Today we are going to break ground to break that cycle of generational poverty and to break that cycle of food deserts," said Aaron "A.J." Johnson, the executive director of the Tulsa Dream Center and a part of EcoAlliance Group.[26]

Hanna Garth sums up the trouble with Project Oasis's messaging. She reminds us how the representation of food access in Black communities "has painted a bleak picture—one of crumbling infrastructure (i.e., no large supermarkets; only liquor and corner stores), dire poverty (hungry children), abandonment (abandoned markets never reoccupied), and violence (fear of leaving the house to shop for food)."[27] These depictions were unabashedly present at the groundbreaking. Garth also reminds us that because "Black communities are a common target of food interventions, ranging from programs that bring fresh fruits and vegetables to corner stores to urban community gardening. Food justice organization leaders imbue their messages" with racist anti-Blackness.[28]

The market cost $3.9 million to develop, and its funding came from a variety of investors. The Tulsa Economic Development Corporation provided $1.5 million, with costs covered by the Tulsa Development Authority through the North Peoria TIF (DISTRICT 4). Tax increment financing, or TIF, is a method of providing public funding that diverts funds from future property tax revenue increases. That funding method, which encourages private investment in districts, has been seen as a critical component in state-facilitated gentrification alongside other processes such as opportunistic (re)zoning, the condemnation of so-called blighted property, and land assembly, which is the purchase and combination of small parcels of land to form a large single site for redevelopment. Through the US Department of Housing and Urban Development's Community Development Block Grant program, the city of Tulsa also provided $1.5 million. The remaining funding came from the philanthropies of the George Kaiser Family Foundation, Charles and Lynn Schusterman Family Foundation, and the Zarrow Family Foundation. The involvement of these partnerships, grantors, and philanthropies brought me back to Billie Parker and left me feeling that the multiple underwriters for the opening had undermined the Greenwood spirit and perhaps the one major aspiration of the Great Gathering: self-reliance. But at least the community could eat.

Healing the Disconnect

While the relationship between community and inequality presents a complex problem for North Tulsa's leaders, a movement began that interpreted that relationship as the best tool for achieving community development. Marlon, in founding a community garden mentioned previously, did so to offer North Tulsa's community much more than food. "So, we do a community garden and an orchard as a kind of farm justice for the people; we're urban farmers, I guess," is how Marlon describes what he and his organization do. But it was how he and his organization went about it that was of interest:

We get to know the people that are coming, you know, coming for the food. They come, and we see them at least once or twice a month. Sometimes they come back and help us, even if they cannot get the food that day. And so you begin to form a relationship. That's part of that thing where I have a lot more connections with the community because just over time, you just get to know 'em. By doing the work, you know, stuff together. It's not perfect by any means, but when they come here, we find out how people are and find out what's going on in their life.

By engaging with the community in this way, Marlon said he was using the community garden to "heal the disconnect." "It's been difficult—has been for a while—for a lot of the folk in the community to connect to what we're trying to do, particularly the younger generation." Answering my question about what they're "trying to do," Marlon replied, "It's all a matter of just creating something that makes life a little bit easier for the people in our area so that they can make better choices." With the food, Marlon had a simple-enough plan for building community. It also happened through the parties they threw, among other services. "We just kind of, you know, if we can reduce that stress in their lives a little bit in different ways, that's really our mission."

Marlon was modest. He later admitted that it was about more than reducing stress. The "disconnect" that needed healing, in his mind, was that North Tulsa's residents were out of joint and out of rhythm with their city, their community, and themselves. Poverty was to blame, plain and simple. But according to Marlon, the garden, nature, and community could be an antidote. "We can connect with them; we can do all these kinds of things to keep their mental health improving—even a little bit—so that they can make better decisions and live and feel that sense of abundance. Out of that sense of abundance, even without having much, they can realize that it is greater than whatever they're facing, especially with that sense of community." "Abundance?" I pondered that idea for a minute. Although Marlon's use of the term seemed casual enough, I also knew enough about North Tulsa to recognize that it was anything but abundant. The abundance that Marlon referred to was a *Christian* abundance. Specifically, he was referring to the Bible, John 10:7–10 (King James Version): "The thief cometh not, but for to steal, and to kill, and to destroy: I am come that they might have life, and that they might have it more abundantly."

The abundance here is about the fulfillment of the spirit. It is the absence of lack and want. It is life's satisfaction in God. It is no coincidence, of course, that "Abundant Life" teachings were pioneered after World War II by local

Oklahoman and internationally renowned televangelist Oral Roberts, who founded Oral Roberts University in Tulsa. Roberts believed that God's abundance was a comprehensive state of blessing, affecting the spirit, the body, and the soul. Through the Holy Spirit, God brings prosperity and health for those seeking an abundant life, removing from that life the ills of poverty, disease, and injustice.

Marlon was making North Tulsa a better place for his community, and it seemed to have helped him live that abundant life. "I get more out of living in the community here than I could elsewhere; I would not trade it for more money. I mean, literally as it is, it's like walking in gifts just all the time. The riches of riches and community." Unfortunately, the same could not be said for the community. North Tulsans' poverty produced ailments of immobility and injustice that were material and measurable, but their resolution was spiritual. Their spiritual orientation, however, was as totalizing as the promise of abundance. It was deep-rooted, though not quite constitutional. The complete commitment to abundance was the consequence of spiritual dislocation. In other words, if abundance was that which Tulsans sought, anticipated, then I needed to understand the spiritual root and shape of North Tulsans' state of scarcity. To be sure, they were mired in a scarce landscape lacking grocery stores and adequately paying jobs with a total reliance on external support.

After lingering on the question of abundance, I asked Marlon what contributed to the scarcity, or, as he put it, the "disconnect," that North Tulsans were facing. He began to answer as if he were profoundly contemplating an existential problem: "The people in the area, right, they still are . . ." He stopped. Thinking quite intensely, he continued, "It's the history, and they don't know it." "History?" I wondered aloud. "Yeah . . . even though they didn't live necessarily through it, the history, it's still impacting them." Marlon began to explain, "For example, it kind of goes *back*. One of the things that we've learned, partly through our experience, [is that] for a lot of younger Black students, it's not cool to be seen growing and being in the garden." Marlon said that he had inquired why this was. In trying to encourage them, he tried to apply the work of Ron Finley, the guerrilla urban farmer and self-described "gangsta gardener" in South Central Los Angeles. There Finley successfully got young Black kids to engage in urban farming—"He does great stuff, especially where he's trying to make [farming] kind of cool again," said Marlon.

To encourage greater participation among North Tulsa's young community, Marlon was creating additional activities and amenities that would help this group and the broader community engage in the outdoor space and with each other. He had built a shaded deck for relaxing outdoors and was planning on installing free-to-access Wi-Fi. "We got that so that people don't have to worry about getting online. They could use it even if we're not open, they can just come in the building and use that. Also, got the electric outlet on the outside of the building so they can charge their cell phones."

Marlon attempted to make gardening cool and worked to increase the amenities that would attract the younger community members, but it didn't seem to work. "You know, we would say, well, growing food's like printing your own money, you know, and what you get here actually will taste better than you can buy, you know, at the store. And it's healthier. We say all these things but still have the same issues." The issue Marlon found was an issue with history. "Part of what we would hear is this whole story of slavery; it really comes up, where the kids are like, 'You want me to go out to the fields,' you know?" I understood how that could happen. In her understanding of Black experiences of time, Deborah Thomas argues that the narrative of slavery is part of the temporal simultaneity of the plantation. In simultaneous time, there is a lived copresence with the past of slavery given its constant referents, such as everyday anti-Black violence.[29]

This was what Marlon aimed to communicate with the example. I was unprepared for that answer. I expected an answer about structural inequality and its rootedness in racism, which, of course, is historical, but Marlon's sense of history was something bigger. It was the history that Michel-Rolph Trouillot has described as "engraved in individual or collective bodies," at once "the materiality of the socio-historical process" and that which "sets the stage for future historical narratives."[30] The issue was also the consequences of that history: "Though we're mostly about providing emergency food, theoretically emergency food, they come all the time. It's a constant food emergency." Healing the disconnect would therefore mean a significant healing of the history. The garden, then, would have to be an agent of reconciliation. Marlon's garden was only part of the plan to heal the disconnect.

This focus was the core difference, as explained to me by Marlon, between many of the existing nonprofits and those like his, whose mission isn't just to provide services to the community but also to eventually support local economic development. Marlon founded the community garden using the philosophy of John Perkins, chairman of the Christian Community Development Association (CCDA), whose notion of Christian community development asserts that Christians should be

committed to seeing people and communities wholistically [sic] restored. We believe that God wants to restore us not only to right relationships with Himself but also with our own true selves, our families, and our communities. Not just spiritually, but emotionally, physically, economically, and socially. Not by offering mercy alone, but by undergirding mercy with justice. To this end, we follow Jesus' example of reconciliation. We go where the brokenness is. We live among the people in some of America's neediest neighborhoods. We become one with our neighbors until there is no longer an "us" and "them," but only a "we." And, in the words of the Prophet Jeremiah, "we work and pray for the well-being of our city [or neighborhood]," trusting that if the entire community does well and prospers, then we will prosper also.[31]

The CCDA essentially embodied the ethics of church and community that underpinned Clifton's message of collaboration. The CCDA's followers engage in the Christian version of putting their money where their mouth is. Called *practitioners*, they commit to living in an underresourced neighborhood for a minimum of ten years. Perkins organized the philosophy and program around three principles: relocation, reconciliation, and redistribution, which Perkins called the three *R*s of community development.

The calling to become a practitioner for Marlon was remarkably tied to geographic notions of social justice. According to the group's philosophy, social organizations that don't have members who live in an area they serve will never know the full depth of that community's experience. "So, some of the groups, whether it's a bigger church or it's a bigger nonprofit, you know, the people live somewhere else. Maybe they got an office, you know, out here in North Tulsa. But they are not, you know, people who are living in the area," Marlon began to explain, indicating the limits of conventional nonprofits. "Granted, I'm sure they do a good job or, you know, like with the health clinics, but where are they when the money's run out? Nowhere, because they never really tried to foster community connections. And that's what happens when they're run by people who aren't living here."

For Marlon and the group, a lack of intimacy between the community and those who provide its services was at the root of so many of the social problems that communities like North Tulsa face. "So many of them, those problems, we believe, can start to be solved by the community," said Marlon. This idea was also the main principle of Perkins's philosophy of community development. It would take the reconstitution of the community; therefore, "relocation" is the first principle or step of the process. And so many of the community garden's employees had moved to North Tulsa with the aim of community revitalization and restoration.

Relocation means living like Jesus, among the poor. While Jesus spread the Gospel, practitioners spread the word of God and their labor to develop communities. "It is the actual practice of loving thy neighbors as you would yourself," expressed Marlon. "The people that own businesses here don't live here. The police don't live here. The teachers don't live here. We see the problem we have because they don't. Imagine if they did?" he challenged me. To be honest, Marlon was also literally challenging me. When I first met him, I was a freshly minted PhD. "I'm sure you could get a job at OSU-Tulsa! The houses here are cheap!" It was a compelling consideration but one that I wouldn't seriously entertain. That said, I wanted to speak to someone who had done it.

I spoke to Kiki, a relatively recent transplant to North Tulsa who worked with Marlon. I wanted to understand how she felt about the group's philosophy of relocation. Kiki had grown up in Texas and went to the University of Texas at Austin to study education. Involved in a Christian group in college, she visited Tulsa and learned about North Tulsa's history. She was later drawn to Perkins's philosophy. The CCDA's website shows local affiliate organizations and churches. Through those contacts, she ultimately got together with Marlon. While not a formal member of CCDA, he was among a growing group of unofficial practitioners. Kiki had gone to school to be a teacher but thought that the conventional school setting was not the best form of education. She wanted to incorporate nature and practical skills into her pedagogy in a way that would not be possible in a typical school setting.

Moreover, she had plenty of reservations about the model of a White teacher like her teaching in minority-serving schools and school districts. "You know, when they talk about trying to get teachers to come out to schools and try to attack the 'achievement gap' and all that kind of stuff, I worry about how you get teachers to have cultural competency, trying to get more culturally competent teachers to come out here." This was a question that Kiki said she had had to grapple with herself because of Perkins's philosophy. "And, you know, my first question was, well, why would you not consider living in the school district where you're going to be teaching so that you see the kids when you're outside, you know, when you're at church or when you're running errands? I mean, that makes such a difference."

This challenge was at the root of the variety of spiraling effects in the community. It was about the absence of professionals or individuals of economic means. Absent such resources and influences—those subjects of abundance—scarcity would mark the landscape. After all, wasn't this effectively the consequence of White and Black flight, the general outcome of any form of "brain drain" in a community or society? The effects of that emptying were what social agencies and nonprofits attempted to deal with. Unless they were in and of the community, though, practitioners saw it as insufficient. "They want to do something for North Tulsa; they have good intentions. We have a lot of people like that. But my question always is, where do you live? You know, come live here. That's number one," said Marlon.

He recognized that the request was, as he called it, a "stark challenge" and fully appreciated that it was not for everybody. He suggested that those committed to these areas, but not willing to relocate, could start by "spending your money here, by visiting, by having family parties, by, you know, just incorporating this community into your life, even if you do, for some reason or another, have to live outside the area. But most people don't even think about that and even less consider relocation when I ask that question, 'Where do you live?'" For Marlon and Kiki, it was a matter of faith. It was a matter of faith as well as a matter of equality and social justice. "So, for those I see that are 'social justice oriented,'" using air quotes, effectively making his position on such people clear, "if you're not actually living with the people that you're saying that you're interested in, that's just kind of a disconnect."

Theoretically, I saw the value in this ideal type of community formation. However, I struggled to see how this wasn't equivalent to gentrification. And so I asked. "Yeah, I knew that was coming up next!" laughed Marlon. "But it's still a fair question," he began his reply. "How do you do this without falling into the 'sin of gentrification?' Well, the way you do it is you can't just move into an area and have that be it. I mean, maybe that is helping in some ways because you're bringing money into an area, but you have to do it—relocation—while also working on reconciliation and redistribution." Apparently, when you don't abide by the other two *R*s, "that's when you get into gentrification." Marlon explained that gentrification was all about the individual, their property value, their lifestyle, and the pursuit to reproduce them; "it is not about connection in community."

Marlon explained that he talked to people about the idea, and they often responded with, "Aren't you afraid that when you talk about relocation, that it would drive out . . ." Marlon's speech turned to a whisper. One could see the approaching laughter in his eyes, ". . . the poor people?" Indeed, he followed the statement with laughter. Marlon found it humorous not that people feared talking about poor people but that they didn't seem to understand that there was no need to fear displacing them. There was a way to live together, and by doing so, those people would cease to either be poor or be perceived as poor because they would be community members and neighbors. He went on to explain, "And so you have to say, well, you know, it's *how* you relocate. You know, it's what you do with the connections that you make." That "how" of relocation was reconciliation. The CCDA has guidelines for how to engage in the philosophy's practice. One approach, as Marlon explained, was to "let the people in community tell you where you're going to live, you know instead of you just picking out a spot. You know, you form your relationships with people before you move into the community. Because if you say, well, I'm going to move in here, you're moving in here to be *with* this neighbor, not to displace that neighbor."

Holding that view and taking that approach would lead to a reconciliatory relationship. "You know, how does a White person move into a predominately African American community and learn from them, not try to replace them with a different kind of culture? Then learning from it, you then serve it." This type of community orientation would ultimately lead to reconciliation by shifting the usual power dynamics based on race and class. Marlon had answered my question about gentrification to his satisfaction. I figured that I wouldn't get much further by pressing him on the economics of choice in these recommendations. So rather than challenge him, I asked how the idea of telling someone where to move in the community would work. And the answer provided an initial insight into the final R, redistribution.

Marlon explained that typically someone would try and find the best house for the least money. However, the philosophy of redistribution meant that a practitioner would be encouraged to buy and renovate a house that needed significant repair, thus lifting the standard of the entire neighborhood. Or there could be a multiunit home for sale that they could then share to house those least fortunate in the community. This framework of service, then, underscores the approach to redistribution, which Marlon summed up, "You know, how can I, instead of moving poor people out, get them more resourced?" But redistribution would bring about reconciliation, and reconciliation would produce community restoration. What I found compelling and curious about Marlon's description of a reconciled community was that it described a return to a former model of community, one particularly framed through the presence of professionals:

> You would have the bank owner living in the community, you know, and the house he had might be a little better or some of the businesspeople who lived there. Maybe. Yeah, their houses were a little better than the other houses. They had a little bit more land. The teacher, the doctors, they had, you know, they lived a little better, but not distinctively

so. But that was fine because everybody was doing their part. And their kids went to school with all the other kids. You had that. And that's what we lost and what we don't have now.

I couldn't ignore the overt similarities between Marlon's description of this community and the target groups in Clifton's "all call for all people": "We also need business owners, educators, and teachers. We need the doctors and the lawyers." At the root of these ideas of community, a particular notion of class seemed to permeate every meeting, every agenda, and every initiative that I encountered in North Tulsa. The relocation that the group and Perkins recommended was a return to what many now-poor and often Black communities looked like fifty or sixty years ago. It was interesting to see the romanticization of this history given that, in many ways, segregation is what made this class diversity possible by, as Reverend put it earlier, "containing" them together. Redlining and urban renewal in the decades since had facilitated the contemporary poverty of these communities and brought about the loss of the mixture of the professional class and working class that had organically made up the community.

Bringing back class diversity to these neighborhoods and the greater proximity to resources that it would represent, especially for those without access to capital in both its material and cultural forms, would be a mechanism for upward mobility. From a structural perspective, I could not disagree. This community would be one of abundance. This, if anything, was the formation of the Beloved Community through the three *Rs*. This approach would bring about the long-term forms of restructuring that could have a generational impact and could do something about the "history" that Marlon mentioned.

Still, I couldn't help but think of Billie Parker. When Billie said "community," it was evident that hers had a somewhat different makeup than that which Clifton had imagined and that which the nonprofits and CCDA members were trying to produce. While Clifton requested an "all call for all people" and Marlon, in a similar vein, wanted to bring the professional class back to North Tulsa, Billie's was a call for *the* people, whoever they were, on their terms. Billie's idea of community was of a significantly different orientation than Marlon's and Clifton's. But while her vision of Greenwood and Black Wall Street had different ethical orientations, the community she referenced was still understood as prosperous, with that prosperity being economic. The narrative of abundance, of prosperity, then, framed the idea of community that North Tulsans wanted to restore and to have repaired.

G.1. The railroad that historically demarcated the line between North Tulsa and downtown Tulsa. Condominium development taking place in Greenwood is visible in the background. Photo by author.

G.2. A sign commemorating the 1921 massacre on Greenwood Avenue in front of the historic Vernon AME Church. Photo by Joseph Rushmore.

G.3. The Interstate 244 highway built through the Greenwood District. Photo by author.

G.4. A man walks in shadow under Interstate 244 where it passes over Greenwood Avenue. Photo by Joseph Rushmore.

G.5. Signage for North Tulsa's St. Andrew Baptist Church, promoting assistance for the community. Photo by author and Joel Wanek.

G.6. North Tulsa's Lewis Avenue Baptist Church. Photo by author and Joel Wanek.

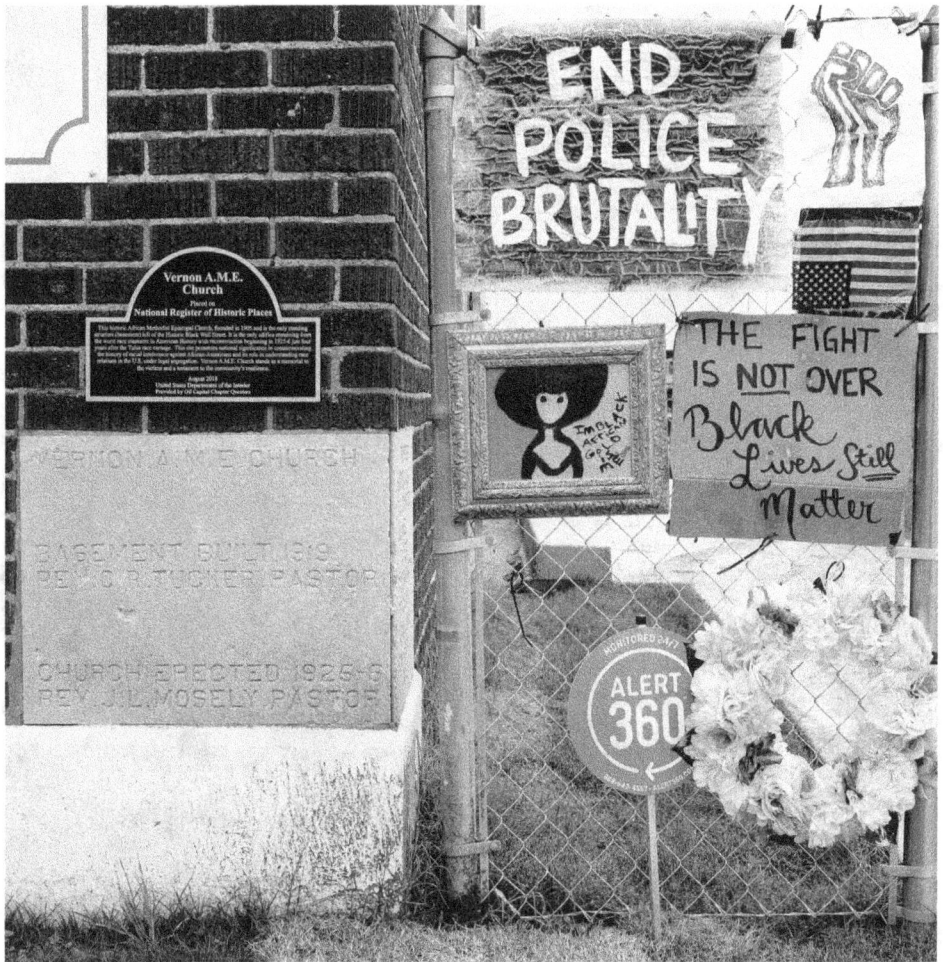

G.7. The cornerstone of Vernon AME in historic Greenwood alongside signs of protest during the 1921 centennial events. The basement of the church is recognized as the only original structure from Greenwood before the massacre. Photo by author.

G.8. Greenwood Avenue with a new street sign commemorating Black Wall Street.
Photo by Joseph Rushmore.

G.9. Souvenir shop on Greenwood Avenue selling Black Wall Street memorabilia.
Photo by author.

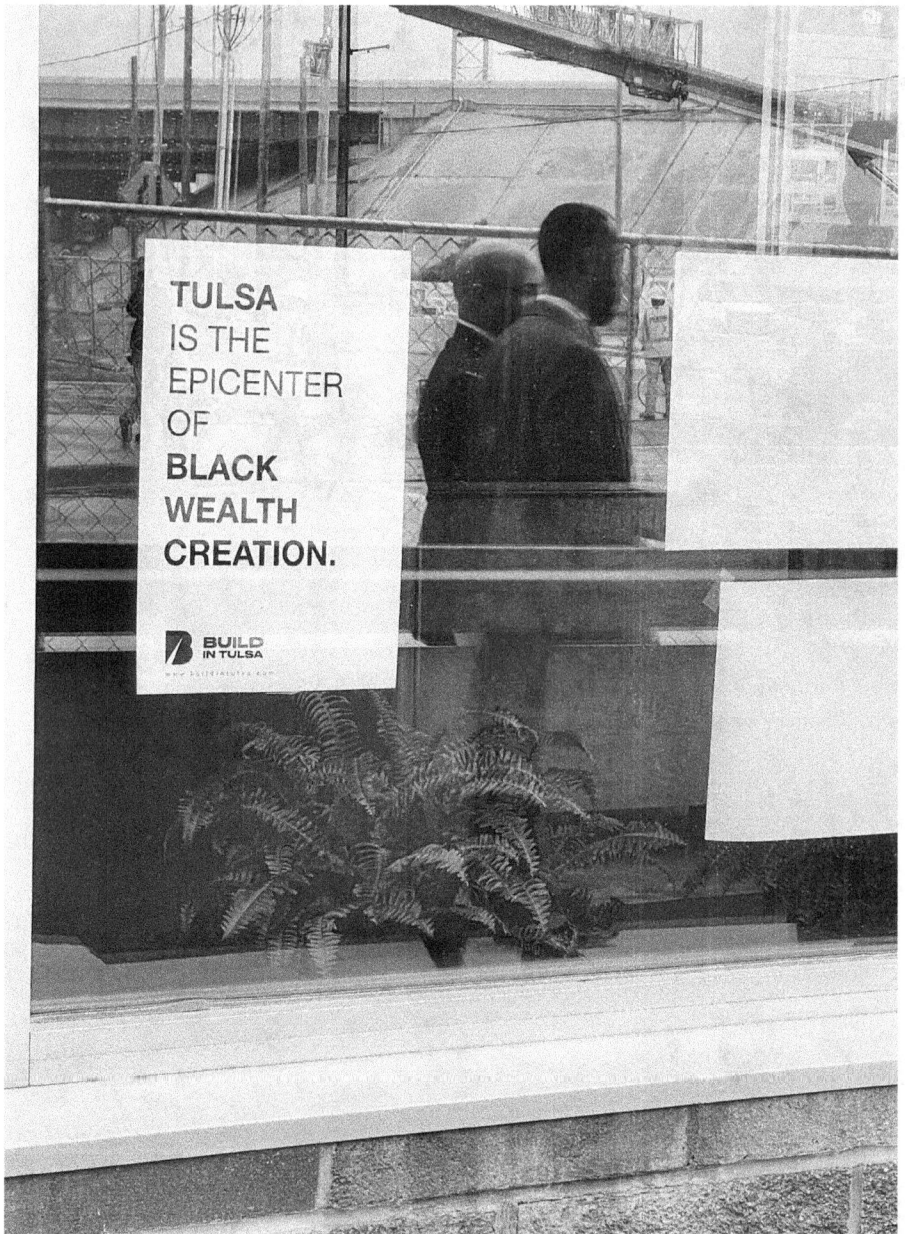

G.10. Organizations like Build in Tulsa aim to utilize the commercial history of Greenwood to encourage new entrepreneurism in the area. In the reflection are two professional men, Interstate 244, and construction equipment for the new Greenwood Rising Center. Each is symbolic of the history and the anticipated future of the area. Photo by author.

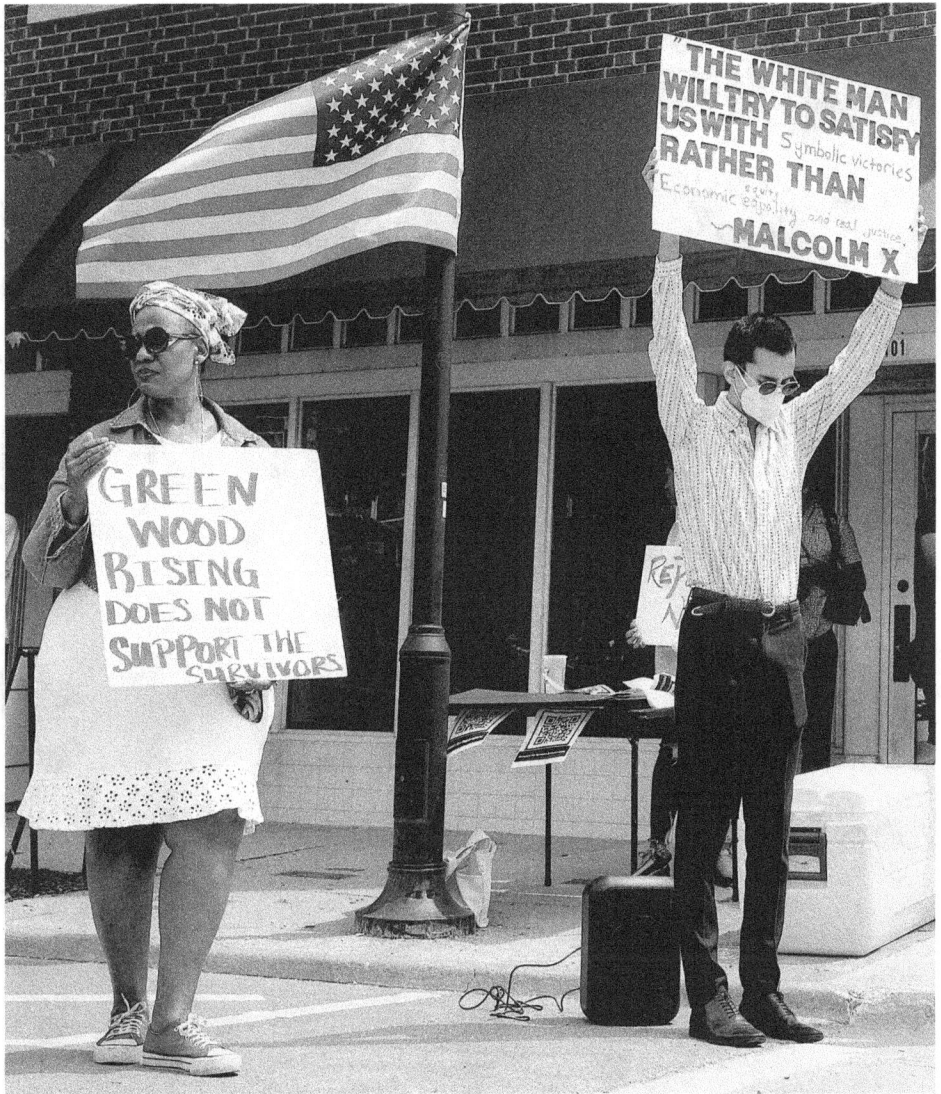

G.11. Two of many protesters responding to the opening of the Greenwood Rising historical center, widely felt to be a project exploiting the history of Greenwood. Photo by author and Joel Wanek.

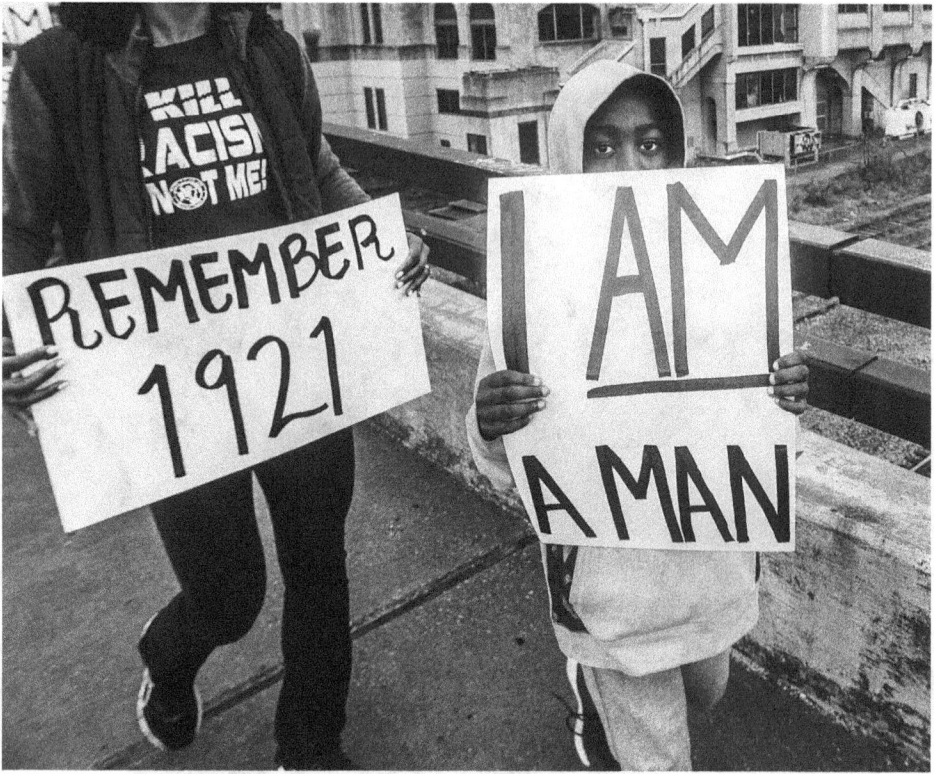

G.12. Two participants in Vernon AME's weekly march to Tulsa City Hall demanding reparations for the 1921 race massacre. Photo by Joseph Rushmore.

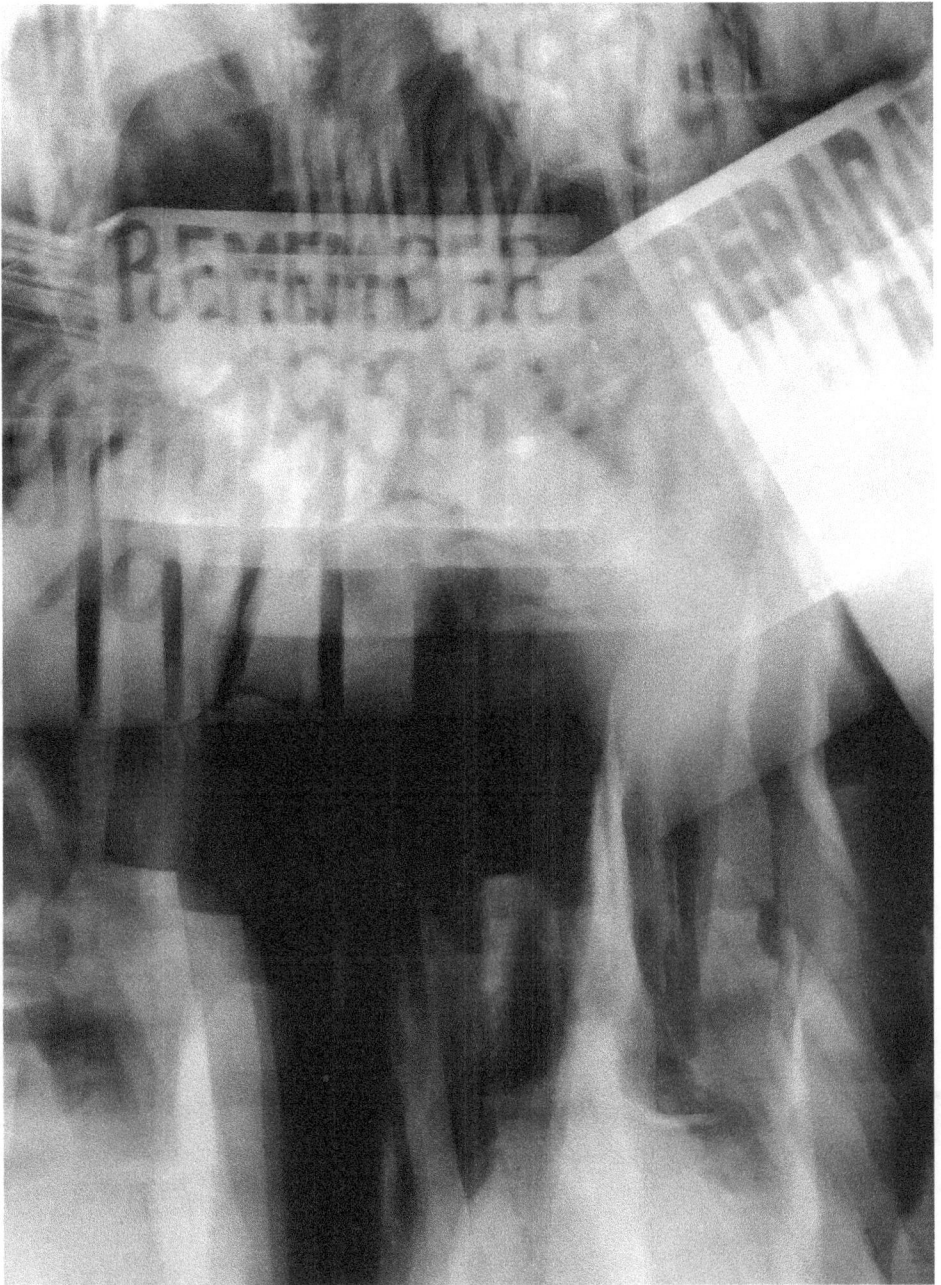

G.13. Signs from Vernon AME's weekly march to Tulsa City Hall demanding reparations. Photo by Joseph Rushmore.

G.14. Tulsa residents in Oaklawn Cemetery, at a location believed to be one mass burial site of victims from the 1921 race massacre, prior to its excavation in 2021. Photo by Joseph Rushmore.

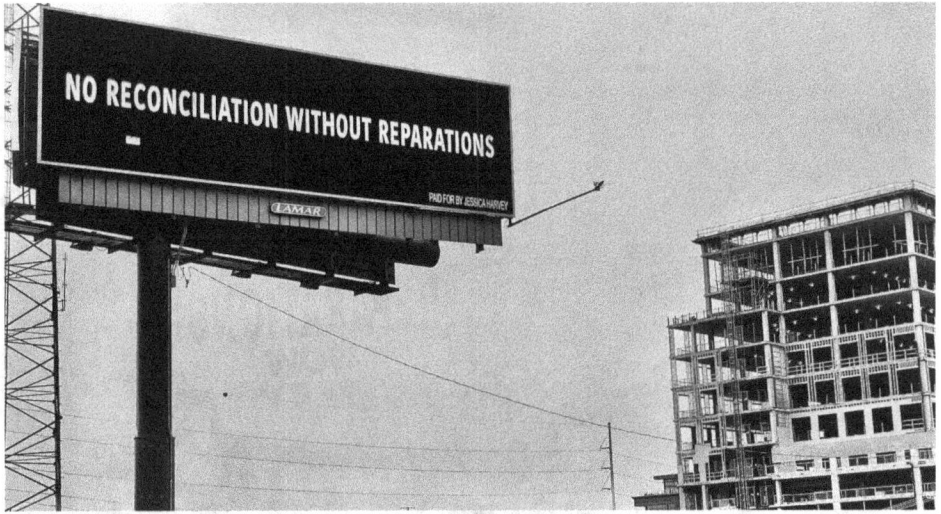

G.15. Billboard over Interstate 244 alongside a new condominium development in historic Greenwood, countering the common rhetoric of reconciliation. Photo by author.

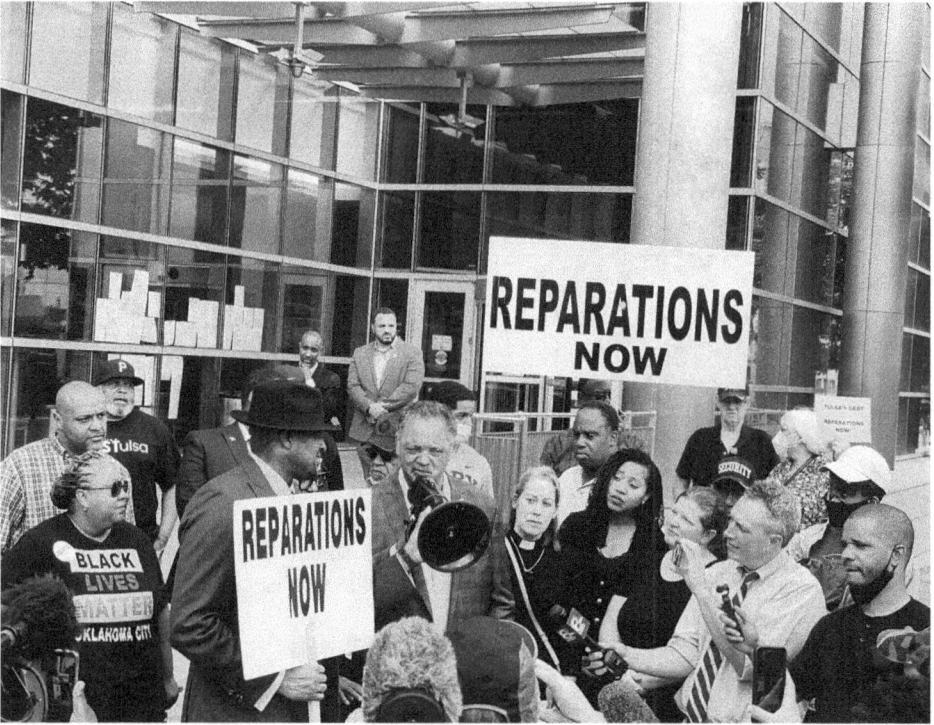

G.16. Vernon AME pastor Reverend Robert Turner, alongside Jesse Jackson, outside of Tulsa's City Hall at a gathering demanding reparations before the city council discussion of reparations. Photo by author.

G.17. The three remaining survivors of the Tulsa Race Massacre, Hughes Van Ellis, Mother Randle (Lessie Benningfield Randle), and Mother Fletcher (Viola Ford Fletcher), being celebrated at the centennial parade. Photo by Joseph Rushmore.

FOUR. **REPAIR**

"Listen, it was 635 businesses from Archer all the way down. Even off First and Brady [streets], those buildings was occupied by Black farmers, brick masons, and all kinds of people.[1] This right here was sitting thirty-five businesses. A dollar bill turned eighteen, twenty-one times, you could write your name on a dollar bill and see it before the day was done!" I was talking with Uwa Anwari, a North Tulsa elder I met at the Greenwood Cultural Center, where he volunteered. We were discussing the history of Greenwood, but I was interested in his views about some of the recent developments around revitalizing Greenwood and Black Wall Street, which included a great deal of interest and investments both locally and nationally.

Uwa was in his early seventies, and though born decades after the massacre, he recollected its history as if he had lived it firsthand. I learned from him that his generation—the first born after the massacre—was directly taught about the event by those who had. "I learned about the massacre when I was a kid, going to church, from people like Vernon White, Julius Williams, Mr. Ben, Fannie May White, Mr. Thompson. . . . All them made sure that we understood what happened to us as a people." Saying their names as an ancestral invocation, Uwa further told me that he and these church members belonged to Mt. Zion Baptist Church in Greenwood. The necessity of recounting that history made sense. Mt. Zion was completed and dedicated on April 4, 1921, mere weeks before it was "completely reduced to charred smoldering ruin during Tulsa's infamous race riot," as stated on a commemorative plaque mounted at the church entrance today. It took another thirty-one years for Mt. Zion to be rebuilt. On October 21, 1952, it was "rebuilt and dedicated as a monument to faithfulness and perseverance."

Uwa continued, "But when the massacre occurred and everything, and they was forced out—now don't think that they didn't fight—they took everything, without giving *us* anything." Stretching out his arm to cast a horizon before us that resurrected a Greenwood that today was materially imperceptible, Uwa told me, "All this is stolen. This goes back more than forty-five blocks, and everything was stolen." Uwa was a master rhetorician, his oratorical skills gained over decades of organizing. He was one of the few true griots left in North Tulsa. Talk long enough with him, and one falls into the rhythm of his narrative flair and timing that reliably catches you off guard when he arrives at his argument's pivot. "So . . ."—and there it was—"what does that mean about what we're trying to build here as a community?" Uwa continued. He knew how to let the question linger to allow its effect to mature fully.

This question about the dispossession North Tulsans have faced, and the ways they've sought to reconcile with it, was the very heart of my inquiry over the years I spent in Tulsa. Again, if the outcome of the two days of the race massacre was the razing of the Black city, then the slow process of dispossession that followed was the salting of the earth. The earth was salted, and little could be sown, much less reaped. This peculiar kind of inheritance showed up in the personal challenges of North Tulsans like Ashley and Keisha and the generalized landscape of hardship that warranted the intervention of nonprofits. The arrangement of Black life in Tulsa continues to suit the societal expectations and norms that depend on the Black relegation discussed in the first chapter. The ordering of White life seems to require and demand the disordering of Black life, as the stark boundaries of life's chances on either side of the expressway demonstrate.

North Tulsans couldn't do it on their own anymore, although they kept trying. A simple grocery store required interventions from across the scales of the state, community, and spirit. What this meant for local North Tulsans and Black Tulsans generally is that their city, and their history, needed repair. Black Tulsans required this repair because the violence of the massacre now manifested as everyday and institutional means of anti-Black racism. It has formed the unspectacular violence of systemic and intergenerational poverty.

In the previous chapters, I've examined how the community—that entity that the previous chapter showed is central to any form of progress in North Tulsa—navigated the stakes and challenges that Uwa presented. In this chapter I specifically seek to answer Uwa's question of *what* this community is trying to build. I do so by examining how they make sense of their fraught legacy, equally defined by triumph and tragedy, and how they work to find repair in their navigation, which is increasingly evidenced as a sense of restoration.

We Are Descendants

What the community was trying to build had everything to do with *who* they thought they were or wanted to be. At the Great Gathering, I saw how the community operationalized itself through collaboration. One attendee most clearly articulated "who" their community was by proclaiming to the group, "I don't want to see us be slaves where we depend on others for food, shelter, and clothing; we gotta have a grocery store that is owned and operated by Black people. *We are descendants of Black Wall Street*, and we are begging someone to sell us groceries?"

Over the past several years, the "descendant" concept has grown in use and purchase. It references being directly descended from victims of the 1921 race massacre while also signaling a generalized sense of belonging in Tulsa. The former definition became ever more important and dominant as the movement for reparations for the massacre gained momentum in the years preceding the massacre's centenary. Justice for Greenwood, an organization associated with a reparations suit filed by Damario Solomon-Simmons in 2021, opened a dedicated descendant hotline and online portal for a class-action solicitation.[2] Still, a generalized descent remained and functioned as a category that also advanced a reparative claim to Greenwood's geography and history. This use is well represented by the North Tulsa hip-hop group Fire in Little Africa—whose name recovers the historically derogatory assignation of the Greenwood District as Little Africa. In their song "Descendants," Fire in Little Africa exclaim:

This is our home, Little Africa, Greenwood . . .
It's in our souls . . .
This is the voice of a descendant of a martyr . . .
From a lineage of warriors who came for ours . . .
From the beginning to end, you'll remember my skin . . .
Since the massacre happened, my people seeking revenge . . .
We are descendants![3]

Fire in Little Africa in this song and across their entire album—released on the massacre's centenary—locate their belonging, their claim to Greenwood's history, and its claim to repair through descent. Their song, Justice for Greenwood, and the Great Gathering attendee each advance a notion of descent identified by inheritance, self-reliance, and perseverance, all qualities that motivate an aspiration for community formation. But each also especially positions these qualities and the claims that they motivate as essentially based on recuperating Black Wall Street's historical success.

The legacy of Black Wall Street's prosperity and affluence, which the community sought to revitalize, was an organizing and driving notion of community—it represented everything that North Tulsa today wasn't. This restorative ethic of prosperity is present in the attendee's counterdiscourse of begging; in other lyrics from Fire in Little Africa's "Descendants," where the group claims that the 1921 White mob was "preying on the prosperous"; and in Justice for Greenwood's pursuit of financial compensation for massacre survivors and descendants to "bolster [the] present-day Greenwood community."[4] The idea of restoration, then, answered *who* the community was and *what*, as Uwa asked me, they were trying to build. Who they were, or specifically who they wanted to be, and what they were building were singularly articulated as a retrospective sense of an economically prosperous community. In other words, they were producing, through the act of "recovery," a descriptive statement of themselves that was based in Greenwood's material past but made available today through the immaterial claim of descent.

Hannibal Johnson's accounting of Greenwood illustrates this assertion well. He advances that "African Americans in Tulsa engaged one another in commerce. In the process, they created a nationally-renowned hotbed of Black entrepreneurial activity."[5] Black Tulsans in Greenwood formed a community where commercial relations meaningfully facilitated and defined their social ties. This narrative stands as a significant model for North Tulsa residents' contemporary framing of their community, which demands the recovery of this narrative past of prosperity.

However, this narrative conveniently overlooks that prosperity's formation. I provided an account of Greenwood's founding and the way it was made possible by African American access to capital and land among "the talented cadre of African American businesspersons and entrepreneurs that helped shape America's Negro Wall Street," according to Johnson.[6] While that access was the beginning of the local economy, its productivity and ultimate success were facilitated by segregation, which "forced Tulsa's African Americans to do business with one another."[7] Johnson argues that the "economic detour" of segregation permitted the Greenwood District to prosper, as Greenwood's "dollars circulated repeatedly within the African American community."[8] While one view might be that segregation gave Greenwood's capital no choice but to operate within the community, to be sure, more than land, capital, and the closed economy were necessary for Greenwood's success, as industriousness, creativity, and productivity also propelled Greenwood's economy. According to Johnson, "'Deep Greenwood,' the first two blocks of Greenwood Avenue, just north of Archer Street, became the hub of Tulsa's African-American business community. Two- and three-story commercial buildings dotted the thoroughfare, housing Tulsa's unusually large number of African-American entrepreneurs and professionals. The clothing stores, nightclubs, cafes, rooming houses, and other businesses lining the streets and avenues of the Greenwood District provided ample opportunity for casual strolls, shopping sprees, and entertainment excursions. Greenwood offered a dab of this, a pinch of that—a little bit of everything."[9]

This depiction of Greenwood's commercial success or productivity stood as the standard of community for the many people I spoke to. Success measured the community's health. Thus, North Tulsa was doing poorly because North Tulsans were poor. In operation was the same tautology found in Clifton's community collaboration model.

In Tulsa's dominant framing of the Black community, Greenwood–as–Black Wall Street is the only narrative that can legitimately be portrayed and celebrated. Hardly discussed is that most of Greenwood's residents lived in poverty, in the shadow of its minority Black middle class. The 2001 Race Riot Commission report notes that during the massacre, the "looting and burning of African American homes was indiscriminate, [in which] both poor and wealthy families lost their homes."[10] However, in celebrating and mourning what and who was lost in the massacre, Greenwood's impoverished never figure as part of Black Wall Street. Thus, there is much similarity between contemporary North Tulsans and the majority of historic Greenwood. Still, the narrative to shape the ethics of community formation emphasizes the prosperous thread of Greenwood's story, perhaps understandably.

To understand how this is possible, it is important to turn to Michel-Rolph Trouillot, who tells us that "history reveals itself only through the production of specific narratives" and that the exercising of power "makes some narratives possible and silences others."[11] As Trouillot shows, "Silences are produced not so much by an absence of facts or interpretations as through conflicting appropriations."[12] The prevailing narrative about Greenwood presents a selective interpretation of its past, one with the gloss of prosperity. That narrative demands that its purveyors work to make its framework fit, which "set[s] the cycle of silences," as Trouillot names the process, that obscures narratives that lack sufficient power to exert themselves.[13] What remains are "conflicting appropriations" or a narrative agreement that "masks a history of conflicts."[14] This agreement in North Tulsa is the collective subscription to the prosperity narrative, despite North Tulsans' challenges reconciling with their existing history of poverty.

The result in real terms is a wrestling with the weight and burden of the narrative of their past, which are too much to bear. We saw this wrestling play out in the previous chapter and the attendee's statement at the beginning of this discussion. It's helpful to return to the attendee's statement. Again, he said, "I don't want to see us be *slaves where we depend* on others for food, shelter, and clothing; we *gotta* have a grocery store that is owned and operated by Black people. *We are descendants of Black Wall Street, and we are begging someone to sell us groceries?*" His pronouncements were more than mere casual assertions. They were declarations of truths uttered to counter the inherent contradiction of North Tulsans' impoverished circumstances. North Tulsans were meant to be neither enslaved nor dependent. The attendee's *gotta* was a corrective to resolve the contradiction of the descendants of Black Wall Street begging for groceries.

But this wrestling was perhaps never more poignantly demonstrated to me than in the quiet declaration of Darrell, the master's student at Oklahoma State University–Tulsa (OSU-Tulsa). We were continuing our conversation in the Tulsa Arts District, just a stone's throw away from Greenwood, and as if talking to himself, he said wistfully, "We're still trying." "Trying?" I asked, snapping him out of a trance. "Oh, yeah, you know, we're still trying, really trying to revitalize the area. To bring *it* back," he said, gesturing toward Greenwood. Maybe it was a consequence of my well-established reputation for pedantry, but I became fixed on Darrell's "trying," meditating on the word and the labor it implied. It wasn't that the community was facing challenges with the government or some predatory developer; those were confrontations at which they had not yet arrived in earnest. The labor of trying was working through the problem of community, and one that found itself wanting when weighing itself against its history. This challenge increased in difficulty as they struggled to carry the burden of Greenwood's historical narrative of success.

The wrestling, to be sure, is not simply a problem for North Tulsa's community but is an intrinsic issue with the general development and operation of the community. Community is complicated, and even more so when it necessitates a stable narrative. Miranda Joseph's argument for community and capitalism's coconstitution clarifies North Tulsa's community problem. To Joseph, the social hierarchism of capitalism relies on and even generates discourses of community.[15] "Communal subjectivity," as Joseph argues, "is constituted not by identity but rather through practices of production and consumption."[16] The demand for production and consumption is why capitalism works "so relentlessly and so explicitly to constitute community."[17] We see in historic Greenwood how capitalist community—rooted in structural inequality, specifically segregation—accordingly produced economic productivity. Joseph's proposition implies that most communities lack the kind of equality they believe the phenomenon of community implies, which is undoubtedly the case for historic Greenwood and contemporary North Tulsa.

Following Joseph's argument that community is a capitalist process, the question remains whether the constitutive presence of capitalism undermines the validity of an idealized community. While the gist of Joseph's argument, this view troubles, or even undoes, the importance of idealized, utopian notions of communal relations inherent in Black ideations of community— the same community that both forms and holds up the ethical expectations of Greenwood and Black Wall Street. However, to Joseph, the community formation she advances depends on "mythic origin stories, on narratives that aim to restore some imagined historical community as timeless."[18] Thus, there is no inherent contradiction between the mythic formation of community and capitalism. Cedric Robinson established this point in demonstrating the interdependence between capitalist development and centuries-old western European mythmaking, forming and facilitating communities of exception and exploitation.[19]

What we see with Greenwood is a presentation of that formula by which the only legible form of community is the one that is produced through capitalism. The remainder of Greenwood, that poverty-ridden majority, is narratively marginalized, if not erased, because the community cannot function, much less exist, without a capitalist mythos or Trouillot's "conflicting appropriations." In Tulsa this tendency is most observable through the institutional reproduction of Greenwood's narrative of exceptionality.

Greenwood Rising

Greenwood and its image of prosperity understandably serve as a lasting source of inspiration for many Black Tulsans who seek to restore the glorious days of Black Wall Street. Efforts to emphasize this influence have done much to identify and counter the absence of Black accomplishment in the chronicling of American life and the established refusal to acknowledge that accomplishment locally.

What North Tulsa's geography and history mean to Black Tulsans is so inextricably tied to this accounting of prosperity that institutions have been developed to advance it. By the 1980s, various social organizations and political coalitions took Greenwood's resurgence as a lodestar for their collective aspirations. One such organization was the Greenwood Cultural Center, which opened in 1995 with a $3.5 million grant from the Economic Development Administration, $100,000 raised by the local Black community, and two and a half acres of land in historic Greenwood and $275,000 provided by the City of Tulsa.[20] The Greenwood Cultural Center's opening heralded the resurgence of the Greenwood District's legacy. The center's website states that its mission is to be "the keeper of the flame for the Black Wall Street era" and "to preserve African American heritage and promote positive images of the African American community by providing educational and cultural experiences, promoting intercultural exchange, and encouraging cultural tourism."[21]

In its effort to promote "positive images" of Greenwood's past, the center protects and preserves the legacy of prosperity that once defined the district through the joint qualifications of community and commerce. As Black Wall Street's legacy survived, and its legend grew, its definition as a community would find itself subsumed into a notion of the "commercial" that became ever more distant as North Tulsa endured successive waves of underdevelopment. This complicated discourse about the community went beyond the stable narratives that formal organizations like the Greenwood Cultural Center could unproblematically advance. Securing this stable narrative of community was needed to facilitate any agenda, such as getting a grocery store built, and this regularly meant invoking the trope of Black Wall Street. However, against the absence of robust commerce in North Tulsa, the legacy of Black Wall Street operated as an uneasy foil that accentuated the distinctive poverty of the community.

North Tulsa was rich with narrative wealth yet lacked the wherewithal to reliably mobilize it for its benefit; thus, the names Greenwood and Black Wall Street became available for broader use. Indeed, Greenwood's history of prosperity was attractive. It became increasingly so during the aftermath of George Floyd's 2020 murder when seemingly countless American political and corporate entities sought opportunities to proclaim—and market—their support of Black life. During the few years leading up to the 2021 centennial of the race massacre, this broader mobilization of Greenwood as a promotional phenomenon was locally well underway. It hit a fever pitch the year before the centennial, following Floyd's murder, which occurred during the weekend of the massacre's ninety-ninth anniversary.

Observing the political and corporate opportunism at play, James Reynolds, a Black Tulsan who works for a North Tulsa nonprofit that focuses on Black male recidivism, worried that Tulsa's politicians would "do the same thing they always do." James and I were discussing the recently formed 1921 Tulsa Race Massacre Centennial Commission. Tulsa mayor G. T. Bynum and Oklahoma US senator Kevin Matthews had announced its formation in 2017. On the centennial commission's website, Matthews, the commission chair, writes that "the 1921 Tulsa Race Massacre Centennial Commission will leverage the history surrounding the events of nearly 100 years ago by developing programs, projects, events and activities to commemorate and inform." Matthews goes on to say that the commission will work to remember the victims and survivors by creating "an environment conducive to fostering sustainable entrepreneurship and heritage tourism within the Greenwood District specifically, and North Tulsa."[22]

The commission, working toward a transparent commercial agenda under the pretense of commemoration, struck James as case of, as he put it, "You know, where you try to cash in on your pain and suffering." A "selfish trap" is how James described the commission's model. To him, the legacy of Greenwood was "not about cashing in as much as it is about building something new." "Building something new" seemed misaligned with the repeated framing of what North Tulsa hoped to become. Indeed, it was counterposed to the ongoing determination to "rebuild" Greenwood. However, I understood what James meant. He was suggesting fresh ideation of Black life and place in Tulsa. However, what was on offer was doing the "same thing they always do," to quote James.

While not with the same intention as James, the centennial commission did plan on building something new. The centennial commission raised over $30 million to fund various projects but specifically to fund its capstone project, Greenwood Rising, a new history center in the Greenwood District. Greenwood Rising was initially envisioned as an expansion of the Greenwood Cultural Center, which had for some time lacked sufficient state and local financial support. The plan was for an operational partnership between the organizations. However, a conflict would develop between the Greenwood Cultural Center board and the centennial commission regarding the structure of the cultural center's board. The centennial commission ultimately built Greenwood Rising at the southeast corner of Greenwood and Archer, just at the all-important marker of the heart of the Greenwood District. Opposing camps and a growing rift in the community of leaders and organizers in Tulsa formed around the centenary and Greenwood's redevelopment.

According to the commission, Greenwood Rising was "located at the single most iconic entrance into the Greenwood District" through donations by the Hille Foundation and 21 North Greenwood, LLC, a developer who had planned to build a mixed-use development on the site with retail space on the ground level and residences on the floors above.[23] I read about the donation on the centennial commission website's "About Us" page. There was a line saying, "Many thanks to the Hille Foundation and 21 North Greenwood, LLC, for this extraordinary gift."[24] A *gift*?

At the Greenwood Rising opening ceremony, Senator Kevin Matthews thanked those same project donors in his introductory remarks: "I love Tulsa, but there is no romance without finance, and so thank those sponsors!" I recalled Uwa's declaration that all of Greenwood was stolen land. And the notion that it could be provided back to the community as a gift was nothing less than perverse. "They talk about this Greenwood thing and rebuilding," Uwa said disapprovingly. Building on his earlier general critique, he was now specifically referencing Greenwood Rising and development along Greenwood Avenue, which included the opening of new Black-owned businesses. I asked him to expand, and he did: "Let me tell you, you can't rebuild if you don't own. We owned! We owned it. Now we renting that! It's a big difference, a huge difference. You renovating somebody else's property? That they done stole? OSU came in, all these different entities came in and took and placed themself here, displaced all the original business that was owned back then. Now they come in with different entities—I know them, the Kaiser Foundation and these other 'foundations.'" Uwa's air quotes struck more critically than I'd ever seen the gesture used before. They signaled an attempt to grasp something that he still deeply longed for: the Greenwood of his ancestors.

"But the thing about it is, how did that land come about?" Uwa asked. I offered what I thought was an obvious answer based on his critique thus far and replied, "They stole it." But Uwa intended another move—I should have known there was something more behind the obviousness of his question. "Look at Drillers Park." He was referring to the baseball park that occupied much of the Greenwood District, formally named ONEOK Field, after the natural gas company founded in 1906. Uwa continued, "They stockpiled *our* bodies during the massacre right there! And now they play baseball and entertain on our ancestors. You know?"

His theory about the location of the mass graves of the massacre's victims had become more prominent among locals throughout my several visits. The location was not formally recognized, like Oaklawn Cemetery, where the remains of nineteen massacre victims were found in 2021. The city sought to hastily rebury those remains without making provisions for properly identifying the victims and their possible relatives or allowing time to hold a reburial ceremony, callously reproducing the initial act of injury.[25] But Uwa was making a broader point: "All this is sacred ground," he said, referring to Greenwood generally. Uwa looked at me as if to produce an empathetic understanding, a sense, of his lived experience, before saying, "They on sacred ground."

By invoking his ancestors—those who taught him about the massacre and about Greenwood before it—and locating them today purportedly in the ballpark, desecrated as the foundation on which contemporary Tulsa both entertains and generates revenue, Uwa advanced a charge of criminality that was about more than just theft of land. He identified the degree, and perhaps the literal terrestrial depth, of the injuries North Tulsans lived with—injuries that were ongoing, unrecognized, but still productive. And to his fellow North Tulsans, Uwa offered an equally weighted charge: in this context of stolen land and desecrated ancestors, what could be rebuilt while merely "renting"?

While Uwa advanced an argument for recovering Greenwood's ancestors, some of whom the city would seek to rebury unceremoniously, the best that the City of Tulsa and the centennial commission could muster was "the Pathway to Hope," something of a walking-tour route that runs between Greenwood Avenue and the John Hope Franklin Reconciliation Park, a block to the west. John Hope Franklin Reconciliation Park set the model by which Greenwood Rising and the Pathway to Hope were developed. Located in the historic Greenwood District at the intersection of Elgin, Detroit, and Interstate 244, the park was intended as a major step toward "reconciliation." It was funded by the state of Oklahoma, the City of Tulsa, seven philanthropic funds and foundations, ONEOK, and the Bank of Oklahoma. Then mayor of Tulsa, Kathy Taylor, hailed the park as "a milestone in our city's path toward reconciliation." The city intended the park to be a promise, with Taylor saying, "We know that we cannot change our history. But we can learn from the mistakes of the past, then work on solutions that translate into a brighter future for our children and grandchildren."[26]

That promise of reconciliation is represented by the on-site Hope Plaza, home to the Tower of Reconciliation. The twenty-five-foot-tall bronze cylindrical tower narratively depicts African American history as one of struggle and literal upward mobility. At its base is a set of Africans holding shields and spears. Going up the length of the spiraling sculpture is a depiction of the migration of enslaved Africans to Indian Territory alongside Native Americans on the Trail of Tears, the immigration of free Blacks to Oklahoma, the all-Black towns, and finally Greenwood and the riot and the efforts to rebuild afterward. Toward the top of the tower is the word "Reconciliation," just below figures helping one another climb toward the sky.

The tower is joined by a sixteen-foot granite structure that contains three life-size bronze sculptures representing images from the 1921 riot. The first figure, titled *Hostility*, shows a White man fully armed for assault. The second, *Humiliation*, depicts a Black man with his hands raised in a manner that is evocative of the slogan "Hands up, don't shoot." The last is *Hope*, showing the White director of the Red Cross in 1921 holding a Black baby. This last statue always provoked quizzical looks and questions from Black park patrons. That a White man and Black baby should symbolize hope smacked of the patronizing framework that had in many ways suppressed the self-determined development of North Tulsa. Moreover, the promise of reconciliation, as represented by the memorial, was now permanently cast in the shadow of a new condominium development erected across the street.

The pathway, like the park, intended to serve as a reconciliatory metaphor is similarly and achingly overshadowed. The path is sandwiched between ONEOK Field—the proclaimed burial site of Uwa's ancestors—and Interstate 244, which had buried the Black community of Greenwood in every meaningful way. Cognizant of the symbolism of the highway, the centennial commission asserts that "the Pathway to Hope will symbolically reconnect a Greenwood District bisected by I-244 during Tulsa's urban renewal phase in the 1960s and 70s. What some locals called 'urban removal' displaced citizens and businesses and plowed through 'Black Wall Street,' Tulsa's thriving Black business district known throughout the land. The Pathway to Hope will acknowledge this history, elevate Black Wall Street icons, and encourage present-day healing of past, yet lingering, wounds." The pathway is effectively a sidewalk with a highway sound-barrier wall. The wall functions as a sparse mural featuring quotes from John Hope Franklin and various images that include yearbook pages from Booker T. High School. Oddly, the barrier is not high enough to entirely block the view of the highway or the vehicles zipping past, as most sound barriers do. This leaves Interstate 244 visible and still imposing, a damning metaphor for the community's inability to entirely overcome the forces of its dispossession.

If the highway represented a previous form of urban removal, contemporary gentrification would signal that there was still more to take from Greenwood. Condominiums, like the one that lurked behind Reconciliation Park, had begun to populate the landscape of Greenwood—all to accompany the growing Tulsa Arts District's ever-expanding array of amenities and activities. Recall that the location for Greenwood Rising, what the centennial commission cited as the "single most iconic entrance into the Greenwood District," was originally slated to become a condominium development. And while it did not, the lot directly across from Greenwood Rising, at that same iconic entrance, had already become a mixed-use apartment complex called Greenarch.

It is tempting to identify these residential developments as purely part of a new wave of gentrification. In Greenwood this process perhaps should include the arrival of ONEOK Field, the stadium home of the Tulsa Drillers baseball team, which opened in 2010. Perhaps we should go further back still and include the campus of OSU-Tulsa that occupied much of historic Greenwood. In 1986 what was then called the Tulsa Urban Renewal Authority—now the Tulsa Development Authority—provided the land to the University Center at Tulsa. A collective of four universities, University Center included the satellite campus of the historically Black Langston University, the University of Oklahoma, OSU, and Northeastern State University. By 1999 only OSU and Langston remained. Today much of the grounds remain vacant.

The fact is that Greenwood has long undergone the process of "regeneration" over the century post massacre that it endured municipal advances to possess its land. Thus, the arrival of the condominium landscape should be seen as a mission accomplished. The Greenwood District has become a site for gentrification that actively mobilizes the memorialization of the massacre to locate, mark, and market the value of the massacre and Greenwood's prosperity before it. Greenwood had increasingly become associated mostly with the adjacent arts district that had for some time been adopting the now-ubiquitous aesthetic of promotional murals, vintage record shops, and chic whiskey bars. Indeed, there is no perceptible shift in amenities and attractions walking along Archer Street from the Tulsa Arts District into Greenwood. But now Greenwood could accomplish the objectives of gentrification through racial accentuation. On the ground floor of Greenarch, several Black businesses operated, such as the popular café Black Wall Street Liquid Lounge, and at the iconic intersection of Greenwood Avenue and Archer Street sat a Black-owned restaurant, Lefty's on Greenwood.

In recognizing the evident and undeniable presence of gentrification in Greenwood and holding constant its dependence on dispossessive violence, which through redevelopment is made visible, how should we account for the presence of Black commerce as party to, or in partnership with, pernicious capital? Brandi Thompson Summers's *Black in Place* provides a helpful framework for thinking through this question by understanding Blackness in the city as a result of urban dispossession.

Summers argues that systematic displacement through gentrification decorporealizes and aestheticizes Blackness to facilitate the development of White capital. The process yields what Summers theorizes as "black aesthetic emplacement," which permits a continuing focus on the significance of Blackness in place while noting how Blackness's qualities—like Black "cool"—can be extracted, disassociated, and utilized.[27] Summers's ethnographic context of Washington, DC, provides an assessment of gentrification as a Black aesthetic that absents the Black bodies that stand as its referent. There, the extracted Black aesthetic is utilized by White capital to appeal to White middle-class aesthetics and ethics. Greenwood is situated differently from Summers's DC, as the function of aesthetics is not at issue. Still, the extractability and productivity of Blackness, or what Summers refers to as Blackness's simulacrum, remains critical to what's happening in Greenwood.

At issue is the usability of Blackness through capitalist interpolation, and not just as it's exercised by White developers and entrepreneurs. The Blackness in Tulsa is facilitated by a historical Black capitalist ethic that complicates and blurs the broader circuits of capitalist development. To be sure, Summers provides an account of Black capitalists aiding in the White utilization of Blackness. However, her analysis focuses on how Black businesses are largely disadvantaged in the commercial landscape of her ethnographic site, DC's H Street Corridor.

As an example, local organizers in Greenwood held an event called Economic Empowerment Day as part of the centenary events. The event's tagline was "From Tragedy to Triumph." The day aimed "to create a collective focal point for the national conversation on the Racial Wealth Gap and the Inequality in Access to Capital," with top-tier sponsorship by the Bank of Oklahoma and J. P. Morgan Chase. The event was organized around three panel-based programs: "Black Wall Street," for "connecting justice-minded investment allocators and policy makers with minority-owned asset management firms"; "Black Commerce Street," for "connecting high potential entrepreneurs and business owners with capital and mentoring opportunities, with a focus on innovation and the importance of entrepreneurship within the Black community"; and "Black Wealth Street," for "providing individuals and families practical advice on building personal and cross-generational wealth." Thus, processes like gentrification are even more insidious than typically believed because of a predisposition toward the notion of development influenced by the history of Greenwood's noted affluence.

Political compromises like "reconciliation" are seen to conciliate the tensions that would otherwise cause capitalist frictions. Throughout, the narrative emphasis on Greenwood's prosperity is regularly articulated and circulated as part of a historical practice of boosterism that goes back to the founding of Greenwood, and Black landholding in Indian Territory, as discussed earlier in the text. There is something fundamentally alluring about the prosperity that Greenwood projects and the potential of its narrative.

Productive Narratives

The circulating prosperity narrative in Tulsa encourages the extraction of Greenwood's commercial affect, or what is effectively its brand. That affect is constituted as an alluring and branded mixture of triumph and tragedy and produces an immaterial "surfeit" of Greenwood. This surfeit is understood as the "excess" of Greenwood's "social meaning" and becomes tied up in the exception of its history of prosperity.[28] The surfeit of prosperity fills the negotiable "gap between materiality and symbolic value," and in the process, the very meaning of Greenwood becomes open, available, and usable.[29] Greenwood carries such representational weight; its surfeit is so semiotically excessive. The challenge with that surfeit of representation is that Greenwood produced more value than North Tulsans have the wherewithal to utilize, much less to control.

"For so long, just being able to talk about the massacre was complex," James told me. Having spoken to other North Tulsans, I was not surprised by this claim. "Most people, even folks living here, just really recently started learning more and talking about it over the last few years, and it wasn't like how it's been recently, you know, like a 'big' topic." Interest in Greenwood grew rapidly, and North Tulsans struggled to keep pace. It is necessary, then, to understand how North Tulsans worked to make sense of their history.

One of those people was Shantell, a community organizer in North Tulsa. She worked on health initiatives, specifically partnering with the North Tulsa Community Coalition. They focus on health for each of the five zip codes in North Tulsa by tying together education and economic development training.

Given her area of expertise and community engagement, I asked Shantell to describe her sense of the history of the massacre of Black Wall Street in the North Tulsa community. Shantell shared that what she had long heard from family and her community was "an ugly narrative." This narrative specifically reproduced the accounts of the violence and the dispossession. But that narrative didn't comport with the perception and feelings she had of her community. "I mean, I lived and went to church in the north and everything." However, she noted that there were inherent disparities. "One thing I realized is that we had to travel a lot. I mean, travel outside of North Tulsa to get a lot of things done."

I thought at first that she was exclusively referring to the structural need to access goods in other parts of the city because they weren't available in North Tulsa. She explained that while that was partly the case, she meant that her family preferred to do their shopping outside the neighborhood. There was, she said, "a kind of dislike" for her neighborhood. The North Tulsa of Shantell's youth would have been fighting the scourge of the drug epidemic of the 1980s.[30] As Shantell got older, she began to appreciate what she called "the rich history of North Tulsa." She gravitated toward it: "I had not heard about the full history and how it affected so many people, quite honestly."

Shantell had not known much about the history of North Tulsa and the massacre despite the Oklahoma Commission to Study the Tulsa Race Riot of 1921 having produced its 2001 report comprehensively detailing that history. That commission and their report had taken up the task of combating the very silencing of Black Tulsa's past that denied Shantell knowledge of Greenwood's history. Despite various organizations in Tulsa that worked to tell the full history of Black life in Tulsa, such as the North Tulsa Historical Society, and the prominent role of Tulsa native and renowned historian John Hope Franklin, the report argues that the history of slavery and Black people in Oklahoma was outright ignored:

> During the World War II years, when the nation was engaged in a life or death struggle against the Axis, history textbooks quite understandably stressed themes of national unity and consensus. The Tulsa race riot, needless to say, did not qualify. But in Tulsa itself, the riot had affected far too many families, on both sides of the tracks, ever to sink entirely from view. But as the years passed and the riot grew ever more distant, a mindset developed which held that the riot was one part of the city's past that might best be forgotten altogether. Remarkably enough, that is exactly what began to happen.[31]

The commission produced the *Tulsa Race Riot* report in 2001 "to develop a historical record of the 1921 Tulsa Race Riot." In its two hundred pages, the report made plain the devastation that the violence caused Greenwood residents and laid out its consequences for members of the Tulsa Black community in the eighty years since. The report demonstrated that the city government had conspired with the White mob that terrorized the Greenwood neighborhood, known colloquially at the time as Negro Wall Street. The commission's recommendations included the provision of reparations for descendants of the massacre's survivors, among other measures. Still, the school curriculum did not teach the riot; neither the city nor state paid the reparations that the report stipulated; and the other recommendations went unheeded. The whole affair went quiet. The most concrete outcomes included establishing the Greenwood Cultural Center in 1995 and the 2010 dedication of the John Hope Franklin Reconciliation Park. This process demonstrated a belief that with recognition came reconciliation, but seemingly at the cost of remembrance.

Perhaps this was the reason for the silence. Silence can be viewed as a mechanism for coping with the racial trauma of the massacre.[32] What was the point of talking about the riot, with so little done in the decades that had passed since? Maybe what was worth talking about was long gone, and talking about it would only bring a painful recollection of the former town.

Historian Robin D. G. Kelley in an interview on the centenary of the race massacre was "skeptical" as to why "we keep repeating the mantra that this story is unknown." Kelley proclaims that "the Tulsa race massacre is the most thoroughly studied and discussed incident of all of the 20th century racial pogroms."[33] To make his point, Kelley lists numerous occasions when the massacre's story has been told over the one hundred years since the event, including in front-page newspaper articles in 1921. He references survivor Mary E. Jones Parrish's 1923 self-published eyewitness account; the 2001 riot commission report; and a 1999 *60 Minutes* special on the event, titled "Tulsa Burning."[34] Kelley also notes that there have been dozens of academic books written on the subject and on Greenwood from scholars like Hannibal Johnson, James Hirsch, Tim Madigan, and, of course, Scott Ellsworth.[35] While Kelley's skepticism was supported by these points, he still did not provide an explanation as to why the mantra that the story was unknown persisted.

Kelley's list of public accounts and analyses was hardly revelatory. In fact, the authors of the 2001 *Tulsa Race Riot* report provided an extensive history of efforts to publicize the riot. Still, they argued, "None of these activities [. . .] was by itself any match for the culture of silence which had long hovered over the riot, and for years to come, discussions of the riot were often curtailed."[36] Unlike Kelley, the report's authors provided an explanation as to why, and without resorting to claims of conspiracy:

> In the days and weeks that followed the riot, editorial writers from coast-to-coast unleashed a torrent of stinging condemnations of what had taken place. For many Oklahomans, and particularly for whites in positions of civic responsibility, such sentiments were most unwelcome. For regardless of what they felt personally about the riot, in a young state where attracting new businesses and new settlers was a top priority, it soon became evident that the riot was a public relations nightmare. Nowhere was this felt more acutely than in Tulsa. For some, and particularly for Tulsa's white business and political leaders, the riot soon became something best to be forgotten, something to be swept well beneath history's carpet. What is remarkable, in retrospect, is the degree to which this nearly happened. For within a decade after it had happened, the Tulsa race riot went from being a front-page, national calamity, to being an incident portrayed as an unfortunate, but not really very significant, event in the state's past.[37]

The authors of the report note that the "historical amnesia" around the riot was nowhere "more startling than in Tulsa itself," helping to explain why, in my early visits to Tulsa over the years that I worked there, the massacre rarely came up in conversation.[38] The consequence of the amnesia is that, as the report notes, "the riot grew ever more distant," and that distance created "a mindset," the authors note, "which held that the riot was one part of the city's past that might best be forgotten altogether."[39] In addition to this orientation to the history, as I discuss later in this chapter, the compromise of reconciliation encouraged everyone to move on.

I have learned that the North Tulsa community holds the accomplishments of Greenwood as the bedrock of their identity. Thus, the massacre's story must have complicated the narrative of their self-perception. In other words, it was only a part of their story. Furthermore, the community of Greenwood immediately went about rebuilding after the riot, despite the destruction and detentions. Why talk about what was destroyed instead of celebrating what was rebuilt? This is the importance of North Tulsa, which has been overlooked with the increased attention to the 1921 massacre in recent years.

Although the massacre took many lives, it did not kill the memory of who this community was. Still, the massacre happened. But while it stands as the most acutely devastating act in the history of Greenwood, it would not be the only dispossessive act that would define the community north of the Frisco tracks. Indeed the massacre was joined by a series of assaults that contribute to the complicated history with which North Tulsans must contend. The massacre represents the constant threat that surrounded communities like Greenwood. In the decades that followed, this community was repeatedly assaulted. These assaults would come in forms like redlining, urban development, and gentrification. While comparatively more benign and insidious than extraordinary and riotous violence, these assaults have had a more lasting effect and consequence for the North Tulsa community.

Despite it all, North Tulsans have held on to their talents, will, and memory and marshal them to continue to look toward tomorrow. *This* is the story of North Tulsa, and this was the history that Shantell wanted to learn. For Shantell, the best bet was to "try to gather any information from conversations with older people in the church." This was easier said than done. "Even the people we went to church with, some of them were older; when we asked them questions, they were just like our family members and didn't want to talk about it."

Shantell explained that it was also hard to learn from those willing to talk because "the information just wasn't passed down." Shantell explained that she thought there was a connection between the disdain for the community and the unwillingness to discuss the massacre. There was, therefore, a geographic relation to North Tulsa that was explained and perhaps produced by these two responses. To me, it sounded as if Shantell's family did not indulge in the forms of nostalgia that are what geographer David Lowenthal calls "memory with the pain removed."[40]

Memory often takes the form of recollecting and forgetting, condensing and transforming, experiences for the past to work in service of the present. The reluctance to entertain an idealized history and memory presented difficulties for recollecting Greenwood's whole story. And for young North Tulsans like Shantell, it's challenging to learn from those who experienced the massacre. The engagements and the interactions that came from these discussions, however infrequent or incomplete, produced for Shantell a "generational gap" where the older generation's reluctance translated into a lack of interest in the young. This then caused a lack of communication about and inheritance of the history.

The intergenerational issue was complicated. Younger Tulsans wanted to know the history and to mobilize it to effect change, framed around justice. However, elder Black Tulsans either hadn't experienced the massacre or couldn't recall much of it. What they knew, they were often reluctant to share. Therein lay the trouble and the challenge. Regardless of the will and interest of North Tulsa's elders or youth, the conditions on the ground made it hard to mobilize. Now, I am not suggesting that individuals and groups have not been working at this. What I mean is that the structure of North Tulsa restricted the community's sense of this mobilization. The community's poverty and lack of infrastructure, the active terrain of nonprofits that, by providing external support and services, effectively siphoned off the internal will and energy for self-development—all these factors created a context that made it difficult to get traction for advancement. This inability for North Tulsans to advance made it challenging for them to reconcile with their history, and it informed how little people spoke of the massacre. When conversations happened, they took place in the intimate settings of the home, primarily as family stories. But seldom was it a publicly told history. The massacre had, for these reasons, felt silenced for a very long time.

Shantell further identified the story of Black Wall Street as the driving force behind the influx of young Black people from outside Tulsa, even outside Oklahoma. In contrast, many younger North Tulsans have historically held less interest. Regardless of interest, though, the elders' unwillingness to share their stories with outsiders impacts any passing down of the history and prevents the youth from accessing it. If the younger generation would need to take up the call, Shantell said that the older generation would have to work with them to keep it alive.

Trying to shift the tone and her mood toward the positive, I asked Shantell what could be done. She replied, "Until you get more numbers and people aware of really what's going on, then those who are fighting the fight are fighting a very long fight that makes it very hard for them to win." For Shantell, that requires educating the younger generation because "not educating the younger generation to kind of get some momentum going in the community with this history, it's going to die off if you don't teach them now or you don't involve them now. You know, eventually, it will die off. And that's something that the older generation has been fighting for years not to happen."

Shantell's framing is a novel theory for what produced the silence of the massacre, but it does not explain the quality and emphasis of the narrative that is shared. This point was critical for determining the conditions on the ground, and I wondered if she saw those gaps in the coalitions that were overtly working to improve the North Tulsa community. She gave an example regarding her experience with the Black Wall Street Chamber of Commerce, whose goal is "to enhance the quality of life for African Americans and the

North Tulsa community through economic development, education, workforce development, community development, and legislative advocacy."[41]

Shantell recounted, "I went to a meeting of the Black Wall Street Chamber of Commerce, which is separate from the historical Greenwood Chamber of Commerce. And basically, the message was 'If we don't come together, we see gentrification happening—people coming into the neighborhood and changing North Tulsa, and if people are not coming together, they [gentrifiers] can come in and cause further divide.'" In this way, the chamber was another promoter of the commerce-collaboration-community complex advanced by many other North Tulsa organizations.

Shantell was also glad to see what she called "the reemergence of Black Wall Street." But to her, it was history that was important. She was bullish on the power of the messaging, and she fervently thought that Black Wall Street "needed to be back." The idea of a prosperous Black district was for her a compelling motivator and signal that North Tulsa could be great. Her concern, however, was for the families directly impacted by poverty: "Particularly those that lost . . . you know?" Shantell paused for a moment to fully compose her thoughts, then continued, "Those families who have carried this on for generations. Some families never came back. People are still living in that. Imagine if you lost someone just like that?" Shantell thought that many of Tulsa's Black residents, even those who hadn't "lost," suffered what she called "post-traumatic slave syndrome." This term, coined by Joy DeGruy, identifies the multigenerational experience of trauma rooted in anti-Black violence that African Americans have encountered from slavery to contemporary police violence and the responding adaptive survival behaviors developed by African American communities.[42]

The diagnosis was fairly straightforward for Shantell: "Those who have experienced, you know, their families have lost everything with the massacre and, you know, generations on, it is still not where they need to be. I mean, redlining still happens. People can't get homes, or homes are very undervalued, schools are undervalued. Those things continue to be a problem in North Tulsa." North Tulsa was living with and through trauma. The massacre destroyed neighborhoods and families and left in its wake a community that desperately needed healing. To Shantell's mind, that healing could only come by way of North Tulsa's revitalization.

"When I think about the church members who tell their stories," Shantell began, "they're in their sixties and seventies. They talk about how North Tulsa was thriving, and even back then, people having their own businesses. . . ." Shantell paused. She pondered, "I don't even know if that [was] like a mentality.

And do we [today] have a certain mentality that keeps us from being our best?" she said, echoing Tony's earlier query on whether the issues North Tulsans faced were cultural. The discussion moved Shantell from feelings of admiration, when she reflected on North Tulsa's past, to disappointment, in recognizing its present. "If you were to walk or drive through North Tulsa, like, there's nothing to do. We survey different groups, and, you know, just hearing from the youth how there is nothing out there and how, you know, they wish that they had things to do. And it can look depressing. It can feel depressing. So you have nothing because it's been wiped away; it never was rebuilt. It's kind of hard to want to thrive in an area that seems gloomy at times."

Shantell's sentiments, her position on North Tulsa's history, were shared by a young North Tulsan, Tameka, whom I met while visiting the site of the Greenwood Art Project, where she worked as a volunteer. "I grew up here. Grew up right on Greenwood Avenue and went to Paradise Baptist Church," Tameka told me, establishing her credentials as a bona fide Northsider. Even though she was a North Tulsan, Tameka confessed, "It's like I never realized how rich my history was." She continued, "Like, I was going to church on sacred, like historic grounds. I'm walking up and down the street, but I'm really walking the path of my ancestors like they grew that whole community." Tameka told me that she first learned of the race massacre in high school, but not as part of her instruction. Instead, it was the result of researching a school report on the Rosewood massacre. "Once I had found that out [about Tulsa's massacre], it blew my mind."

Learning that history was a revelation for Tameka. For her, it opened an entirely new, even radical, framework for viewing her community and herself:

> I grew up on the north side, so it connects to me deeply because we still have all these disadvantages, even if you looked at me and used my high school as an example. I went to McLain. When I went to college, I felt like I was failing, and I didn't finish. And then I see my counterparts, the people I went to school with; they also went to college but didn't finish. So I see that disadvantage, that deep-rooted disadvantage. It comes from our history, and we fled out there [north], and that's where we were kind of forced to go, you know? But we're not worried about where we come from. We're just trying to get on to the next thing and trying to survive. The cycle is continuing, and if we don't speak up against it, it's gonna keep happening.

For that reason, to "speak up against it," she had gotten involved in community organizing that could work to interrupt the cycles of that history. "How are you going to learn about that history? Because we all need to see where we come from, and we need to plan for the future. We need to make a change," she told me.

> I knew a woman. She's an older woman, out by where I grew up out north, out by McLain, and she was telling me that us young people need to go to our communities, and not just doing this type of thing, but also like right in the heart of where we're from. I've actually like marched around in my neighborhood where I'm from. And we had a police officer that was also the head of 100 Black Men of Tulsa, and he showed us some markings on their houses. Why are they like this? And he talked about the drug dealers and gangs, and I lost a classmate like five days before we were supposed to graduate high school.

Tameka took a second to remember her friend; it was one of those moments of fleeting and fluttering grief that are especially familiar for those who have unexpectedly lost someone. I couldn't help but scale that sense of grief out to qualify the sense felt by the entire North Tulsa community. "From my community . . . ," Tameka started again as if in midsentence, a sentence that I imagined began with "She was . . ." Tameka continued, "That type of stuff is why I'm out in the community and do my community service because I want to help North Tulsa. I want to help where I'm from. Not just talk about it, you know? I don't want to just talk about this and not do anything more for where I'm from."

"Doing something" wasn't as straightforward as it appeared. North Tulsans like Shantell and Tameka were finally reconciling with a history that was silenced far too long but were also nowhere near deciding what they could do with it. For North Tulsans, the challenge would become greater still as their history had become open for interpretation and use beyond the boundaries of their community. Their narrative would become just one among competing demands on Greenwood's history because that history, however difficult, represented one of the few opportunities to narrate the promise of Blackness.

James attributed the recent uptick in interest in the riot to the centenary being on the horizon. "And, of course, Floyd," he added, referring to the murder of George Floyd. "You know, even the language has changed. We stopped calling it a riot and started calling it a massacre," James said, noting how quickly even the framing around the massacre was developing.

Surfeits of affect, like the excess meaning produced by Greenwood, "open up new performative spaces, possibilities, social relations, and material forms that exist in tension with, and beyond, the brand even as they emerge through it."[43] From that space emerges new profit opportunities. The result is that Greenwood's Blackness becomes increasingly available to and is actively mobilized by Black actors, including street-level entrepreneurs, local Black politicians, and nationally recognized Black celebrities, and non-Black entities looking to benefit from Black causes by appearing to provide benefits to them.

For that reason, as Greenwood's story became increasingly popular over the couple of years just preceding the massacre's centenary, there was an excess of narrative, as it were, that could be taken up and used by outside entities. The consequence was external influence over how the story of what occurred in historic Greenwood was told, without any regard for the contemporary community of North Tulsa. For example, what is presented is a narrative fixation on the exceptional violence that meted out Black bodily and community death, which reduces Tulsa's racial history to the massacre.

Starting with the 2019 release of HBO's *Watchmen*, greater national and international interest has been paid to the city's history.[44] This attention grew the following year when George Floyd was murdered on the anniversary weekend of the riot. As a result, Greenwood became a new symbol of both Black accomplishment and anti-Black violence. In many ways, the HBO series, while bringing unprecedented attention to the 1921 incident, overshadowed the efforts of many local and locally affiliated community organizers, academics, and politicians to not only tell that story but, more important, articulate the contemporary concerns of Tulsa's Black community. As a result, Tulsa's story has focused on the exceptional violence that Greenwood suffered. What has gone overlooked is the unexceptional, everyday will for advancement that mostly defines the community of North Tulsa. The retelling of the massacre's story, the decision to open *Watchmen* with Greenwood's devastation and not its brilliant development and success, reproduces the narrative that is now an American pastime—its fascination with Black death and community destruction.

This flattening of Tulsa's racial history counterposes the *other* story told about the community, that of the thriving Black Wall Street destroyed by that violence. Black Wall Street, as a trope, a model, and a lodestar of Black ambition and aspiration, has, as I've been discussing, experienced a resurgence in the everyday narratives and imaginaries of Black Tulsans, especially in the lead-up to the momentous centenary of the 1921 massacre. It, without doubt, is a memory worth celebrating and a platform for generating a

Black-directed regeneration of North Tulsa. The regeneration, however, has, in many ways, also been done without the community.

Today the symbolic power of Black Wall Street is evident. It portrays an often undepicted example of what African Americans can and did accomplish despite the impact of White supremacism in Jim Crow America. In the current culture of "Black excellence," premassacre Greenwood offers an unparalleled model. For this reason, alongside local activities to promote the narrative of Black Wall Street, outside parties have picked up the narrative for their purposes. One example that comes to mind is the "Black- and Brown-owned" Greenwood Bank founded by former Atlanta mayor Andrew Young, rapper Killer Mike, and media executive Ryan Glover. The bank's "about" page explains, "It's no secret the current financial system has failed at keeping wealth in the Black and Latino community. Our communities suffer from a lack of wealth, money circulation in the Black community, and generational transfer. That is why we created a new Black-owned financial institution. A mobile banking platform inspired by the early 1900's Greenwood District, where recirculation of Black wealth occurred all day, every day, and where Black businesses thrived. Today's Greenwood is a Black-owned banking system developed by us, for us. This is our time. Join us now. *Greenwood. Modern Banking for the Culture.*"[45] Involved and invested Black executives and celebrities, including *Grey's Anatomy* actor and activist Jesse Williams, signal the kind of Black accomplishment the Greenwood moniker is meant to represent. What is not present across the various pages of the website is any mention of Tulsa.

Another example is then US presidential candidate Mike Bloomberg's Greenwood Initiative. As the story goes, Bloomberg visited Tulsa, Oklahoma, in December 2018 to announce that the city had won Bloomberg Philanthropies' Public Art Challenge. The winning proposal, which came from the 1921 Tulsa Race Massacre Centennial Commission, focused on the tragedy of the 1921 massacre. The initiative, which received $1 million from Bloomberg Philanthropies and was supplemented by a $200,000 grant from the George Kaiser Family Foundation, became the Greenwood Art Project. Run by Rick Lowe, renowned artist and Macarthur Fellow, the project sought "not only to raise awareness of the destruction and loss of life associated with the massacre, but also to celebrate the resilience, healing and recovery of the community, in ways that resonate in today's world."[46]

Bloomberg was "moved by the story of how a predominantly Black neighborhood had become one of the country's most prosperous communities— and was appalled and angered to know that its destruction at the hands of a racist mob had been whitewashed from history books."[47] As a result, in the spring of 2020, during his presidential campaign, Bloomberg "announced an ambitious plan to accelerate the pace of wealth accumulation for Black individuals and families and address decades of underinvestment in Black communities."[48]

That plan was called the Greenwood Initiative as a "remembrance of the hundreds killed in Greenwood, and in recognition of how racism has prevented Black families from building wealth."[49] The initiative was ultimately folded into the general programming of Bloomberg Philanthropies, which works to "fulfill Greenwood's mission of reducing wealth disparities in Black communities." The initiative's initial investment of $100 million went to America's four historically Black medical schools, none of which are located in Oklahoma.

In both these cases, these organizations use the message and moniker of Greenwood ostensibly to honor its past accomplishments. However, they do so while overlooking the contemporary community of North Tulsa. This presentation sets up a complicated negotiation between the "homology between the oneness of the group or 'people'" understood through a general Blackness and "certain kinds of objects in which they see their identity as residing," which here is the represented object of Greenwood.[50]

These organizations presume an easy commensurability between Black Tulsans and Black Americans generally. There is a framework of identification between these groups, within which Black Tulsans expectedly qualify as part of the broader category of Black Americans and have access to that designation's meaning and claims. However, there is a question about the claim making ability of non-Tulsan Black Americans on Black Tulsa's history. *Their* history, made material, has become marketable and produces a tension that can only be seen as anxiety around what Michael Brown, thinking about contestations around cultural property, calls the "resistance to the uncontrolled proliferation of signs."[51] At play is Greenwood's surfeit as an accessible form of general Blackness.

The other way to understand Greenwood's use in these cases is as an excess of value. The issue is that Black people's value has always exceeded the limited and impoverished imaginations of those that have attempted to make it productive. This has meant that there is always an excess of value, and that excess has been ordered by using exception. Or another way to put it is that exceptions are valuable. In the end, Blackness is qualified value made useful. It is thus what AbdouMaliq Simone has termed "generic blackness," which "points to the uninhabitable in all that makes itself known as exemplarily inhabitable."[52] In my interpretation, I see it as working to make Blackness workable, useful, inhabitable, in Tulsa's case through the device of Greenwood. That value must be contained, regulated, given utility, but the issue is that local Tulsans and North Tulsans do not have the means to make it useful for themselves.

Through an analysis of its history, the stakes and the challenges North Tulsans faced were laid bare. Greenwood's prosperity, beginning with the 1921 massacre, has remained under assault by those seeking to benefit from the community. They were confronting gentrification, a recent history of post-urban-renewal impoverishment responded to not with state support but with philanthrocapitalist initiatives, and a legacy of violent dispossession from which they were trying to procure a narrative of promise, which was simultaneously being taken up and exploited by people were not community members. This general workability of Blackness in North Tulsa, accounted for by its history of extractive dispossession, has formed around a general condition that is preoccupied with Greenwood's prosperity and its injury.

Reparation

Many locals working to bolster Greenwood's reputation welcomed the national interest in Greenwood and its ability to bring attention to the community. This attention was perhaps the only means to attract capital to be used for locally directed development. Attracting capital would mean coming to terms with Greenwood's story becoming a national one. The prosperity of Greenwood should be heralded, then, especially where it could serve to promote local Black entrepreneurism, such as with the Build in Tulsa campaign. With the taglines of "We are fighting for the future of Black America" and "Unleash Black America's Infinite Value and Potential," Build in Tulsa seeks to "create a scalable, tech-forward business and entrepreneurship ecosystem to catalyze the creation of generational Black wealth." Effectively, the group, which secured funding from various venture capitalists and the ubiquitous George Kaiser Family Foundation, aimed to re-create Black Wall Street. Randolph Wiggins, Build in Tulsa's managing director, believes that "when it comes to racial and economic justice in America, Tulsa is ground zero—not only for the problems of the past, but also for the solutions of the future."[53] Wiggins illustrates how Greenwood is being utilized as a model, a medium, even, for advancing and advocating for Black success on a broad scale. The existence of the Black millionaires who over a century ago had built Greenwood from nothing meant that it was possible. Greenwood would be the utopia of Black excellence.

The events of the centennial celebration briefly realized the utopia of Greenwood. National celebrities and politicians could be seen moving along Greenwood Avenue among the throngs of Black folks—many of them out-of-town tourists—who had come to drink in the promise of prosperity that was and would be Black Wall Street. Public events, such as a "survivors and descendants town hall," had registrations at capacity, with entry into event venues like the Greenwood Cultural Center and Vernon AME so in demand they had to be managed by local police. Despite the police presence, the atmosphere was electric. Greenwood Avenue was brought alive by DJ sound systems, vendor booths, Pan-African flags, Black Wall Street and Greenwood murals, and vibrant outfits; multigenerational Black joy spilled out of coffee shops, restaurants, and stores. Perhaps this is what Greenwood *felt* like over a century ago. The attendance was the full effect of Greenwood's narrative power. It conveyed the story that Black people want to be told of them, that they need to tell themselves; a story that helped them to remember, or perhaps learn for the first time, who they were and who they could be.

The narrative representing Greenwood's past and future promise and the general Blackness that it attracted held reparative potential. The community's aspiration for and efforts toward Greenwood's restoration presented a novel model of reparations. The 2001 Oklahoma Commission to Study the Tulsa Race Riot of 1921 recommended a program of reparations. Over its two hundred pages, it made its case for reparation by presenting in narrative and visual detail the atrocities Black Tulsans suffered over the two days in 1921 and their aftermath. The case to the commission was clear. They wrote, "There was murder, false imprisonment, forced labor, a cover-up, and local precedence for restitution. . . . The 1921 riot is, at once, a representative historical example and a unique historical event. It has many parallels in the pattern of past events, but it has no equal for its violence and its completeness. It symbolizes so much endured by so many for so long."[54]

The commission called reparations "a moral obligation."[55] The morality of the cause was in the balance, given the severity of the massacre. This includes the claim that Tulsa was the first US city to be bombed from the air and the way that the community suffered from what they called "vigilante violence."[56] Reparations here were about something more than being compensated for the crimes of the massacre. The race massacre reparations would be a means of healing the entire city. It would bring about interracial reconciliation. The desire for reconciliation spoke to a deep and meaningful investment in Tulsa, unlike most reparations programs, which call for benefits for the injured community. A fuller presentation of the report's reparations rationale illustrates this point more clearly.

To materialize reconciliation through reparation, the commission recommended five points of reparative restitution: (1) direct payment of reparations to survivors of the Tulsa Race Riot; (2) direct payment of reparations to descendants of the survivors of the Tulsa Race Riot; (3) a scholarship fund available to students affected by the Tulsa Race Riot; (4) establishment of an economic development enterprise zone in the historic area of the Greenwood District; and (5) a memorial for the reburial of any human remains found in the search for unmarked graves of riot victims. They made this recommendation on the basis that their study of the Tulsa Race Riot of 1921 demonstrated "a continuous pattern of historical evidence that was the violent consequence of racial hatred institutionalized and tolerated by official federal, state, county, and city policy."[57] They further asserted that "government at all levels has the moral and ethical responsibility of fostering a sense of community that bridges divides of ethnicity and race." Thus, reparations "in real and tangible form" would "be good public policy and do much to repair the emotional as well as physical scars of this most terrible incident in our shared past."[58]

The 1994 passage of legislation in Florida compensating survivors of the 1923 Rosewood massacre inspired Oklahoma state legislator Don Ross, a native of Greenwood, to submit a joint resolution seeking similar compensation for the survivors of the Greenwood riot and supportive programming for the community of survivors in North Tulsa. The bill's failure prompted Ross to request an investigative commission to study the event and consequences of the 1921 race riot. The commission comprised eleven members selected by the Oklahoma governor and the mayor of Tulsa; over half of the commission was Black.

Nevertheless, as Charles Henry notes, internal strife undermined the commission's objective. Moreover, Henry states that the "racial conflict" present among the commission members was also taking place in the public sphere, with only 12 percent of the Oklahoma population supporting the idea of reparations.[59] The result, he advances, stemmed in part from Ross's unwillingness to endorse the commission's recommendations, even though he wrote the report's introduction. Henry explains, "Perhaps reading the polling data and listening to the objections of his fellow legislators convinced Ross a reparations bill could not succeed."[60] As a result, Ross proposed "a largely symbolic bill that called for low-income student scholarships in Tulsa, an economic development authority for Greenwood, and a memorial." Ross called the bill, which allocated no funding, "at best, an opportunity; at worst, smoke and mirrors."[61]

Henry conducted a comparative analysis of Rosewood and Greenwood in his 2007 text *Long Overdue*. He offered critical insight into some of what might have led to the failure of the Tulsa commission's recommendations. For Henry, these included several factors. First, Oklahoma's Black political bases were comparatively weaker than Florida's; and second, the Oklahoma report requested a significantly higher amount of reparations, at $33 million. Even the composition of the commission undermined the credibility of the Tulsa report, according to Henry. He writes that the "Tulsa Race Riot Commission was composed of politicians and/or political activists rather than scholars. Their meetings quickly took on an adversarial character, and their final recommendations were lambasted by both Black and White commissioners as either too little or too much."[62]

Significantly, albeit somewhat controversially, Henry advances that the framing of reparations itself provided a disadvantage. In Rosewood, he states, "the claims bill was presented as a property issue rather than a racial justice issue," in which "the case's social and racial aspects" were downplayed to maintain "that Rosewood residents won 'compensation' from the state for the loss of their property, not 'racial reparations.'"[63] Moreover, although Tulsa had a significant number of survivors who could have buoyed a reparations case, there were no survivors' associations or meetings that could strengthen the moral claim. As a result of all these shortcomings, Henry claims that the commission report received little support and that "Ross, who had done much to frame the issue in racial terms, backed away from the final recommendations and submitted a bill focused on 'reconciliation' rather than 'racial justice.'"[64] The commission report ended its introduction with "Let justice point the finger and begin the reconciliation!"[65]

Justice for Greenwood

In 2005 the survivors of the massacre sought reparations. Two years after the commission released its report, prominent civil rights attorney Charles Ogletree Jr. and his associates sued the state of Oklahoma, the City of Tulsa, and the city's police department on behalf of riot survivors and survivors' descendants. Based on these parties' inaction and negligence during the riot, they argued a case for restitution and repair for the injuries to body, emotion, and property caused by the events of those two days. The suit asserted that during the massacre, the City of Tulsa, the chief of police, and the Tulsa Police Department were guilty of deprivation of life and liberty (first cause of action), of property (second cause of action), and of their right to equal protection under the law (third cause of action). The suit alleged:

> With respect to the deprivation of life and liberty claim, certain Plaintiffs allege they had relatives killed in the riot or that the Plaintiffs themselves were physically or emotionally injured during the riot. With respect to the deprivation of property claim, certain Plaintiffs allege they had real and personal property burned, looted, or otherwise destroyed in the riot. With respect to the equal protection claim, all Plaintiffs claim they were denied their equal rights under the law because Defendants "routinely under-investigated, under-responded, undercharged, mishandled and failed to protect Plaintiffs from a series of criminal acts or prosecute those responsible for such acts."[66]

Alongside asserting that the city and state were negligent because of their deputizing actions and the provision of ammunition during the riot, the remaining "causes of action" contended that the plaintiffs were "deprived of their federal rights pursuant to Defendants' longstanding official policy, practice or custom of racial discrimination and their reckless or callous indifference to Plaintiffs' federally protected rights." Given the decades that had passed since the massacre, the lawyers needed to counter Oklahoma's two-year statute of limitations for civil actions. They contended that there was a conspiracy to silence the history of the riot, which had prevented the survivors from suing.

The court acknowledged the limitations in obtaining the facts necessary to bring the case at the time and the general legal apparatus of Jim Crow in addition to the heightened threat of racial violence. The seventh cause of action sought to counter the defendants' claim of a statute of limitations, "estopping" the City of Tulsa "from asserting the statute of limitations because of promises made in 1921 and 1999 regarding restitution for damages."[67]

Though recognizing that Jim Crow had prohibited bringing a suit for decades, the courts countered that there had been an opportunity to do so since desegregation. The case was thus dismissed based on the statute of limitations, a decision that an appellate court upheld. Moreover, the United States Supreme Court declined to hear the case. With the statute of limitations, the case had succumbed to a version of the "delay until death" response to reparations described by scholars William "Sandy" Darity and A. Kirsten

Mullen. In their formulation, delaying reparations until all legitimate claimants are dead is "a convenient barrier to making payments" for reparations.[68] While many legitimate claimants, both numerous massacre survivors and their descendants, were alive, the delay in bringing the claim had accomplished the same outcome. For any suit to be successful, then, it would have to overcome the challenge of time.

Fifteen years later and twenty years after the report's release, Tulsa approached the centenary of the massacre following a summer of global revolt and protest in the wake of George Floyd's murder. It was then that local Tulsan lawyer Damario Solomon-Simmons filed a suit for reparations. In a *Los Angeles Times* op-ed, Solomon-Simmons asserted, "For a long time, the word 'reparations' was a non-starter, but it is finally losing its taboo [as] the urgency of the protests across America shows that reforms won't last unless we pay for the crimes of the past."[69]

Solomon-Simmons's legal team included members from Ogletree's 2005 case and lawyers from a New York firm who joined pro bono. They represented plaintiffs that included the three known still-living survivors—Lessie Benningfield Randle, Viola Fletcher, and Hughes Van Ellis Sr.—and several descendants of massacre victims. They also represented North Tulsa organizations, Vernon AME Church, and the Tulsa African Ancestral Society, a nonprofit whose membership includes descendants of massacre survivors. The lawsuit named the City of Tulsa, Tulsa Regional Chamber of Commerce, Tulsa Metropolitan Area Planning Commission, Tulsa Development Authority, Tulsa County, Oklahoma Military Department, and Tulsa County sheriff Vic Regalado.

The suit claimed reparations on account of the events of the massacre and its long-term repercussions. The complaint's central claim was that the massacre produced an "ongoing nuisance," materialized as the continuing structural disparities experienced in North Tulsa. The nuisance encompassed high unemployment, a lack of leadership, and the absence of infrastructure. Moreover, the suit contended that Tulsa officials were now "enriching themselves by promoting the site of the Massacre as a tourist attraction," with no plan to distribute the profits among the residents of North Tulsa.

Solomon-Simmons referred to how, while the public, private businesses, and politicians in Tulsa have come some way in acknowledging and addressing the race massacre, their progress is indicated by partnering to develop several ventures that utilize the history of Greenwood to their gain. These include the Greenwood Rising Center and Tulsa mayor G. T. Bynum's support for locating the suspected mass graves of Black Tulsans left in the wake of the massacre, seen by many in the community as a politically opportune and hollow gesture.

Massacre survivor Mother Violet Fletcher most strongly made this charge during her testimony before Congress: "My country, state and city took a lot from me. Despite this, I spent time supporting the war effort in the shipyards of California. But most of my life, I was a domestic worker serving white families. I never made much money. To this day, I can barely afford my everyday needs. All the while the city of Tulsa has unjustly used the names and stories of victims like me to enrich itself and its white allies through the $30m raised by the Tulsa Centennial Commission while I continue to live in poverty."[70]

Despite this increased engagement with Greenwood's opportunities, the city has been reluctant to acknowledge the intentional dispossession that the state-supported massacre facilitated. The framing of the massacre as an ongoing nuisance was aptly described by James, unprompted, while we discussed the dispossession caused by the city and the White citizens during the massacre. James asserted that this history deprived the very landscape of North Tulsa of closure: "There's a lot of current standing [White-owned] structures that benefited from that incident. Like the actual grounds, the actual buildings, and things that were destroyed. Black people no longer own them and operate out of those buildings—that's intense. That gets factored into the whole question of reparations, right? Especially with the fact that there's been an intentional lack of closure in the situation." Little did James know that his rationale was the driving force behind Solomon-Simmons's reparations argument.

During the 2021 centennial activities in Tulsa, Solomon-Simmons's legal team held a press conference at the Greenwood Cultural Center, which I attended. US president Joe Biden had been in the same room the night before, visiting with massacre survivors Mother Randle, Mother Fletcher, and Hughes Van Ellis. According to Mackenzie Hayes, a lawyer on Solomon-Simmons's legal team, "For one hundred years, survivors and descendants have tried and tried again to seek access to justice in the courts, and they have been denied repeatedly." She continued, "They said it was too late; they said, 'Sorry, your claims, we can't hear them, it doesn't matter that you have not obtained justice, we're just going to let this pass.' And that's not OK," Hayes told the press conference audience. Because they were in Oklahoma, Hayes considered her team to be "blessed," precisely because in Oklahoma, while there is no domestic terrorism statute, a fact that I found odd given the 1995 Oklahoma City bombing, there is a statute for public nuisance.

Moreover, the state recently used the statute in 2019 to successfully win a landmark opioid case against pharmaceutical companies, including Johnson and Johnson, who paid $572 million for intentionally emphasizing the benefits and downplaying the dangers of opioids. In his decision the presiding judge, Thad Balkman, stated that the companies' false and misleading marketing satisfied the first element of Oklahoma's public nuisance law, which is that "a public nuisance is one which affects at the same time an entire community or neighborhood, or any considerable number of persons, although the extent of the annoyance or damage inflicted upon the individuals may be unequal."[71]

The advantage of pursuing a public nuisance claim in the reparations case was that the public nuisance law has no statute of limitations in Oklahoma. Regardless of when the incident occurred, the nuisance statute expressly permits a claim to be brought if the system producing the nuisance is ongoing. The team argued that this ongoing nuisance was precisely the case with the continued poverty in North Tulsa, which began with the race massacre and, as stated by Damario as part of his press conference address, "cuts across every aspect of life here in Greenwood."

The opioid litigation provided the reparations team with a test case, and they planned to use the same principles and methods the state had used to bring their suit. In establishing the basis of the nuisance for the audience, Hayes charted a history of violence and dispossession that began with the massacre and carried through to the current condition of North Tulsa:

> So when we talk about why we think this is a public nuisance, on May 31st, 1921, the white mobs came in and they murdered [the people of Greenwood]. They destroyed, they killed, they looted, they rioted, and a public nuisance was created. After that moment, it continued and continues to this day, we believe that the massacre ignited the nuisance that exists today in Tulsa, specifically in north Tulsa, and all of the policies and practices that have been implemented by the defendants have elevated and exacerbated the public nuisance. For example, urban renewal: these policies pushed black people out of their homes. It made them poorer than their white neighbors. A highway was constructed, cutting north Tulsa away from south Tulsa, taking resources, opportunity. The health disparities that have continued as a result: there's no hospital, by the way, as all of you know, I'm sure in north Tulsa. That was I think it's probably the most profound thing

that I recall is just that there's no hospital in this vicinity. But there was in 1921, and it has not been rebuilt.

And that is a nuisance. There are so many other things that have happened, the educational disparities; all these things are part of the public nuisance. It continues today. And because we have a test case, because we have the state and the city of Tulsa who has demonstrated that acts such as these societal injustices that can be remedied through the statute. We believe that we are right on the law in equating the societal injustice of the massacre and its continuing harm.

By describing the massacre as setting the foundation of the public nuisance, Hayes is pointing to what legal scholar Melissa Fussell demonstrates as the function of race riots:

> Race riots resulting in real property takings, like race riots themselves, are not as rare as they might seem. Quite a few incidents are infamous, but many others are relatively unknown, buried by decades of fear and secrecy. Although they occurred in different places, and different events were blamed as triggers, common threads exist among them. Generally, the takings happened after there had been a substantial accumulation of wealth in the black communities. The black citizens typically fled from their communities under threat of death, too afraid to return; their aggressors either seized their property without compensation or gave them insignificant compensation.[72]

What occurred in Tulsa was part of an established practice of profiting through violent Black dispossession. Within the first fifty years following emancipation, Black farmers in the United States held over sixteen million acres of land.[73] The crop-lien system of credit, partition sales, redlining, and other means saw the rise of Black land dispossession.[74] Also at play was the role of outright violence, as "murders of African American landowners, for the purpose of appropriating their property, and coerced public sale of family land resulted in a rapid decline in black American landownership in the twentieth century."[75]

This "taking" amounted to "a grim and extensive . . . catalog of the damages visited upon blacks."[76] As demonstrated throughout the preceding chapters, this catalog includes the havoc wrought by Jim Crow, urban renewal, the prevalence of the nonprofit sector, and the various forms of demolition and removal that they enact. As Darity and Mullen in their consideration of the case of Greenwood note, "The black population of Tulsa, Oklahoma, had witnessed the destruction of its prosperous Greenwood community in the white rampage in 1921. In subsequent years, the community saw significant progress in rebuilding the black business district that had been erased during the white riot, only to witness that progress wiped away, beginning in 1967, by an urban renewal program that destroyed the resurrection effort in the former black stronghold. Thus, the Greenwood community in Tulsa was subjected to both a white massacre and a 'slum clearance,' approximately half a century apart."[77]

A critical function of the nuisance is the delay in acknowledging the harm. And while the recognition and repair are delayed, the perpetrators enjoy a prolonged period of accumulating benefit.[78] Accumulation happens through the material increase in property acquisition, the generation of capital as revenue from the state and federal governments in development projects, and municipal budgets in response to poor neighborhoods. Furthering the nuisance claim is the assertion that the community is disadvantaged through the defendants' unjust enrichment through Greenwood's dispossession. "There is a new museum coming up, and the names and the stories and the images of all of these descendants and survivors and their stories are being told, and the people who have suffered are not reaping any of the benefits, as a result," argued Solomon-Simmons.

The argument was that a cultural tourism industry was being developed around the narrative of the massacre while denying the survivors and descendants compensation. To Hayes, this development was particularly egregious. Hayes declared that the team was asking the defendants "to give up all of the resources that they have achieved or received as a result of using the likenesses and names and images of survivors and descendants and give it back to the people who it belongs to." This charge in truth merely demonstrated the way that the nuisance had most recently materialized.

The suit demanded the nuisance be abated through a victims' compensation fund for the "survivors and the descendants to have the opportunity to be compensated for the harm they have endured for the last hundred years and continue to endure"; they want a hospital built in North Tulsa, educational resources for the community, and, most critically, tax suspension, with Hayes elaborating: "We want the folks in the community, the black Tulsans, who live and endure the continuing harm to not have to pay any more state and local taxes because they have been denied justice for so long, their economic justice has been taken from them, and we believe that it is only fair to not have them have to spend their resources, to give it back to the state or the city or the county that has taken so much from them."

Even though the legal team based their case on a solid and recent precedent and even though there had been much progress in public discourse acknowledging the tragedy of the massacre, there was still significant resistance to the specific framing and claim of reparations. As Solomon-Simmons told it, "The mayor is one of the loudest and strongest opponents to reparations, he made that very clear, so anything that the mayor is supporting, we know is fraudulent. Anything the mayor is supporting, we know is not really moving us forward towards actual reparations because he stated, 'I don't believe in cash payments, I don't believe in direct reparations.' And we don't support anything that doesn't say reparations." Solomon-Simmons went further in establishing the basis of the reparations claim:

> The city of Tulsa mayor, Bynum, said yeah that the city of Tulsa shouldn't have done this [facilitated the massacre]; but it was not a full-throated acknowledgment that [reparations] needs to happen. He's still talking about we can't be responsible for what criminals did a hundred years ago. Well, these people did criminal acts, but they were acting under the authority and the direction of the city. They were acting within the scope of their employment with the city. So yeah, there were criminals, but legally they were doing what they were told by the city. So, he's still trying to give the city cover. They have no cover. They are responsible. We will not accept any empty resolutions. We will not accept any empty rhetoric, empty promises. We need to see justice.
>
> The survivors, descendants, and black people of Tulsa who suffered the massacre had a right to reparations, respect, and restitution.

Much about the team's case left me wondering about the scope of repair they were advocating. "Nuisance" was a direct charge for the current circumstances of poverty and inequality that the North Tulsan community faced. It was an apt and, I would say, elegant way of putting the experience of impoverishment. It is a nuisance that hinders any further development. It was also ongoing. However, the 1921 massacre was an assault on the general community, and that nuisance qualified as a community-wide experience. But there was significant slippage between the general quality of the notion of injury from the nuisance and the exclusivity of the plaintiffs. The nuisance was public, but the discourse was overly concentrated on the "survivors and descendants," which seemed exclusionary. Perhaps limiting the scope was necessary for the sake of the case. Nevertheless, I had trouble reconciling their reparations claim and the scale of the injury that was the nuisance.

I brought these questions to Hayes, who cautiously replied, "If we make it past a motion to dismiss, it would be the farthest that a reparations case for Black people has gone in the country." She hoped that it would have what she called "a domino effect." I appreciated her candid uncertainty when she continued, "You know, I don't know. It always goes back to buzzwords and how do you sell something. It's really hard to sell people in Congress on this idea. It's impossible, it's never happened. Ever. And so, any idea that we will get there, perhaps cynical, but I don't think it's going to happen in that way. Not as long as White Republicans are who they are. So how do we make it more creative in order to solve systems? I think things are going in the right direction; we have to just shift hearts and minds." Shifting hearts and minds and getting anywhere close to convincing people in Congress, she said, required creativity "in exploring and reimagining what reparations are, and how they could be applied and reapplied and multiplied."

"I think it's just, you know, the more creative evaluation of what we can do," she said of the approach. But it was an approach that was limited because while most states have nuisance statutes, they're all unique. Oklahoma's law was particularly broad, which gave the team some leeway in making their case. "So the nuisance statute, I think, is particularly interesting because when you try to abate a nuisance, you can do so in a way that is broad based and in a way that you're asking other methods or systems to be remedied in order to abate this nuisance," Hayes explained.

The "abatement of a nuisance," in other words, demanded providing whatever solutions were necessary. To Hayes, it created "interesting opportunities to think of other ways that you can solve the racial injustice in America. Because it is beyond just money. It's systems. Systems have to be destroyed and re-created, to be rebuilt from the ground up." "The abatement was a broad tool then?" I asked. "Whatever it takes to create the equity is how you abate the nuisance," Hayes replied. To her, nuisance abatement could be broad enough to transform the reparations debate, which she thought had to move past being "we want our due; we want our cash," as she put it. "I believe in cash," Hayes admitted, "but I think we narrow ourselves when we think of it [reparations] that way."

Nuisance was a model for creatively framing reparations in a legally convincing way and, most important, in a way that accounted for the continuing experience of racism's Black inheritance. And while Hayes convinced me of the breadth of the reparation through the nuisance abatement model, it still didn't satisfy what I saw as a need to qualify the slippage of the claim's register. I thought of those Black folk who *today* lived on Greenwood

Avenue, in the Tulsa Housing Authority's public housing, like the Pioneer Plaza and Sunset Plaza apartments. What of those individuals' claims of repair? Again, they, as much if not more than anyone, experienced the nuisance of anti-Black racism. Yet they, as part of the community, were not named as plaintiffs.

I shared my critique with Hayes, who replied, "If I were to have it my way, I would give every Black person in America their due. Because this country was built on our backs. It's continuously built on our backs. And we are victims of the horrible injustices that continue today. And we should be duly compensated for it. But it doesn't always work that way. And the law is not favorable that way."

I was unconvinced. I agreed that nuisance was a powerful charge. Indeed, nuisance could sustain a claim of injury, from the violence of the massacre to urban renewal's dispossession of the nearly 250 Black-owned businesses operated in Greenwood by 1942, rivaling pre-massacre Greenwood. Nuisance could connect urban renewal back to how Oklahoma statehood undermined Black town development in Indian Territory. In other words, while this was not advanced by the legal team, nuisance was another way to operationalize White state development. It was the other side of the coin of American progress. Its responsibility for carrying the claim of repair was broader than the narrow lineage of survivors and descendants. At the opening event of Greenwood Rising, Kevin Matthews asked for a moment of silence to "recognize the 160 descendants of the Tulsa race massacre." Asking to do so among the crowd of thousands, which was comprised mostly of Black Tulsans, illustrates the narrowness of the category.

For nuisance to be the comprehensive and transformative tool that Hayes and her team argued it could be, those categories—survivors and descendants—would need broadening. All of Black North Tulsa were survivors. They survived the nuisance and anti-Black violence daily. The collective claim in Fire in Little Africa's "Descendants" feels ever more impactful and necessary: "This is our home, Little Africa, Greenwood . . . It's in our souls . . . We are descendants!"[79]

Qualifying only the formal survivors and descendants for repair while holding constant the condition of life in North Tulsa as the nuisance was, as I have argued before, a loophole of reparative liability. This loophole functions as a reparative logic whereby individuals benefit from a collective claim.[80] When I made that argument, I referred to the loophole as a cynical, opportunistic strategy; however, the same cannot be said here. Instead, the loophole in the reparative framework at play is a product of the same exceptional narrative that I have spent this chapter outlining. As Hayes noted, when it comes to making a successful claim for reparations, "It always goes back to buzzwords and how do you sell something." Indeed, the narrative is for sale here: again, the story of a prosperous Black community, devastated by the massacre in 1921 and ravaged ever since. But again, what is left out are the inconvenient actors and their inconvenient stories of poverty and nondescent. Yet today they carried most of the burden of the nuisance. Recall, as Trouillot shows, that "silences are produced not so much by an absence of facts or interpretations as through conflicting appropriations."[81] Over a century ago, the primary patrons of Greenwood's commercial district were that ever-growing poor majority who came to Greenwood for an opportunity.

The focus of the reparations case is those deemed capable of helping exercise the power "that makes some narratives possible."[82] The survivors, deserving of every ounce of repair and every cent of reparations, are part of the narrative influence. Elders Mother Viola Fletcher and her brother Hughes Van Ellis at ages 107 and 100, respectively, testifying before Congress alongside their public appearances ahead of the centennial, connect us to premassacre Greenwood. Their testimonies of the violence experienced in their youth and the trauma they've endured since can, as Hayes put it, "shift the hearts and minds" of those who too willingly cast a blind eye at the everyday and therefore inconsequential suffering of Black folks. The takeaway is that reparation is secured through sympathy and in Tulsa. That sympathy is gained through recognizing Greenwood as the site of prosperous Blackness.

Reparations are not a new question for North Tulsans, but they had only received "reconciliation" as an answer. Today they ask the question again, but it has become complicated by the expectation of what a repaired and restored Greenwood must be and for whom. What complicates that expectation is the attachment to Greenwood's representation as a Black site of prosperity. It's understandable why that narrative is so alluring. Over the past century, Greenwood has gone from a once-exceptional community to yet another blighted Black space. In the wake of Jim Crow, racism, discrimination, and dispossession have created and reproduced circumstances of limited opportunity, or what Solomon-Simmons's team has identified as the nuisance of anti-Blackness.

What, then, are reparations for those who fall outside of the recognized categories of survivors or descendants? James told me, "People are crying out for help. And that's why I believe in reparations. But that word is a trigger word because what monetary value can you place on someone's life, let alone generations that have been affected by it, still being affected by it?" To James, a better future would come from better allocation of existing opportunities and more equitable incorporation, which was in line with the general prescriptions for advancement that many Tulsans advocated. James insisted that reform required "really trying to reprogram the next generation." I wanted to understand what reparations meant in James's framing, especially since reparations, as conventionally understood, are about compensation for an injury. "A check is quite honestly just the beginning," he began to say, almost dismissing the importance of direct payment. "What does healing look like?" was his concern, which I found encouraging, as it signaled an emphasis on the total sense of repair. His answer brought me back to Uwa's question of what the community was trying to build and to Marlon's project of healing the disconnect.

As I thought more about what each was proposing, it became evident that what James, Uwa, and Marlon suggested was repair as a form of autonomy. It was an autonomy with a self-repair sensibility that had, in fact, long been part of the ethics of Greenwood and of Black people in Oklahoma. Their ideas drew on a narrative about repair that is central to the longer framing of Black life in North Tulsa. It wasn't prosperity but this autonomy that the community was trying to build back. The disconnect that needed healing was the need to rethink the terms by which their community understood itself.

Lester Shaw, a young native North Tulsan who had recently returned home from Atlanta to start a marijuana dispensary, "the Motherland," off of N. Peoria and Apache in the heart of North Tulsa, shared this sentiment: "It's a mindset that's missing," Lester began. "I hear a lot of complaining about what we did, what we had, but I still gotta drive south to eat clean food; we don't even have a grocery store out here." Lester's critique struck at the heart of the nostalgia economics that had permeated much of the discourse around development in North Tulsa. To him, the past was that, and he appeared not to require it to qualify his or his community's abilities or future. "So when are we gonna start building? When are we gonna start teaching people how to at least build?" he asked rhetorically, yet in impatient anticipation of his community members. Lester's proposal went against the affiliations that sought to celebrate and profit from Greenwood's past of prosperity. His "we" included only his community; they had to do it for themselves.

"That's why they're talking about resolutions and reconciliation, instead of reparations!" Uwa declared. Reconciliation was the compromise that left open the terms of engagement between North Tulsa and those external to the community who sought to negotiate their future. Uwa continued, "They talk about reconciliation because they don't want to use the word *reparations.*" Reparations would foreclose the possibilities for profit and thus to Uwa seemed like a more radical demand: "Reparations means, OK, we finna repair what was done, and, you know, they don't wanna talk about it. They go around the back." Indeed, reconciliation was a workaround justice. "They don't want people of political influence to use the word *reparation*, like [Mayor] G. T. [Bynum], so it's just *reconciliation.*" Following Uwa, reparations would mean undoing the entire apparatus by which North Tulsans had eked out what little opportunities they had found for themselves. It meant, in principle, going against the nonprofits, the declarations of support by the state, and, most recently, the commitment to and increasing profitability of Greenwood's promotional narrative.

"You can't reconcile something that is totally corrupt," Uwa declared, before continuing, "You have to destroy it and come up with something that is totally new. You know, everybody is talking about reform; you can't reform, you've got to destroy that totally and come up with something new. I can't be a reformer." Uwa was uncompromising in his abolitionist declaration.

Moreover, he was illustrating the limitation and possible danger of a principle of reformation put forward by Angela Davis, who argues that reforms "produce the stultifying idea that nothing lies beyond" what in Davis's argument is the prison but for North Tulsa is the current corrupt system of Tulsa politics that had brought the 1921 massacre into its circuit. The result, as Davis asserts, is that talk and the pursuit of reform ultimately marginalize the strategies that might bring about real structural change.[83]

As we talked, he seemed to be working something out. "It's the same thing, to be honest," he said to me but really to himself. I asked him what he meant. "Repair, you can't repair . . . you can't repair this, not really. How the hell you gon' repair anything, when you got over three hundred Black lives, thousands really, that's really not accounted for; how are you going to repair that with money? It's not enough money to repair one life, much less hundreds, likely thousands." Uwa had understood the limitations of the narratives of repair that circulated in North Tulsa and beyond.

His demand for an account was more inclusive than much of the rhetoric and framing of "survivors" and "descendants" had been. He was asking that all Black North Tulsans be brought into that number. Otherwise, how would they repair anything, when those injured, excluded in the calculus of reparations' qualification, would ultimately serve to disqualify the satisfaction of repair? Uwa continued to make the case: "You know, my thing is that either we organize ourselves to confront these forces that affect our lives on a day-to-day basis, as a collective whole, *as a people*, or we going to fall.

And keep on falling and keep on going for the same thing that we've been going for, for over a hundred years now." Uwa was pushing himself, and thus me, past the goal of reparations, and it was simultaneously challenging and exhilarating. "And you see what we got?" Uwa concluded. "Do you see what we've got? Nothing. Because nothing is owned; everything is rented."

His point was sophisticated and straightforward. "Going for the same thing that we've been going for," was Uwa's warning that with reparations must come a complete reordering of the frameworks by which North Tulsans understood themselves. Because everything being "rented" meant that North Tulsans, despite all they had accomplished over the past century, had failed to fully realize the self-determination of Greenwood. And fixing that couldn't be done through reform or a purely reformative notion of repair.

Uwa had come back around to his initial assessment and had come to realize what was at stake. He seemed to have confronted just how far away his community was from where they were and where they needed to be. Uwa seemed resolved about what it took to get there. His prescription was effectively a refusal of what Greenwood had come to mean over the past century. His notion was too radical to be practically taken up within the political, cultural, and economic landscape that was Tulsa, a fact that I believe he accepted. This acceptance is perhaps why he seemed so at peace as he went about his volunteer work at the Greenwood Cultural Center. But I feared that without Uwa's principles guiding the philosophy and policy of reparation, the best North Tulsa might achieve was reconciliation.

For North Tulsa's community, restoration as repair is the mobilizing of nostalgia in the construction of a materially revitalized future. Indeed, North Tulsa's politics seemed wholly engaged in the principles of repair as a form of restoration, ever focusing on the past as the community charts a path forward. David Scott has warned that when the future ceases "to be a source of longing and anticipation," the past becomes "a densely animated object of enchantment."[1] This condition is why Black political subjects regularly seek legible frameworks of claim-making that are often retrospective assertions—the future is too often burdened by the injuries of the past. And while this retrospective politics is certainly at play in North Tulsa, it is complicated by the past serving as a model for the future Black North Tulsans aspire to. Therefore, reparations in North Tulsa are as much about the restoration of Greenwood as about justice for the massacre.

Mainstream reparations discourse in the United States today is often anchored to the moment of slavery, which qualifies the injuries produced thereafter from Jim Crow, mass incarceration, to the racial wealth gap. This framing advances slavery as the origin story for the Black experience, the phenomenon around which Blackness as an identity and position in the United States is forever oriented. Greenwood offers an innovative alternative reparative framework by virtue of the temporal signals of what it permits North Tulsans to claim. Black Tulsans' ideals of reparations are unique because their reparative reference is the injury of the 1921 massacre. And so the hardships, many of which are the same as the mainstream narrative, and which Tulsa's reparation suit has framed as a nuisance, follow from the massacre, not slavery. What's also important to note is that Black Tulsans do not count the 1921 massacre as one of slavery's injuries. In establishing their terms for reparation, North Tulsans have established a model that obviates plantation slavery as the basis of a legitimate reparations claim and thus as the overarching narrative of their Black lives. Reparation accomplished through the "abatement" of the nuisance of the massacre will for North Tulsans produce the restoration of pre-massacre Greenwood. It is there that they place their ontological anchor; it is pre-1921 Greenwood that serves as their origin story.

As I have described, North Tulsans have approached this process through individual and community means but have undertaken this negotiation of identity and restoration principally through the commercial redevelopment of North Tulsa as a renewed Black Wall Street. I focused the last chapter on the complicated use of Greenwood's and Black Wall Street's narratives and the way they are mobilized, from everyday commercial use to a basis for reparations claims. Looking to Greenwood and seeking to revive Black Wall Street is a critical and innovative move in shifting the politics and representation of Black accomplishment. It is a story that must be told and made commonplace in our general landscape of Black narratives. However, there are certain vulnerabilities in that strategy, namely, how that narrative can be used outside the control and beyond the benefit of the North Tulsa community.

I want to suggest that there are limits to what a focus on Greenwood and Black Wall Street can accomplish for the material and even reparative revitalization of North Tulsa's community. The story of Black Wall Street is often too neat and too narrow to accommodate and account for the full breadth of the Black community in North Tulsa today, as evidenced by my discussion around descent. In fact, the story, as told, is much too narrow to account for the breadth of the community before the massacre. Rather than fixate on Greenwood, I want to propose that North Tulsans' repository of meaning, of inspiration, of orientation goes much deeper, though not all that much farther back in time, to the geography of freedom that was Indian Territory.

Counter Orders

In the public imagination, reparations often take the form of the figurative "forty acres and a mule," based on General William Tecumseh Sherman's Special Field Orders, No. 15. Sherman ordered the confiscation of 400,000

acres of land along the Atlantic coast of South Carolina, Georgia, and Florida and parceled it into forty-acre allotments for settlement by formerly
enslaved families. Andrew Johnson returned the confiscated lands to Con-
federate plantation owners, and Black people received compromised citizenship and a new form of contract bondage instead. Though a temporary
remedy, this was a concrete and executable plan for what reparations could
have been, as argued by legal scholar Katherine Franke in her book *Repair*.
In a colloquial sense, forty acres and a mule appear as possessions that are
compensatory for the labors of slavery. According to Franke, land-based
reparations following slavery looked like the extension of the provisions for
self-determination: land, tools, and independence.[2] In other words, reparations were the means for self-provisioning. Compensation was not the objective, and neither was incorporation; instead, it was what I can only call
sovereignty.

A version of this ideal played out in Indian Territory through the development of all-Black towns, including early Greenwood. Black landownership in
Indian Territory—accomplished through a process of complicated, and at
times dispossessive, Black-Native relations, which I discuss in this chapter—
was complemented across the country by growing Black landownership, although those landholders elsewhere may not have enjoyed the same early
political freedom as those in Indian Territory.

Indian Territory represented what George Lipsitz offers as a Black spatial
imaginary. This spatial imaginary revalorizes Black spaces that have been de-
valued or abandoned through solidarity, the generation of community and
congregation, and the reinscription of value into that community.[3] Indian Territory's legacy produces a viable alternative for organizing Black Tulsa's order
and existence. The ability to reach for this alternative, rooted in the Black experience in Oklahoma and specifically in Tulsa, from the Indian Territory
settlement has been present but silenced right up through the centenary of
the 1921 race massacre. Neither the riot nor Greenwood's prime were the
history made quiet or obscure; rather, it was the geographic liberty of an
open-ended freedom-making that the all-Black towns accomplished. And
the will to look elsewhere. Thus, more than repair, Indian Territory stands as
primary reference for the ethics and identity that form and inspire the North
Tulsa community.

Having Indian Territory as a geographic reference for anchoring Black
life and subjectivity is a significant departure from the often-referenced
plantation. Indeed, the plantation as an ontological geography, meaning a
place that had helped to fundamentally define what it means to be Black, has

been seen as instrumental to Black cultural formation and social life. The plantation represents the identifiable intersections of capital, labor, and territory, coherently and cogently understood as a racial capitalist formation.[4] The co-constitution of the labor regime of slavery, the geography of the plantation itself, and the subject of the enslaved, has produced a totalizing and violent phenomenon. To support this assertion, Katherine McKittrick argues that "the plantation uncovers a logic that emerges in the present and folds over to repeat itself anew throughout black lives."[5] Therefore, the plantation presents a means through which "racial geographies and violences make themselves known."[6]

Within this formula, blackness serves as a peculiar quintessence of subjugation that Charles S. Johnson argues is "rooted in the soil," forming a tradition in which enslaved Africans saw themselves as twinned, however violently, with the land.[7] The violent disciplining, and its cultural and institutional conjoining and reproduction, provides what Cedric Robinson has advanced as the "historical agency" of racial capitalism, the result of which is a geographic twinning of racial subjectivity and the tradition of the plantation.[8] As a result, the plantation has become a central analytic in understanding the operation of both contemporary capital and the ever-present reality of anti-Blackness.

While the plantation serves as a meaningful and legitimate geographic prototype for the experience of Blackness, it is not the only form. The history of Blackness in Indian Territory reveals a meaningful alternative to the racial ontology of the plantation. In North Tulsa's case, the local contemporary "black sense of place" could be seen as yet another product of a plantation inheritance.[9] However, Indian Territory operates as a referent from which Black Tulsans can draw for a map of their liberation that serves as a redescription outside the "descriptive statement" of the plantation.[10] As Sylvia Wynter explains, breaking with the "specific idea of order" requires abandoning "the need to map its ordering principle" by making that order irrelevant.[11]

Around the process of emancipation in the United States, Black people responded to the "geographic orders of freedom" by "negotiating, disrupting, and countering controls over their location." What resulted through that process, Ikuko Asaka states, "were alternative visions of black freedom that articulated aspirations for economic independence and complex understandings of the relationship between race, place, and labor."[12] As Judith Madera puts it, "It is not about the relation of law to land (jurisdiction). It is about the relation of land to territory."[13] There is no better analytic framework for doing this unsettling than Madera's use of "deterritorialization."

In *Black Atlas*, Madera illustrates how African American writers in the mid-nineteenth century, at the start of the "golden age of Black nationalism," rewrote the boundaries, territories, and place of Blackness.[14] During that period, the idea of territory had begun "entering into nearly all domains of life," with Madera asserting that it "stood for an altered relation to land" and "harkened to something outside the story lines of slavery."[15] In this moment, that altered relation meant that place could be more than a property relation, especially for those who were at the very time wrestling directly with the property and properties of their subjectivity.

North Tulsa's history illustrates how that process of world-making through deterritorialization worked in a community that endeavored to realize its freedom in the postemancipation era. It's that world that North Tulsans have sought to return to for some time. But to get there, they seek to make their way back to the notion of Greenwood before its destruction. To circumvent the powerful framing of the plantation as the very composition of Blackness, and especially of Black freedom and thus reparation, North Tulsans can look to Greenwood as a symbol of the geographies of freedom outside of, and not just after, slavery. Moreover, in their history they have a model for how the emancipated sought various ways to make a new life for themselves in the country and beyond, which I argue Indian Territory, more than Greenwood, represents. Indian Territory offered new beginnings and, critically, a novel geography free from the tyranny of the still-potent specter of the plantation. Thus, North Tulsans can look there to find their way through ongoing currents of violence.

Although, as in many other Black communities throughout the United States, North Tulsans' everyday experience is one of too-common marginalization and recurrent exploitation, they can call on a narrative of historical accomplishment between settlement and 1921 to give them hope and their promise for the future. This articulation points to a form of repair that extends beyond the violence in 1921, urban renewal, and the direct injuries they as a community and as individuals faced as a result. North Tulsans in their desire for the restoration of the Black Tulsa that existed before the riot provide a broader geographic model for a reparative horizon.

An analysis of this history and the popular notion of Indian Territory that its Black inhabitants had at the time reveals a novel but material notion of Black utopia centered on the intersecting meanings of land, autonomy, and futurity. These migrants organized their possibilities around a concept of territory and ideas of freedom that disrupted the prevailing postemancipation narrative of Black placemaking. In this narrative Black place is already and always contingent and determined by existing racist structures. Instead, through settlement in the territory, Black Oklahomans thought of a racialized geography as a particular kind of freedom dream made material. Black settlement in the territory introduced a differently racialized geography. This geography served as a specific kind of freedom dream that materialized Black futurity. In other words, it produced a radical Black orientation to place, one untethered to the plantation. Indian Territory land served as the basis for notions that southern Black people would fold into their imaginaries of freedom.

Judith Madera shows how Black geographic formation could interrupt and dissent against racist orders. For my argument, Madera illustrates how the "spatial teleologies of Northern freedom and Southern bondage" could be seen beyond and through the authors' "black territorial imagination."[16] Through their territorial imagination, Black people "politicized the idea of territory" to not only "get out from behind white ownership—from being the object of property"—but unmoor territory from its "significations."[17] This rearrangement, which Madera calls "positive deterritorialization," opened up territory as a novel spatial production that could reconcile both contestation and affiliation.[18] As such, spaces like Indian Territory became part of Black people's "search for meaningful worlds" of possibility.[19] By contrast, "negative deterritorialization" is the reconstitution or reterritorialization of a geography "in such a way that it impedes further lines of flight," becoming a "'conjugation' in a system of capture."[20]

As a process of opening, positive deterritorialization creates "productive connections that flow from a reserve of freedom" and "increases freedom and increases connections."[21] As part of this process, Madera advances that territory cannot be "a settled state of affairs or a bounded culture" but is inherently unstable and denotative.[22] Madera elaborates further: "Territory is embodied. Identities are bound up in known spaces of belonging that overlap with sites of uncertainty. At the same time, territory is polymorphous; it is idiosyncratic and contingent. Spaces can change us, and they can change our intentions. . . . Territory is composed of multiple, unstable signifieds[;] it is entangled in its subjective undoing."[23]

Embodied, uncertain, polymorphous, idiosyncratic, contingent, multiple, unstable, and entangled: these are just some of the characteristics that make up territory. And before we think that this is some adjectival overload, note that these qualities index the relations within the material space of land and open the ethical "action" of Indian Territory's geography. That action and opening are shown in Madera's defining of *deterritorialization*, which is a "dislodging of geographic contexts and descriptors. . . . [I]t can be about presenting a world and presenting how to undo it. It can also be about posturing in one world and moving an agenda forward in another or passing through the codes of a given space outside the modalities that systemize control. Deterritorialization partitions territory. It moves boundaries. And so, it has the potential to be generative since, by realigning territories, it can alter the overall map."[24] As a geographical-ethical discourse, deterritorialization provides an alternative to White territorial frameworks, which could "decode and reconstruct" space to inscribe representation into place.[25] As a simultaneous means of placemaking and subject making, deterritorialization produces Black self-positioning by "the elasticity" of emplacement. As such, "territory for midcentury African Americans," Madera asserts, "was something physical, something at the juncture of power/knowledge systems, and something textual [that] reads as a frame of reference for attainment and a frame for sequencing action."[26]

This process of deterritorialization then propels what Kendra T. Field calls a "continuum of flight" of Black people's mobility into Indian Territory and elsewhere.[27] Robin D. G. Kelley writes, "The history of black people has been a history of movement—real and imagined."[28] Field asks us, in thinking about this continuum, "in a single transnational frame, to hear 'Liberia' and 'Oklahoma' in a single breath."[29] Rather than merely fleeing persecution, Black people actively imagined the geographic possibilities of what could lie and be made at the horizon. That horizon should be seen as one that was inherently uninvested in the promise of American empire.

Ralph Ellison, in *Going to the Territory*, writes, "For the slaves had learned through the repetition of group exercise that freedom was to be attained through geographical movement, and that freedom required one to risk his life against the unknown."[30] Through deterritorialization, Indian Territory came to represent a countermapping through which, Sylvia Wynter notes, a "counter order" could be imagined.[31] Its geography provided a powerful countervoice through which Black people could speak back to subjugation's narrative framework. In other words, freedom came through geographic formation, turning the unknown into the known. In that process both freedom and geography were defined on their own terms and through their own frameworks. This geographic reinscription also had consequences for the development of Black subjectivity in Indian Territory. Indeed, if the plantation could produce a particular—and violent—twinning, then human geographic relationships and senses of the self would likewise form in Indian Territory.

Through the Black framing of territory and *the* territory, territorialization, the process by which space and land operate as and facilitate social relations, offers a philosophical challenge to Black and Native studies. It does so by troubling the geographic assignments often ascribed to Blacks and Natives. These studies seldom tie Blackness to the land on productive terms. Instead, they maintain its abstract function, which intersects only at the level of culture.

Meanwhile, Native association with the land is a given and is analytically reproduced. This approach produces and reifies tropes that only allow for a similar incorporation of Blacks and Natives through racialization. Black and Native history in the territory reconciles what it means for Indian Territory to be the site of both Black freedom and Native dispossession because the Dawes Act allotments discussed in the introduction allow for a way to understand the "antithetical but complementary histories" of Black and Native people.[32] Native dispossession semiotically produced the abstraction of Indianness. This brought Native identity, as a cultural sign, into closer proximity to Blackness. Indianness was constructed by deconstructing the myriad of constitutional identities, cultures, and relations that made up the vast diversity of Native subjectivities. As noted earlier, these subjectivities were underpinned by kinship systems, communal ideas of land, and ontologies. These suffered massive disruption and upending by federal and, later, state policies that secured the rise of the White supremacist order in the territory. This disruption made available the literal lands in the territory that would serve as the foundation for Black freedom's ideologies and practices and subjective formations.

According to David Chang in his *The Color of the Land*, allotment facilitated a core transformation of individualization in Indian Territory among Native peoples. However, Chang argues that the Creek resisted the process and that this resistance limited the impact on Creek kinship. Ironically, the Creek used the allotment of land to form the basis of that resistance: "The way they chose allotments and the ways they used them demonstrate that Creeks were determined to try to use the new land system to sustain kinship and community ties rather than to embrace the economic individualism that allotment was meant to accomplish. On maps of allotments, surnames appear in clumps on the landscape. Most Creeks tried to select parcels that related to existing settlement patterns, where members of kinship groups lived in rural neighborhoods."[33] In addition to how the Creek reproduced kinship on allotted land, they also resisted how they labored on it.

One of the intentions of the allotment policy was to civilize Native peoples by encouraging them to become yeoman farmers. However, many Creeks decided instead to be landlords, leasing out their property, or even selling it once the federal government lifted sale restrictions, and then domiciling with relatives on their allotted plots. This land use would severely impact the existing small-scale agricultural practices among the Creek but would represent the "most spectacular failures" of allotment in seeking to transform Creek subjectivity.[34] Ultimately, "allotment disrupted and altered but did not succeed in fully replacing the way Creeks used land and settlement to sustain community and kinship," writes Chang.[35]

Allotment, however, had significant implications for notions of community and kinship among the Black people who had and would come to call Indian Territory home. Allotment made possible the promise of land discussed above. Patrick Wolfe makes the case when writing that "the 160-acre allotments with which the Bureau of Indian Affairs sought to break up Indian society could seem to represent a much better deal than the forty acres and a mule with which black people hoped to establish an independent social basis for themselves after the Civil War."[36]

Indian Territory contained a sizable and growing population of African Americans who would benefit in varying degrees from access to allotted land. This population composed a relatively diverse group. Black Creeks, Cherokees, Choctaws, Chickasaws, and Seminoles—all of whom descended from the Black people who had arrived in Indian Territory as part of Indian Removal—possessed a Blackness that had been interpolated by the various adopted Native senses of being and was developed over generations of living as part of their respective Native groups. "State negroes"— those who came from the United States across Indian Territory's border— would in meaningful ways qualify as possessing a distinct form of Blackness. What made these Black people distinct from the Exodusters who migrated to Kansas immediately following the end of Reconstruction is that, unlike in Kansas, which had a mostly White population, Indian Territory's sizable settled Black population meant that there was a cultural counterpoint to Black Natives.

The results were "complex negotiations of race between Black Indian citizens and Black newcomers from the South."[37] These racial negotiations were so complex that Chang argues that there was a veritable "rift" between the two groups. One Creek Freedman summed up the rift by noting, "I was eating out of the same pot with the Indians . . . while they were still licking the master's boots in Texas."[38] At the root of this animosity was access to Indian Territory land, as Chang notes:

> Prior to statehood, newcomers lacked citizenship rights in the Indian nations, and therefore they could not make the land their own by clearing and tilling it. African American settlers who wished to farm could either squat on the lands of the Indian nations or work as tenants for an Indian landlord. Both of these choices placed them in conflict with black Creeks, who had worked with their conservative allies in the 1880s and 1890s to put a halt to squatting and the taking up of the commons by tenants who worked for large landholders. Thus, before allotment and statehood, the politics of landownership separated black Creeks from African American newcomers.[39]

Between 1904 and 1908, bankers, land speculators, and other interested parties lobbied to lift the restrictions on the sale of both homestead and surplus portions of allotted lands. As a result, the restrictions were lifted for those enrolled as Freedmen in 1908; however, those restrictions would largely remain in place until the early 1930s for "full-blooded Indians," who were able to sell their land only through an exceptional application. This led to the view that Freedmen's land was more secure because it was harder to challenge the transferred titles. Therefore, Freedmen's allotments were preferentially sought out by new Black and White arrivants to Indian Territory to those of so-called full-blooded Indians owing to their comparatively reduced restrictions. As it would turn out, rich oil deposits would be found on many of these Freedmen's lands, which increased the desirability of and competition for Freedmen's land.

Allotment access produced the "complex" quality of race relations undergirded by class distinction, which demonstrates what is possible when race enters market relations. For instance, Chang notes that "African American newcomers charged Freedmen with disloyalty to the race if they sold their lands to whites," with Freedmen retorting that "the newcomers were 'white man's Negroes.'"[40] As I have argued elsewhere, the work of race in the market produces "an expectation of equitability," and when that equitability is not experienced, race logic produces "a reflexive critique whereby problems in the market are located within themselves and [the Black] community."[41] One of the Black newspapers at the time entered the fray, writing, "when a colored man approaches his Native brother and proposes to buy land off him he is turned away as if nothing had been said."[42]

Of course, Native Freedmen sold land to arriving southern Blacks. Without those transactions, many of the all-Black towns that dotted Indian Territory would have been impossible. The early resentment between the Freedmen and the later arriving Blacks would eventually transform into solidarity as Whites who moved to the territory gained greater influence and shifted cultural norms toward anti-Blackness. Indian enmity and aggression also grew toward all Blacks, which necessitated solidarity between the Freedmen and the southern Blacks. The Oklahoma Historical Society notes, "In the last two decades of Indian Territory Indians and freedmen faced complicated choices about citizenship and land ownership that ruptured any remaining ties between the two. Both Cherokee and Creek freedmen waged lengthy challenges through the United States courts for their rightful share of tribal monies gained in land sales. Both cases were decided in favor of the freedmen."[43]

It recalled an earlier battle for recognition as Freedmen who were not present in Indian Territory at the time of the Dawes Act were often disqualified from enrollment.[44] To establish their claim of belonging, they had to prove their literal emplacement, once again tying their Native identity to land. Moreover, by statehood in 1907, there was blanket recognition of US citizenship. This recognition bound together the two previously discrete categories of Blackness that operated in Indian Territory into the singular formulation of "negro."

As Melissa Stuckey argues, "Anti-Black racism in the Creek Nation was one factor that pushed formerly enslaved and other African-descended tribe members to forge closer bonds with African Americans who emigrated to the Creek Nation."[45] These relations, of course, raise the complicated issue of how settler colonialism and freedom in this context produced notions of the territory. The political and legal flattening of Black identity did not foreclose the retention of heritage, which would pose challenges to the broader process of Black racialization as a coherent political and even cultural project. Black arrivants, and therefore Blackness, sought and struggled to make a way through that process. The result was a reductive determination of Blackness that required new terms of relation. Reconciling the simultaneity of dispossession and freedom, violence and utopia, required wrestling with racialization and its operation through geographic becoming.

Both Native and Black subjects became disassociated with their normative relational terms of geographic belonging. Both groups were taking part in a very similar set of processes. Black subjects were becoming untwinned with the plantation and were able to plot a sense of emplacement on their terms. Native subjects became disaggregated from their sense of place, one of intimate relationality. I use *disaggregation* because *aggregation* implies a collectivism that better classifies Native epistemology and identification. This formation is what Edward Sampson calls "ensembled individualism."[46] This identification is interpreted by Marilyn Strathern as "dividualism," in which persons are "individually conceived [but] contain a generalized sociality within." These persons, Strathern continues, are "constructed as the plural and composite site of the relationships that produce them."[47]

Disaggregation and untwinning are coeval processes of transformation. These two groups experienced the simultaneity of transformation but with disparate relational positions within the territory, where one became separated and the other rooted. However, through Oklahoman statehood, the two groups ultimately experienced the similar fate of enclosure and land recession, undermining the project and the Black sense of place that the territory made possible.

Karla Slocum has noted among contemporary Black town residents a "seeming reluctance to claim American Indian identity," which Slocum asserts helps explain "why the Native American bases of Black towns are now practically invisible and why some might say that Black towns are 'just Black.'"[48] My assertion is that this also has much to do with the way that land worked to orient and reorient racial subjectivity. Land, transforming into an object of anxiety for Natives and promise for Blacks, became the central modality by which settler colonialism reconfigured Indigenous and Black life. This refiguring was the product of racialization.

Racialization's imperative objective is disassociation, as disassociation makes available the impacted subject's material resources—those resources often being land and bodies. For Native peoples that disassociation through racialization resulted in a settler logic of elimination from land.[49] Patrick Wolfe argues that "the separate destinies that race inscribed harmoniously reproduced the foundational structures of U.S. society, simultaneously providing for both the elimination of Indians and the exclusion of blacks. As such, the two disparate racializations together served a unitary end."[50]

There are convincing critiques that complicate what they claim as Wolfe's emphasis that settler-colonialism by definition is a system of native elimination.[51] What he outlines is what Tiffany King notes as the required dehumanization of Black and Indigenous peoples in the facilitation of White "conquistador humanism."[52] However, for Black people, as noted by the above discussion on twinning, this "exclusion" took the form of a violent incorporation to land. And yet land, and specifically Indian Territory land, was perhaps the best opportunity to pursue the long vision of freedom from that violent incorporation.

Transit of Freedom

Tiya Miles and Sharon Patricia Holland, in the introduction to their edited volume *Crossing Waters, Crossing Worlds*, suggest that broadening the historical imagination requires thinking through the articulations produced in the space "where black experience meets Native experience."[53] "Perhaps more than any other space in the United States," they write, "Indian Territory, broadly defined, has held out the promise of home to black slaves and their descendants. By the late nineteenth century and early twentieth century, many African Americans had come to see the Western lands called Indian Territory as a refuge in America, and more, as a potential black space that would function metaphorically and emotionally as a substitute for the longed-for African homeland."[54]

Indian Territory "shone like a beacon at the end of a long tunnel of racism and exploitation," but for it to do so, producing the "concept of a black Indian Territory" would require that Indians function as "a vehicle for black identity formation and racial uplift."[55] Miles and Holland's invocation of Native people in Indian Territory as a vehicle would be taken up a few years later in Jodi Byrd's notion of "Indianness" as a form of "transit." As such, "Indianness becomes a site through which U.S. empire orients and replicates itself by transforming those to be colonized into 'Indians' through continual reiterations of pioneer logics," with those pioneer logics located in "cacophonous" and thus "discordant and competing representations of diasporic arrivals and Native lived experiences."[56]

Put another way, the formulation, framing, and functioning of Indianness were available means by which settler colonialism could materialize. Moreover, this process was available to people beyond White settlers. We can see Byrd's notion of transit historically at play in the Black imagining of Indian Territory's possibility. As Miles and Holland write, "In imagining their paradisiacal home, black town settlers envisioned a place where Indians were necessary but peripheral. They were necessary because it was the Indian presence that differentiated Indian Territory from the states, and it was also the complex history between Indians and their former black slaves that had opened the door for African American settlement; they were peripheral because blacks located Native people at the margins of their new communities."[57] To be sure, Byrd recognizes the challenge with reconciling how Black people in Native spaces fit within the settler paradigm, given that they were "forced into the Americas through the violence of European and Anglo-American colonialism and imperialism."[58] As a solution, Byrd offers the term *arrivants*, which she borrows from Caribbeanist scholar Kamau Brathwaite.

Through the framework of "cacophony," Byrd identifies "the competing interpretations of geographical spatialities and historicities that inform racial and decolonial identities" and that "decenter the vertical interactions of colonizer and colonized and recenter the horizontal struggles among peoples with competing claims to historical oppressions."[59] The result is an approach to "arrivant colonialism" that "focuses not only vertically on the interactions between the colonizer and colonized, but horizontally between different minority oppressions within settler and arrivant landscapes."[60] This allows the "settler, Native, and arrivant [to] each acknowledge their own positions within empire and then reconceptualize space and history to make visible what imperialism and its resultant settler colonialisms and diasporas have sought to obscure."[61] In trying to tease out and account for the actual messiness of colonial relations, Byrd goes a long way in disrupting that which has long obscured those relations, namely, the neat binaries of settler and Native.

To undo this binary, Byrd uses the Indian Territory example of the Cherokees' own institution of African slavery "within their own colonized nation" and the Cherokees' later decision in 2007 to disenfranchise Black Cherokee Freedmen by refusing to recognize their tribal membership. The Freedmen's status makes clear the disutility of conventional and "hierarchical models of racial and colonialist imagining."[62] Byrd's point was further supported a decade later—several years after the publication of her text—when in August 2017 the US district court ruled in favor of the Freedmen descendants and the US Department of the Interior, thus reestablishing the Freedmen's full rights to Cherokee Nation citizenship.[63]

Similarly, Tiffany Lethabo King, in her text *Black Shoals*, attends to the contradictions of the settler colonial relations that exist between Black and Native peoples, writing, "Under relations of conquest, Black and Indigenous people made difficult and agonizing choices when it came to negotiating and fighting for their existence. Claims of innocence on the part of Black or Indigenous people are disingenuous and deprive Black and Indigenous life of the agonizing texture and horrific choices that often had to be (and have to be) made to survive under relations of conquest."[64] In comparison to Byrd, whose depoliticized use of *arrivant* signals involuntary presence and subjugation, King appears more comfortable in acknowledging the possibility of Black people occupying the role of the settler. But suppose Blackness can occupy the settler category. In that case, King suggests that we need a more forceful term for the White settler: "Even if people of color (or non-Black and non-Indigenous) can over time occupy the structural position of the 'settler,'" King writes, "then critical social theory needs another name for the position previously held by the white settler."[65] She suggests the term *conquistador-settler* to attend to the violence of White settler histories.[66] This growing comfort with the notion of the Black "settler" has shown up more recently in the work on Indian Territory of Alaina Roberts, who opens the category even further:

> In Indian Territory, I identify settler colonialism as a process that could be wielded by whoever sought to claim land; it involved not only a change in land occupation but also a transformation in thinking about and the rhetorical justification of what it meant to reside in a place formerly occupied by someone else. This means that in my definition, anyone could act as a "settler," despite previous status as say a slave or a dispossessed Indian, as long as they used this process—composed of rhetoric, American governmental structures, and individual action—which may have aided in their efforts to acquire land or protection, but which ultimately served the goals of spatial occupation and white supremacy: the dual nature of settler colonialism.[67]

Roberts concludes that the basis of her claim is that "power did not emanate from only one person or governmental agency."[68]

In securing any advancement, anyone who drew on the power of the settler colonial state was a settler, even if non-White. An example of this settler Blackness can be found in a different Indigenous context: the African American emigrationist "colonization" of Liberia. In articulating the position of those migrants, Robert Murray in *Atlantic Passages* advances the figure of the "black-white settler" to advocate for the notion of race and the settler figure to become more functionally fluid and practice oriented. Murray argues Black settlers in Liberia represented a "whiteness divorced from the phenotype and presence of people of European descent," what he calls a "'whiteness' without 'whites.'" [69] In Liberia, Whiteness was produced by the Black settler's "Western cultural practices."[70]

Ultimately, the "freedoms and opportunities" acquired by Black settlers in Indian Territory were "begotten by impeding the freedoms and opportunities of others."[71] For Byrd, King, and Roberts, there is a recognition, in order of growing confidence, that Black people who arrived in Native spaces, like Indian Territory, occupied a settler position bearing meaningful consequences for Native people, even corroding Native sovereignty.

The politics that each of these authors assigns to the designation, or its nominal alternative, vary. This produces the settler as a stable position for which one either qualifies or does not. Byrd's notion of cacophony perhaps goes furthest by allowing for multiple meanings of *settler*. And yet, with her use of *arrivant*, Byrd's analysis ultimately reproduces the stability of the settler referent, as it pertains to accounting for Blackness within the process of settler colonialism. A similar criticism can be made of King's notion of the Black "shoal." While doing the important work of theoretically reconciling Black studies and Native studies, King's analysis still reproduces and is occupied by the referent of White settler-colonial studies, even as she disrupts it.

As statehood arrived, there was a significant belief that landownership and the all-Black towns it enabled could become the basis for political power within Oklahoma. Obtaining and exercising this power would require both land and racial unity. Economic boosters and political boosters like J. E. Toombs, editor of the *Muskogee Comet*, encouraged Black unification. Toombs wrote, "There is no time for denominational contentions among us . . . for while we contend for the rights of this denomination or that denomination, the white man is busy buying land."[72]

I am not attempting to counterposition Blackness to Nativeness but rather to meditate on their respective and simultaneous relationships to land in Indian Territory. To be clear, what I mean here by Blacks is those who arrived after the opening of Indian Territory to settlement in 1889. I am also not arguing that Native dispossession facilitated Black freedom. Such an argument would be disingenuous because of the many racial entanglements and exchanges of dispossession and exclusion between the groups. However, it is evident that the territory provided a broad opening for the Black people who arrived later, many of whom had arrived from the South. That opening was a critical opportunity to break from the plantation.

Tiya Miles most forcefully, and perhaps most honestly, asks the question, "What do we do with the black 'settler'?" Miles elaborates:

Or rather, what do we do with the more than one hundred thousand African Americans who moved north and west onto violated and usurped Indigenous lands in the nineteenth century? We have sidestepped this question in studies of the American Midwest and West even as settler colonial frameworks of analysis have reshaped Native American history. We still reach for the familiar and now especially charged term settler when describing black residents, with all of the conceptual baggage that word carries in our present historiographical moment as indicating agents or subagents of the settler colonial state beset with a "recurring need to disavow the presence of indigenous 'others'" in the interest of controlling Native lands.[73]

Miles quickly dispenses with the effectiveness of the notion of the Black "pioneer," noting how the term still echoes the discursive historiography of White settlers who tamed and civilized the wild frontier. Moreover, "the terms *black settler* and *black pioneer* referentially pack African American experience onto the offensive end of the settler colonial playing field."[74] That imagery doesn't comport with the experiences of African Americans "who came to dwell in the house of settler colonialism" and who "struggled to emerge whole from a proximal past of stolen lives and labor."[75] Miles situates African American presence in Indian Territory as not necessarily guided by "choice," writing, "African Americans had but two choices as the young United States solidified its hold over the central portion of North America: make homes on Indigenous lands or die."[76] As a result, Black survival came through forming alliances or engaging in dispossession, which was enacted and facilitated through "the U.S. nation-state or its white citizens: the squatters, soldiers, and land speculators who formed the advance guard of settler colonial intrusion and entrenchment."[77]

Miles asserts that the intricacies and nuances of this phenomenon of Black presence in Indian Territory call us "to carefully consider gradations of difference in positioning and interaction."[78] She especially emphasizes the variability of this notion of choice that complicates the stability of a presumed one-dimensional notion of Black positionality. Paying attention to this allows us to "see spaces of difference and complexity that also exist in African American histories of westward migration and homemaking in the first generations after emancipation and to invent or rediscover a language for writing about them." It can "encourage us to resist falling back on familiar phrasing that reinforces blacks' location on the settler side of a conceptual boundary without examining gradations of relations at and around this line."[79]

Accomplishing this, Miles asserts, requires new "thought-acts" to refine our understanding of the multiple intersecting histories at play here but also to challenge static settler colonial forms.[80] Miles frames the challenge as one of how to "get our words around" Black residence in Native lands, "without flattening their realities, protecting them from critiques of power, or reproducing boldface lines between 'settler' and 'Native.'"[81] Miles references Byrd's notion of arrivants and the use of *ambiguous settlers* as offered by Zainab Amadahy and Bonita Lawrence regarding the similar role taken up by Afro-Canadians as viable options.[82] These options provide what Miles considers is a necessary "third category" for Black people on Native land that is "separate from Native and settler" and that "recognizes the difference enslavement makes and expands our ability to perceive a spectrum of relations."[83] Whatever the option, its purpose is to disturb "the fixed boundary line between Native and settler, pushing us to trace and represent the past with exactitude and imagination," but also to fully appreciate that at the root of this relational spectrum is the particular ambivalence of this Black form of settlement, which Miles frames as "a situatedness of subjection."[84]

"The Exoduster, ambiguous settler, arrivant, [and] exiled settler" are some of the third-position options that Miles ultimately identifies.[85] But the notion of the *exiled settler*, to me, represents the "sharper and brighter formulations" of how to approach this question.[86] Miles convincingly situates Black arrivants in Indian Territory as engaged in a "desperate flight from slavery, racial violence, and economic exploitation."[87] Unapologetically, Miles continues, "Yes, they settled on Native lands appropriated by a colonial state; yes, they made choices to invest in that state in ways that we must examine and expose." But it is critical to remember, according to Miles, that "they did so in a state of near-permanent exile that always shaped their relationship to settler colonial social and political structures." In this moment Miles gives us the category for understanding the Black settler in Indian Territory when she writes that "the Afro-settler is an exo-settler." While she doesn't elaborate on a particularly overt theorization of the exo-settler, she continues the general thrust of her argument by operationalizing the category as one "pushed by exigencies of exodus and exile and (almost) always exogenous to the settler state."[88]

At the root of the politics behind Black settlers' subject positions is the relational position they have to land. To be sure, each of the above referenced scholars understands the power and meaning of land for Black settlers. Tiya Miles, Kendra Field, and Nell Painter most ardently appreciate and advocate for land in Indian Territory as a means of Black settler freedom, with Miles coming closest in my view to apprehending the poetics of Black people's geographic relations to and in Indian Territory land. Other analyses are primarily critical, such as with the underlying geographic politics of Byrd's notion of transit, and Roberts's claim that the land that permitted southern Black people in Indian Territory to become property owners "was part of the broader theft of Indian land that also led to the loss of much Native sovereignty, culture, and language."[89]

King makes a different move altogether, stating that "settler colonial studies becomes primarily preoccupied with the settler's relationship to land," which King claims "disappears the settler's relationship to violence."[90] More specifically, King asserts that "a focus on settlers and their relationship to land displaces how settlers also become conquistadors/(humans) through Native genocide and Black dehumanization," which King charges amounts to a conceptual sleight of hand.[91] King's recourse to this very real problem is to analytically decenter land in the hopes of revealing but also marginalizing the violence inherent in its White settler constitution. This, she tells us, moves past "where Blackness appears or fits within (White) settler colonial discourses or [placing] Blackness at the center of settler colonialism." She resists the "political economic rubrics of land, labor, and settlement" through concepts like "Black porosity," which, "like Black fungibility, slows down the tempo of the homogenizing force of humanist and Marxian regimes of labor."[92]

King also decenters, through a turn to metaphor, the meaning that land has for Black people. It is a necessary sacrifice for accomplishing the coalitional goal of her project. It is important to remember and keep at the fore of our politics, as King does, that "Black healing and Indigenous healing are associated."[93] Still, we must resist sacrificing understanding Black relationships to the land on material terms. Moreover, when we do attend to that relationship, we must do so beyond merely metaphorical and functional analyses. We must not just understand the relations to the land but the relations *of* the land. In other words, we must pursue a deeper sense of placemaking than the ways Indian Territory provided economic opportunity and land through Native dispossession. After all, in agreeing with King, I view that framing as too reproductive of a White settler narrative. The understanding is also both too obvious and too convenient. Moreover, it allows only for the fashioning of Black people, as we have seen above through compromise or critique, as capable only of occupying some variation of the White settler position. This occupation emphasizes and privileges Black arrival and emplacement in Indian Territory owing to subjugation—*fleeing oppression*—which again moors Blackness to a plantation regime, even where the plantation per se is absent. This occupational arrangement demands the now-common, even overrepresented, reference of Black fugitivity and fungibility in Black studies analyses of Black freedom.

The referenced scholars have sought to advance where available, recover where not, and resuscitate where possible the object of freedom while still attending to a mostly liberal moral notion of rights. This notion of rights should be understood as reconciling a competing set of claims, which, when reconciled, produces moral order. This order is effectively the accomplishment of reconciliation, which can be seen in Byrd's cacophony and in the drive for Black-Native "forms of sociality and futurity," understood as coalition, of King's Black shoal.[94] There is much to be admired about this pursuit, but for all its political need—toward solidarity or recognition and the sense of satisfaction that underlies them both—it still limits the on-the-ground understanding of what is happening relationally in the subject-object association of Blackness and land/territory. A framework is needed that adequately gets at the scalar register of freedom, not just as a liberatory (or literary) idiom, or as the presumed anchor and aspirational lodestar of anticolonial, anticaste, and antiracist struggles.

We can accomplish this framing through an unsettling of the settler to allow for an appropriate qualification of settler Blackness that goes past theorists' attempts to reconfigure and effectively reconcile the subject and subjectivity of Blackness. What is required is to understand the geographic relations at play in the ethical formation of the settler. When I say *ethics*, what I mean is attending to the strategies and rationalizations by which one recognizes and makes sense of one's circumstances, environment, and relationship to both, especially through practice. Following Michael Lambek's notion of "ordinary ethics," I assert that the Black settler relationship to land, territory, and Indian Territory specifically must be "grounded in agreement rather than rule, in practice rather than belief," as doing so allows appreciating "the inevitable cracks and ruptures in the actual and the ubiquity of responses to the ever-present limits of criteria and paradoxes of the human condition."[95] This practice, as an ethical form, is best understood as sovereignty.

Sovereign Blackness

Thinking from Indian Territory, the question of colonialism often turns to Native notions of sovereignty. Mark Rifkin has argued that the "geopolitical imaginary" of the United States as it concerns sovereignty and European racial hierarchy is understood as the settler state's "presumptive absorption of Native peoples."[96] This process not only unsettles, or even outright undoes, claims of Native political sovereignty through "limiting possibilities for (Indigenous) self-determination by presuming the necessity of transitioning to particular forms of self-organization, narration, and governance" but also becomes the means by which frames of Native self-reference are translated.[97] There is an unfortunate tendency to omit the United States from the various nationalist political projects that we recognize as "colonial," beyond the limits of Native-oriented settler colonialism. This tendency is partly responsible for foreclosing Black subjects' access to a claim of sovereignty in the United States.

Whether directly or indirectly, scholars have recognized the settler impulse of Black arrival in Indian Territory, a point with which I effectively agree. However, the challenge with their identification is that that scholarship fails to identify or, at the very least, recognize the sovereign quality or drive of the Black settler. Scholars, as I've demonstrated, are willing to identify the dispossessive act of Black settlement that transgresses Native sovereignty. They are also willing to acknowledge that Black settler transgression is made in the pursuit of freedom. However, the recognition of a sovereign imperative behind settler Blackness is overlooked. Manu Karuka argues for seeing settler claims to land as being articulated against a recognized native sovereign belonging, what he calls "counter-sovereignty," a process that establishes "political and economic space for the settler sovereign."[98] While directly leveled as a critique against White settler practice, again, with a mind to the ethical we can perhaps find some utility in his formula for understanding the Black settler.

I want to assert that North Tulsa's community has access to a framework of sovereignty. Their effective disposition is that of a people who have a history of political and economic self-determination. However, that disposition can present as seeking freedom from within the context of self-determination's historical absence. That position I believe qualifies as what Rinaldo Walcott argues is Black life lived within what he calls the "long emancipation."[99]

In meditating on being "still in the time of emancipation" in anticipation of freedom "yet to come," Walcott asks, "What, then, is freedom? How do I demarcate why and how Black peoples do not yet have something called freedom?" In answering his questions, Walcott situates emancipation as "always embedded in the juridical and thus as always orienting and delimiting freedom." Walcott argues that this process, which facilitates the "time of the long emancipation," works to "tie Black people to the regimen of slave and plantation logics and economies." The freedom he attempts to articulate "is one that imagines a break with those logics."[100] To break with those logics, Walcott advocates dwelling in the "fleeting moments" of Black freedom, to advance his work's "central conceit," which is "to grapple with a desired sovereignty of Black being."[101] Walcott's notion of sovereignty takes the form of what he calls "bodily sovereignty," which permits "ways of being human in the world that exist beyond the realm of the juridical."[102]

This "dwelling" is the everyday recognition of North Tulsans' own "fleeting" moment of the sovereignty of their Black being: pre-massacre Greenwood and, as I've argued in this chapter, the possibility and accomplishment of Indian Territory. They are the living forms of Walcott's central "conceit." But they are not always fully aware of this sovereign possibility because their sovereign history, for all intents and purposes, was fleeting. There were only eighteen years between post-Reconstruction Black arrival in Indian Territory and Oklahoma statehood, which brought the formal onset of Jim Crow. There were but fifteen years between the founding of Greenwood and the 1921 race massacre. These moments are reminiscent of W. E. B. DuBois's meditation on the failure of Reconstruction, in which he still found the words to reflect on and recognize the promise it held when he wrote, "The slave went free; stood a brief moment in the sun; then moved back again toward slavery."[103]

To be clear, this dwelling is not some fixture of the past but an active repository for collective memory, aspiration, and *action*. This is how I choose to interpret the Great Gathering: not as just *another* meeting but as part of the slow act of return. It bears returning once again to the attendee who was perplexed why descendants of Black Wall Street were begging for groceries. This process, this "returning," is made possible by North Tulsans' sheer commitment to recalling, "dwelling," and working to build on their available legacies.

What I am suggesting is what Deborah Thomas and Joseph Masco argue for as a sovereignty "unhinged from master narratives, unhinged from normative disciplinary frames, and unhinged from pragmatic developmentalism and utility." In their articulation, sovereignty is "diffuse, uncertain, [and] complex."[104] This formulation opens sovereignty up and away from state-oriented frameworks, though, to be sure, that configuration was firmly a part of the Black imaginary of freedom in Indian Territory, as evidenced by the Black statehood movement pursued by Ed McCabe.

I advance that North Tulsans themselves today are not required to recognize that they are engaging in sovereign practice. This position is especially important since what they have is a received, inherited sense of sovereignty, a form that has passed the stage of intentional ideation. Their sovereignty presents as a sense of place, whereby that sense and its relationship to place figure as a more reliable determinant of sovereign relations than political independence. Indeed, I follow and extend Adom Getachew's resistance to what she calls the erosion of "the moral and political significance of sovereignty" through its increasing framing as "responsibility."[105] Getachew has identified an "instrumental and paternalist" political shift by which the notion of responsibility, which demands material resources after all, "displaces more expansive accounts of sovereignty that emphasize ideals of self-government and independence."[106]

Sovereignty as a sense of place, as an open configuration of Blackness and place, has its basis in Indian Territory and its legacy in North Tulsa today. Establishing this point during the period of Indian Territory is straightforward. It only takes returning to the formation of all-Black towns and early Greenwood. When one listens to North Tulsans' articulations of their aspirations, it is undeniable that, to them, North Tulsa represents a geography of more than freedom. The presence of ethical identifications that indicate such is meaningfully illustrated by North Tulsans' narratives of dispossession. While there is recognition of the cause of injury, as well as a demand for reparation, there is also a clear and robust sense of inalienability, self-reliance, and what effectively can be qualified as ownership inherent in those narratives. In other words, the contemporary "feeling" of Blackness in North Tulsa is the full experience of what I would call *sovereign belonging*, which is defined by the terms of inalienability and ownership but effectively by a sense of emplacement.

Native peoples, Rifkin says, "remain oriented in relation to collective experiences of peoplehood, to particular territories . . . , to the ongoing histories of their inhabitance in those spaces, and to histories of displacement from them. Such orientations open up 'different worlds' than those at play in dominant settler orderings, articulations, and reckonings of time."[107] What Rifkin offers is a framework to assess and determine the relationality to place as the basis of sovereignty, for which I argue North Tulsans qualify. Put differently, sovereignty looks like a commitment to place, irrespective of the violence, the dispossession, and the attempts to fracture a semiotic or material sense of belonging.

To think through this possible application, Deborah Thomas's work in Jamaica proves instructive. Thomas asks, "What does modern sovereignty feel like?" to work out the relationship between postcolonial violence and community formation. Her answer is to assert that community is a physical space that "evokes an affective disposition," which, for her purposes in Jamaican garrison communities, encompasses "submission to a set of dictating norms and forms of violence."[108] To Thomas, this affective disposition to geography produces simultaneous "denigration" and "celebration" of Blackness.[109] Thomas's formula applies to the context of North Tulsa, especially because Thomas uses it to theorize the problem of sovereignty as read within the circumstances of racialized dispossession. Thomas writes that such consideration "forces us to generate more complex accounts of the historical and social relations through which notions of sovereignty are produced, experienced, and circulated across time and space."[110] Critically, it encourages a full appreciation for "the complexity of how visions of the present, the future, and social change are inhabited and expressed in extremely complex and often contradictory ways by people who are operating in networks that encompass many scales simultaneously."[111]

Thus, North Tulsa "feels" like sovereignty because the sovereign effect from the geography of Indian Territory as sovereign can still be sensed. It orients, through simultaneity, the relationship that North Tulsans have toward Greenwood and its legacy. This orientation can easily be confused with the idolization of and attachment to "prosperity," which one would not be criticized for assuming. But even for the referent community during that period, Greenwood, despite being given the moniker of Black Wall Street, did not see itself as exceptional. It saw itself as self-determined. Consider this quote from James O. Goodwin, the owner of the *Oklahoma Eagle*, a legacy Black newspaper in Tulsa: "The significant thing about Greenwood is it was not just a Black thing. It was quintessential America. It was like any other developing neighborhood, whether that's Irish, or Greek, or Jewish. These people embraced faith, they believed in education and hard work. They believed in capitalism and freedom. People should look at Greenwood as a part of Americana and not some aberration or a freak of nature."[112] Goodwin points to the quintessential Americanness of Greenwood, people like any others who believed in "capitalism and freedom," which I would hesitate to conflate with "capitalism *as* freedom." In denoting the ordinariness of Greenwood, Goodwin advocates for its representational qualification "as" America, which is undoubtedly a claim of recognition.

In *None Like Us*, Stephen Best searches for "a way around the dark brood of 'negative allegory,'" which he identifies as part of "the melancholic turn" in studies of Blackness. This turn, he continues, is obsessed with "displacement, erasure, suppression, elision, overlooking, overwriting, omission, obscurantism, expunging, repudiation, exclusion, annihilation, [and] denial."[113] Instead, his interest lies in the "effort to determine political goals according to a model of representation."[114] Best ultimately concludes that "the pursuit of recognition expresses an aspiration to *sovereignty*" and that "the politics of recognition involves us in efforts to escape the condition of non-sovereignty."[115]

Best's model of sovereignty comports with the *historical* narrative of Greenwood, by which I mean the sense of the district as represented by Goodwin. This can also be seen in the accounts that I presented throughout the text as well as that which can be detected in the presented debate around Black settler praxes. As Best argues, the sovereign claim is rooted in and established through recognition, and thus it cannot be seen as an aberration. If it is an aberration, it cannot be representative and thus is rendered illegible. Settler sovereignty, following Manu Karuka and Tiffany King, should be seen as just sovereignty. Sovereignty is a codified Western form of recognition both present in and presented as what Sylvia Wynter determined to be the "real real" and "normal normal," within the "the world system in which we now find ourselves and to the single history within whose dynamic we all now live."[116] The sovereign is not aberrant. However, what we saw with the assault on Greenwood was its being made aberrant. And in that aberration Greenwood became reordered as marginalized.

Sovereign Territories of Freedom

The geography of Indian Territory serves as a meaningful intervention into the debate of Black placemaking. The plantation twinned with the people who live in its wake and is a foundation for Black culture in the United States. This means that slavery's impact, whether as memory or, as I've described, as the continued experience of poverty, continues as a contemporary phenomenon that lives in economic and cultural, as well as emotional, ways. And yet, while it dictates so many of the circumstances of Black existence, it is not without its alternatives. And if one draws on the alternative narrative that Tulsa's Black history offers, what becomes available is a reparations framework that can accomplish the necessary act of "un-twinning." This act is a liberatory repositioning that enables Blackness unbound by the plantation.

Repair, as a result, could be the freedom to progress without the anchor referent of slavery. One's geographic emplacement can then produce other narratives and more meaningful merits beyond the pursuit of the accomplishment of freedom. Far from the perspective that viewed Native lands as terra nullius, Indian Territory was a geography of possibility.[117] It was not only a geography of possibility but also one of resistance. The possibilities for freedom conjoined the notion of territory with Black freedom. Despite the conditioning or twinning that resulted from the plantation system, the Black people who arrived in Indian Territory experienced both a material and a symbolic shift in their positioning. Through geographic relocation, and the geography's distinct association or disassociation with their history of enslaved labor, Indian Territory allowed for a revolutionary recasting of freedom. In Indian Territory, freedom was possible because, in a profound way, it was a land that did not comport with existing Black notions of territoriality. Indian Territory offers a necessary framework for reconsidering the plantation as the principal referent for Black geographic relations. Indian Territory provides us with new relational terms.

In *Repair*, Katherine Franke asks the crucial question, "What would freedom mean to freed people?"[118] Using the examples of how freed refugee Black people exercised their freedom at Port Royal in the Sea Islands of South Carolina and Davis Bend, Mississippi, during the Civil War, Franke locates two exceptional cases for freedom's analysis. In these cases Franke describes a radical experiment with freedom; the freed populations were to a varying degree left to form their own communities and engage in agricultural development. "Their vision of freedom," Franke asserts, "provides a model of what could have been" and, for her, represents what reparations could be for African enslavement in the United States.[119]

These experiments began early in the war, when the enslaved, having crossed Union lines during the Civil War, became refugees and occupied the position of "contraband." The Union Army held them in "contraband camps," which were limited in the degree to which they could sustain a swelling Black refugee population. Ultimately, "visionary military officers and abolitionists from the North" determined that the freed Black population could be granted property on confiscated southern plantations, where their economic labors could also help to generate revenue for the North's war effort.[120] It was on these sites that what Franke calls "utopian experiments in Black emancipation" were developed.[121] Franke states that these experiments had multiple objectives, which included "proving that freed labor was more efficient than slave labor; exploring methods of reparation for the indignity and theft of Black peoples' labor while enslaved"; and, perhaps most important, generally "civilizing" the formerly enslaved in preparation for their lives as citizens.[122]

The freed people who would form the communities at the Sea Islands and Davis Bend centered their freedom on land. Moreover, they wanted their communities to be exclusively Black. "What most of the freed people imagined freedom would look like," Franke says, was "land, tools, and complete independence from white people."[123] While this was a relatively straightforward formulation of what freedom would mean—after all, the United States mainly comprised communities through access to land, the use of tools, and the relative exercising of independence—Franke suggests that, had the practices of Port Royal and Davis Bend been allowed to set the model for postemancipation Black freedom, it would "likely have produced a quite different, more just, and less unequal present."[124]

Of course, what Black people received instead was "freedom on the cheap," semiotically marked by "the dangling 'd' at the end of 'free' [which] stood as a kind of residue of enslavement that bound freed people to a past, and marked their future as freed, not free, people. It served as a racial mark that structured the kind of freedom formerly enslaved people received as something less than that with which white people were endowed as a matter of natural, or God's, law."[125] For Franke, a freeman was "understood as the opposite of a slave, as a man with robust civil and political rights and status. A freedman by contrast was not a slave but was also not the opposite of a slave." The letter *d* represented the "immanent ability to be enslaved, enjoined for the moment by questionable operation of law." The freedman, the bearer of the letter *d*, "was a refugee from slavery occupying a precarious place."[126]

The development of all-Black towns in Indian Territory in the postemancipation era was aided by collective Black freedom, racial identity, and the internal geopolitical climate of America. Moreover, they fit the template for freedom, which involved few to no White people, tillable land, and the ability to form self-government.[127]

A sense of Black nationalism and Black self-determination created a "hybrid identity" of collective Blackness that fueled Indian Territory's Black promise. Stuckey writes that it was a "self-determinist culture" that led African Americans in Indian Territory to articulate the destiny of Black people through town building, to fulfill their "racial destiny."[128] To them, landownership served as the bedrock of "Black civilization-building" and significantly facilitated a Black collectivity through "post-emancipation placemaking."[129] Indian Territory represented Black freedom after emancipation by being a site for the racial *and* sociospatial formation of a communal African American future.

While most settlers in the Indian and Oklahoma territories did not achieve great wealth, their ability to live and work on their terms was an important difference from what they had found in the South.[130] Following Reconstruction's defeat, freedom in the South reproduced the sensation of antebellum Black life. Through Jim Crow and the denial of rights, there was little in the way of life to be made, at least for those seeking it elsewhere. To make possible their freedom, Kendra Field argues that "African Americans turned toward ideologies of economic advancement, self-help, and racial solidarity."[131] Similarly, David Chang argues that southern Blacks held forth a holistic strategy that included "the goal of racial uplift through economic 'self-help,' the call to political action, and emigrationist nationalism," which was held together with the promise of landownership.[132] Indian Territory made this possible.

As Ralph Ellison mused in *Going to the Territory*, "As slaves, they had long been aware that for themselves, as for most of their countrymen, geography was fate. . . . And they knew that to escape across the Mason-Dixon Line northward was to move in the direction of a greater freedom. But freedom was also to be found in the West of the old Indian Territory."[133] Returning to Chang's "holistic strategy" of "economic self-help," "political action," and "emigrationist nationalism," we see the inputs for sovereignty, which is critical to fully appreciate freedom as both imagined and exercised in Indian Territory, which is as emigrationism. The kinds of ethics that emigration signals in the context of Blackness in the late nineteenth and early twentieth centuries, I would argue, are foundational to the general ideation of and possibilities for liberation envisioned by emancipated Black people. For scholars like Nell Painter, Kendra Field, and others, emigrationism is, as defined by David Chang, "the belief that mass migration was a viable strategy for African Americans to achieve prosperity and self-determination."[134]

From the Exodusters immediately following Reconstruction, to the migration to Indian Territory beginning the decade after, to the Great Migration in the second decade of the twentieth century, the postemancipation era saw several waves of departure from the South in the pursuit of freedom. It was what Carter Godwin Woodson identified as "a century of negro migration," during which he found Indian Territory to have "conditions" that were "unusually favorable."[135] To be sure, this was part of a much longer tradition of fugitivity and marronage during the slave era that qualified Black people's pursuit of geographic, if not legal, emancipation that began even as they crossed the Atlantic.

Indian Territory, like some of the other final destinations of emigrating Black people, followed several previous attempts to settle elsewhere, the most common locations being Kansas, Arkansas, Texas, and the Oklahoma

Territory.[136] But the ideals behind the emigrationism that brought Black people from the South to Indian Territory did not end there. The push for African emigration in Oklahoma reached a crescendo when P. J. Dorman founded an emigration club in Mantee, Oklahoma, in 1909. In 1912 Dorman came across an advertisement by the Akim Trading Company in an issue of the *African League*, with the heading "Agricultural Lands in Africa and How to Obtain Them."[137] Dorman inquired with the man behind the advertisement, Chief Alfred Sam.

Dorman's letter to Sam "expanded Sam's pan-African interest," and he arrived in Oklahoma in 1913. Alongside Dorman, he earned the quick interest—and investment—of over sixty Black Oklahomans in their "African movement."[138] Comparing the violence of America with the promise of Africa, Sam spoke to this group and many others of "the golden opportunities that awaited them at Gold Coast Africa," saying that there was "plenty of room in Africa for the American Negro" and that they would "go home and build up a powerful kingdom."[139]

The timing of interest in Sam's movement was not coincidental, nor was Dorman's founding of the emigrationist club in Mantee. Hundreds of similar clubs had formed over the previous two decades; the American Colonization Society reported in the 1890s that "one million or more of the people of color are seriously considering the matter of an early change of residence from the United States to Africa."[140] Following statehood in 1907, the political outlook for Black Oklahomans immediately dimmed as Jim Crow segregation was introduced—an all-too-familiar state of affairs for Black people, who only a couple of decades earlier had left behind Jim Crow's subjugation in the South.

Matters grew direr when Black Oklahomans, who were accustomed to exercising a relatively liberal amount of political will, faced the prospect of disenfranchisement in 1910. The Oklahoma grandfather clause sought to introduce literacy requirements for voting access exclusively for Blacks. The clause was ultimately struck down in 1915, but in the intervening years, the political promise of their landownership had seemingly expired, causing Black Oklahomans to look for a new vista of freedom.[141]

A group did make it to Ghana, the majority of whom ultimately returned due to a lack of provisions on arrival and other hardships mostly caused by delays on their journey. Kendra Field and Ebony Coletu explain that "the movement faced a series of governmental roadblocks extending from the Boley courthouse and the Oklahoma state house to the U.S. State Department and numerous British officials in London and the Gold Coast."[142]

For Field and Coletu, researchers who have ancestral connections to members of the movement, the sixty passengers aboard—only a fraction of the entire movement—"carried the dreams of thousands of African American Exodusters" with them as they looked to Africa.[143] Indeed, as Field and Coletu write, they were "animated by a higher motive," which linked African Americans and Africans on the continent, at least on the Gold Coast.[144] The literal repatriation of Black Oklahomans didn't materialize through Chief Sam's efforts, however, but the movement helped to spawn an even greater sense of Pan-African political identity and organization. Following the demise of Chief Sam's movement, nearly thirty chapters of Marcus Garvey's Universal Negro Improvement Association would be established in Oklahoma, leading the organization to ultimately eclipse Sam's movement.[145]

The Chief Sam movement signals "the symbolic power of black emigration during this 'golden age' of black nationalism," in which the movement's members' "unwillingness to listen and determination to migrate against all odds . . . highlights the gravity of black political and economic life in Jim Crow Oklahoma."[146] Indeed, "African-descended peoples led bold political lives in Indian Territory," Field writes, "and when faced with the emergence of statehood and Jim Crow segregation, many refused to acquiesce and chose instead to emigrate" thus "challenging the notion of a static and withdrawn African-American political life."[147]

Karla Slocum examines the historical appeal and the social and economic legacy of Indian Territory freedom through her analysis of all-Black towns, which I would argue she extends to Greenwood. It is the capacity of geographic freedom, I believe, that made them, as Slocum notes, "alluring places" for remembrance *and* Black futurity.[148] Slocum shows how Black towns' formation and their socioeconomic successes and failures relied on their geographic, social, and historical meaning. Indeed, these historical accounts and memorialization have manifested through the abundance of scholarly literature and mainstream resources that she relies on for her analysis. Moving beyond their mere symbolic value, Slocum argues that all-Black towns offer a framework for connecting *Black* sociospatial pasts to futures. In advancing the temporal relations at play in her point, I want to emphasize the consequence of stating that relation in reverse. The Black futures that the all-Black towns represent, at least for North Tulsans, are about the recovery of their pasts. Black towns represent Black self-respect and self-sufficiency and show that despite racism—that interfering force—people of African descent could thrive.[149]

In this way, all-Black towns represent postemancipation possibilities. To be sure, Slocum determines that this sense of place may be complicated by all-Black towns' being caught between a celebrated Black past and a neoliberal Black future. We can see that easily with the various Greenwood "initiatives." Indeed, Slocum identifies the inherent limitations, and I would add vulnerabilities, of this possibility owing to these towns' and North Tulsa's economic fragility and the various agendas of those invested in them. Resisting symbolic fixity is complicated for all-Black towns, primarily because of residents' reliance on heritage tourism as a form of economic and cultural reinvestment, and this has quickly become the case in Greenwood.

Furthermore, the threat of rural gentrification of all-Black towns and of historic Greenwood that is underway looms over their Black residents. Slocum positions twenty-first-century all-Black towns as prime for articulating a current and ongoing Black sense of place as an alternative to Black geographic futures. Despite how arriving Blacks saw Indian Territory as "a potential black space," as Tiya Miles and Sharon Holland note, Slocum asserts that "a Black place is not a utopia."[150] She reminds us "that being an alluring Black place has its challenges, and this is the reality and conundrum of a twenty-first-century Black town."[151] Despite those challenges, and even the challenges of navigating their problematic history of Native relations, Black towns represent the powerful narrative of place-based freedom and its broader possibilities, possibilities that extend beyond the form and even the limits of their means.

The Americanization of the Negro

The long journey of freedom and recognition undertaken by Black people in the United States has produced what Nikhil Pal Singh has called the "Americanization of the Negro," by which the "meaning of freedom had been distorted in its subordination to patriotic cant and fear."[152] The result of that process of unequal incorporation through the stunted and deferred promise of integration has been a narrowing of the imagination of the myriad forms that Black life took in the conceptualization of postemancipation freedom. Contemporary political discourse would lead us to assume that a geographic attachment to North America has been consistently present in the self-fashioning of postemancipation Blackness.

The notion of opportunity as geography became especially prominent as the clearer horizon of emancipation created urgency around the expulsion of Black people in North America. Asaka argues that understanding the Black relationship to territory during this period requires adopting "a larger geographic scope" because the "spatial imaginings" of Black people at the time were not geographically limited to North America and "entailed mappings of the Atlantic."[153] And while these mappings "undergirded racially hierarchical relations of labor and land use" that "thrust free populations into struggles over geography," this moment produced a "mode of enacting meanings" that saw Black people become "engaged in a politics of mobility."[154] While "rigidifying," it also "disrupt[ed] the association of whiteness and settler status through different figurations of black movements."[155]

The history of postemancipation emigrationism facilitated the broader geographic imaginary that underpinned Black history in Oklahoma. The failure of Reconstruction led to the Exoduster generation of emigrationism that brought southern Black people to Kansas and Indian Territory.[156] Robin Kelley, like Nell Painter, aptly uses the notion of exodus to frame the moves Black people made post-Reconstruction, including to Indian Territory, which is meaningful because exodus "provided black people with a language to critique America's racist state and build a new nation." Kelley argues that this movement's "central theme wasn't simply escape but a new beginning," and it "represented dreams of black self-determination, of being on our own, under our own rules and beliefs, developing our own cultures, without interference."[157]

Emigrationism, like Chief Sam's movement, signaled the rejection of the United States. "What attracted African Americans to Indian Territory in the first place," writes Field, "was its momentary status as a political and economic space on the margins, if not beyond the bounds, of U.S. oversight."[158] As Kelley argues, "Emigration not only rendered African Americans 'transnational' people by default, but it remained at the heart of a very long debate within black communities about their sense of national belonging."[159]

As emigrationist movements before his did, Chief Sam's movement illustrated that the conditions in the United States brought about such pessimism in Black people that they looked elsewhere for their freedom. Kelley notes that such movement could be counted as a questioning of Black "allegiance to and identification with the United States."[160] This desire to move has long stayed with Black people in the United States because their belonging has always been in question, except for when it explicitly wasn't. Even then, it was certainly debated. The results were not promising around the mid-nineteenth century when the Fugitive Slave Law and the *Dred Scott* decision made clear that Black people did not qualify for citizenship. "While some black leaders insisted on their right to citizenship during the mid-nineteenth century," Kelley writes, "others such as Mary Ann Shadd Cary, Jermain Loguen, James T. Holly, Samuel Ringgold Ward, Paul Cuffe, and Martin Delany called on black people to find a homeland of their own."[161]

Whether it was "Africa, or somewhere other than here," Black people recognized that there was a choice in imagining, identifying, and claiming "a new beginning, a beautiful, peaceful, collective life where needs were fulfilled and poverty was a thing of the past."[162] Kelley, in *Freedom Dreams*, published in 2002, wrote:

> Few scholars or activists today take proposals to leave America and return to Africa or some other "homeland" seriously. Back-to-Africa proposals in principle are almost universally dismissed as "escapist" or associated with essentialist, romantic ideas about black cultural unity. Critics dwell on the impracticality of such schemes, or they point to sharp cultural and class differences that keep the black world divided. They are not wrong to do so, but any wholesale dismissal of the desire to leave this place and find a new home misses what these movements might tell us about how black people have imagined real freedom.[163]

Repatriation to Liberia and Sierra Leone. Flight to Canada. Escape to Haiti. The great Kansas Exodus. The back-to-Africa movements of Bishop Henry McNeil Turner and Marcus Garvey. The 49th State movement. The Republic of New Africa. The Rastafarian settlement of Shashamane, Ethiopia. These are all moments and movements that evidence Field's "continuum of flight" assertion.[164]

While many Black people today, twenty years after Kelley's publication, may no longer frame their desire for freedom in these terms, the relationship to the United States is effectively little different from the sentiments that drove the creation of and undergirded those movements. Black people once again must shift their gaze, too often fixed on the horror of everyday Black life in death toward promise, understood as an elsewhere. It is no coincidence, then, that the figure of Greenwood as Black Wall Street has come into focus in such a way. It represents a Black space that evidenced many of the qualities of what emigrationism promised, such as self-reliance and economic uplift. However, the silences around Greenwood leave a troubling vulnerability in the narrative. The exceptionalism that holds the story of Greenwood together belies the poverty, vulnerability, and isolation that defined much of the community and that today still work to undermine the very quality of the Black lives too often under threat.

What Greenwood points us to instead are the emigrationist imaginaries that made the district possible. What O. W. Gurley and J. B. Stradford had in mind when they founded Greenwood was a Black autonomous space, which it was until a year after its founding, when Oklahoma gained statehood. We know that autonomy was further restricted after its annexation to the City of Tulsa four years later. To fully appreciate Greenwood, to fully grasp its power, requires understanding it, like the dozens of other autonomous Black spaces founded in Indian Territory. Indian Territory during that period, in the age of Black nationalism, prepared and provided an opening. It was a conjuncture in which not only Black freedom but Black sovereignty was being imagined and pursued at a scale not seen since perhaps the Civil War–era experiments at Davis Bend and Port Royal.

By thinking through deterritorialization, the ethics of geographic imagining exercised by migrants to Indian Territory—those transnational, emigrationist exo-settlers—we can, as Miles suggests, "catch some of their fire" and consider what Black freedom means today.[165]

Returning to the notion of ambivalence in the Black settler relationship to the act of "settlement," I want to think about the relationship inherent in settlement as an act of settling in and settling down. Given the ambivalence, the willingness to move, one can argue that Black people didn't have the same settler attachments as their White counterparts. They may have had the same dreams, human dreams of security and satisfaction, but within those ideas was not the same insistence on violence for their guarantee. They were willing to move, to sell, to start again.

They produced a geography of transience, one that complicates the notion as put forward by Saidiya Hartman, where she states Blackness is "living in a country without exercising any claims on its resources. It is the perilous condition of existing in a world in which you have no investments. It is having never resided in a place that you can say is yours."[166] Rather than put up with perilous conditions, Black people packed up, again with their eyes cast upon the horizon of geographic freedom.

That sensibility is also identifiable in what Neil Roberts has called "marronage as a vocation." Roberts writes, "Marronage is neither reducible to fleeing from states nor to movement within state borders. It is perpetual flight from slavery and an economy of survival."[167] Roberts provides useful definitional qualifications of marronage, especially his "sociogenic" variant classified as "the supreme ideal of freedom" that "denotes a revolutionary process of naming and attaining individual and collective agency, non-sovereignty, liberation, constitutionalism, and the cultivation of a community that aligns civil society with political society."[168]

Roberts's formula is useful for the case of Black freedom in Indian Territory, because black people there achieved both individual and collective agencies. However, for Roberts, "flight can be both real and imagined," and he affirms that this "pronouncement bolsters a central maxim of the theory of marronage: Freedom is not a place; it is a state of being."[169] Indeed, this pronouncement, too, is valid. Yet Black freedom in Indian Territory, like notions of Black freedom before it, was very much about place. Perhaps the best and most genuine way to read Roberts's pronouncement is that freedom is not *only* a place, and that is true.

But what we've learned from this moment and these movements is that geography is the basis of freedom. This history has taught us that the exercising of nonfreedom, of violence, has occurred primarily through rending Black people's relationship to place. Rather than see Black movement as flight, we must appreciate Black mobility as an ongoing, exhausting, yet inexhaustible praxis of placemaking. And through that placemaking, Black people developed a lexicon of freedom that is as varied as the sites that Black people have made freedom and worked toward what lies beyond it. Black people are neither bereft of liberation nor foreclosed of freedom. The trouble has been holding on to the tools, the geographies, and the relations therein to exercise it.

The massacre has perhaps produced much of what today is North Tulsa's "Black sense of place," made only more pronounced through the iterations of geographic violence that have taken place since. Such a history makes for a complicated association between Blackness and its material mooring. Indeed, these complicated geographies of belonging are formative for the many crises of Blackness. However, North Tulsans also draw on, or at least have access to, an alternative racial geographic referent. This is a Blackness not fashioned in the plantation but rather in Indian Territory. While not absent of violence, which took multiple forms, the geography of Indian Territory provided new terms of territorialization and the means for untwinning from the plantation and the ontological violence that it produced. An ontological alternative was made possible by a geographic reorientation.

Thus, North Tulsans' struggle, however complicated or compromised, has been in *defense* of their land-based freedom, not its acquisition. Their roots in Indian Territory, while indeed plagued by many challenges and inequalities, were framed with a particular notion of geographic-based liberty, literal entitlement, and perhaps even rights—so much so that they not only dared to imagine but built all-Black towns and aspired to create an all-Black state, exercised self-determination, and, for a fleeting moment, experimented with and embodied sovereignty.

Only a few months after the centennial, Uwa's forewarning of reconciliation would be realized. I learned that Reverend Robert Turner, Vernon AME's pastor, who advocated for reparations through his weekly marches to City Hall and who became a national spokesperson for the community in the process, had left Tulsa for another church in Baltimore. Surprised about his departure, I reached out to friends in Tulsa. I ended up in conversation with James, who, when I asked about Turner's departure, simply replied, "Yeah, people are getting out. I don't blame 'em." I was stunned to hear these words, and honestly couldn't believe them. I asked James to explain further. "It's demoralizing around here," he said. "Tulsa has become really quiet these days, not a lot happening; the whole town feels asleep. . . . There is a feeling here like we've reset and gone back to how things were a few years ago. Sorta like whatever progress was being made is just . . . " James lacked the words to fully describe the sentiment he was feeling, but I sensed its familiarity. "I dunno," he continued as if surrendering to the feeling, "like folks are tired. Which they are; everyone is tired, I think."

To not come away wholly disheartened by the conversation, I had to maintain perspective around what James was saying. While community members have organized around the massacre for decades, the near two-year period that began with the release of HBO's *Watchmen* in 2019, the murder of George Floyd in 2020, and the massacre's centennial in the summer of 2021 was likely the most active in North Tulsa's recent story. It was an electrifying time to be in Tulsa and, especially, to be *from* there. After the centennial, things were bound to feel quiet in comparison. But demoralizing? Reset? Those terms stuck with me. It was as if James was telling me that the town had been evacuated of its energy and enthusiasm. I had a more troubling revelation, however. Perhaps it had all been extracted.

I could see the makings of James's statement in what I had witnessed over years I worked in North Tulsa: how it went from a quiet town with a remarkable history that had been remarkably quieted and then had suddenly and exceptionally been thrust into the grand narrative of dispossession and prosperity that would represent that process for all of Black America. Indeed, North Tulsa had gone from a place of relative anonymity to carrying the mantle for Black uplift and Black excellence. It was burdened as it was boosted.

Although I didn't want to, I understood, then, how James could get to a place of demoralization. People took from Greenwood, and they had taken from North Tulsa repeatedly in the one hundred years since the massacre. The centennial, in a way, represented another taking. As much as it was a celebration of North Tulsa's resilience, it was a consumption of the will and energy that produced it. The past couple of years created Bloomberg's Greenwood Initiative, Killer Mike's Greenwood Bank, and Black Wall Street projects and programs that popped up across the country. Public intellectuals and activist influencers who, before the ramp-up to the centennial, had never stepped foot in the city were telling the town's history as if it were their own, as if they had the right, the authority, to tell it.

That story produced so much for these programs and their promoters, but what had it produced for Greenwood? The Greenwood Rising history center was impressive. However, its development was effectively nullified because it came at the cost of the relationship with the Greenwood Cultural Center, arguably one of the few North Tulsa institutions that had been long invested in Greenwood's development and representation.

Of course, the fight continues across North Tulsa from committed community members like Damario Solomon-Simmons and Tiffany Crutcher, heading the local movement for reparations and justice for anti-Black police violence, to Billie Parker and Lester Shaw, among many others, who are leading by example through their grassroots entrepreneurism. The Greenwood Cultural Center. The North Mabee Boys and Girls Club. The *Oklahoma Eagle*. And of course, all of the organizers who support the collective envisioning of North Tulsa's future in community meetings like the Great Gathering. These people and organizations have done and continue to do the work. Also, the opening of Oasis Market, which stands to finally provide North Tulsa with reliable grocery access, must be acknowledged. There is much to appreciate about the accomplishments of North Tulsa's long fight for a quality life.

Uwa's warning haunted me because hearing this account from James recalled David Scott's analysis of the expenditure of political energies, arguing how "emancipation has given way to accommodation, and reconciliation has displaced revolution as the language of social and political change where the future has been reduced to a mirror image of the present."[1] This was the reset that James mentioned. Greenwood had quickly found itself in the domain of accommodation and reconciliation, in the reform that Uwa foretold.

Uwa's was not the only critique of the reformative model. The North Tulsa hip-hop group Fire in Little Africa (FILA) has a song, "P.O.D.," on its eponymous album released for the centenary. When I first heard the song it seemed anachronistic against the backdrop of the centenary festivities and the promise that Greenwood Avenue oozed. Its lyrics accurately relayed the sentiment that emerged out of North Tulsa's decades of struggle, but they again seemed timely in the wake of the centenary:

Hey yo, it's something in the air, I feel like it's the last days
Adamant on my journey, I walk over mass graves

Generational trauma, I'm stuck on the last page
Tryna rewrite the story, I look at the gas gauge

It's empty, just like the north shit, we barely got gas stations
Rollin' on up the porch, I think back to the past days

As soon as we tried to ball, they came and they castrate us
Burnin' down n***** cities, put kids in gas chambers
Funny how it was missin' from history class papers

If you gon' write us out, we need to see a check
They eatin' greedy, got me feelin like I'm DMX
Excuse me, but we need some reparations, fuck a BMX

My generation never got to really see success
My n***** see a judge before they see a jet

They lit the match and they keep askin' us why we upset
It's all good just sit back until you see what's next

Now we a threat 'cause they don't like the way we mentionin'

The fact these n***** dirtier than ice in Flint, Michigan
But everything is us and FILA came to get it lit again
Walkin' thru my city like I'm A. J. Smitherman

Dammed if I let you n***** take over our shit again
I need bands, I'm talkin' grants and Benjamins

New game plans to pass down to apprentices
Black owned brands, schools, banks and businesses

Hey, I'm from the city full of broken hearts
The nights cold, all we know is dark

So many tears through the years, might need Noah's Ark
We had it lit then they stole the spark

To all my n***** in the Town that just wanna rebuild but
    don't know where to start
The time's comin', n**** keep ya' heart.[2]

In "P.O.D.," FILA illustrates the yearning that North Tulsans have to reconcile their contemporary conditions with their historical production. Indeed, what does "walking over mass graves" represent, if not the simultaneity of the destruction of Greenwood and the lived experience of contemporary poverty? Throughout the song, there's a constant and necessary critique of the structural processes that produced those conditions and the empty gestures offered as a response.[3] Of all the heartrending accounting throughout the song—only half of it is reproduced here—these verses most poignantly represent where North Tulsa seems to be at the present moment. In these lyrics are the ethic of restoration, which qualify so much of the community's ambition, but here they are mediated by a sharper, more radical claim for repair. Nevertheless, they are still the words of a community seeking the satisfaction of what their history has proven to them is possible.

Ruth Wilson Gilmore asked, "How do we find the place of freedom? More precisely, how do we make such a place over and over again? What are its limits, and why do they matter?"[4] Gilmore prefaced these questions with her now-seminal and oft-cited declaration that "freedom is a place."[5] Gilmore qualified that declaration, however, by asserting that to come to that conclusion, "one need not be a nationalist, nor imagine self-determination to be fixed in modern definitions of states and sovereignty."[6] Over a decade later, Gilmore calls the "homely premise" of place-based freedom, as part of abolition geography, the "still-to-be-achieved work" of "unfinished liberation."[7] The abolitionist work and imaginaries that Gilmore inspires are alternatives for the nationalist, self-determining, and sovereignty-seeking forms of freedom that have been central to many of the processes and philosophies of Black freedom movements throughout the world. In a sense, the abolitionist call that Gilmore offers seems necessary in the face of those frameworks' limitations, if not outright failures. For Gilmore, abolition shows

> how radical consciousness in action resolves into liberated life-ways, however provisional, present, and past. Indeed, the radical tradition from which abolition geography draws meaning and method goes back in time-space not in order to abolish history, but rather to find alternatives to the despairing sense that so much change, in retrospect, seems only ever to have been displacement and redistribution of human sacrifice. If unfinished liberation is the still-to-be-achieved work of abolition, then at bottom what is to be abolished isn't the past or its present ghost, but rather the processes of hierarchy, dispossession, and exclusion that congeal in and as group-differentiated vulnerability to premature death.[8]

The people of North Tulsa know all too well that freedom is a place, and so is unfreedom—a point that Gilmore would not dispute—and both of those places are inhabited by them. The critical distinction in the shared notion of place-based freedom is that it is made possible through struggle, activism, *and abolition* in Gilmore's articulation. It is of the form that Tasneem Siddiqui, in work on postemancipation Black self-determination, argues "revolves around the revolutionary transformations that formerly-enslaved communities envisioned and materialized through a socially-just vision of social organization."[9] While I appreciate Gilmore's 2005 "opening" of the imagining of freedom as a place, I fear that it comes too close to resembling a foreclosure of the sovereignty that underpins North Tulsans' sense of belonging and freedom. This sense pushes the notions and strategies for community restoration and repair and has driven my analysis throughout this book.

Karla Slocum's analysis of all-Black towns in Oklahoma is instructive on how to tell the complex story of how Greenwood's history shows in North Tulsa's present. Slocum writes:

> Telling and profiling Black-town histories as triumphs allows for an attractive Black success story, but the story is not complete. The success story not only does the opposite of stripping Black people of their humanity but also limits understanding of their struggles with structural racism. Publicly profiling how Black people built economically engaged and socially inclusive communities might, on the one hand, appeal to a Black consumer who is drawn to a narrative that vindicates

Blacks as deficient and without agency. On the other hand, down-playing histories of Black trauma can promote forgetting or ignoring Black struggles. The Black-town story that incorporates traumatic beginnings is more complex and includes remembering a variety of experiences.[10]

As Slocum shows of Oklahoma's Black towns, Tulsa's Black history is a complex experience of racial-geographic incorporation, exclusion, marginalization, and responses to articulations and practices of hope and aspiration. In North Tulsa this experience plays out through profound community considerations about how to effectively "restore" its ideal form, represented by Greenwood. Greenwood holds enough symbolic power for these community members to counter the violent anti-Black social order and its maintenance through the restriction of Black life as an everyday experience. Tulsa's story enables us to identify racist violence's unexceptional impact through structural and systemic processes and their operation in contemporary poverty. Identifying how these processes are executed beyond exceptional violence garners a more productive and robust understanding of how Blackness is formed by racialism and racism, yet still resists and imagines life beyond these forces' universal operation in the United States.

This aspiration is recognized, but not overprivileged, in the twin legacies of the terrorism enacted in 1921 and the narrative of prosperity that it is seen to have undone. Overprivileging the race massacre obscures the many acts of violence produced in its wake. The violence of the 1921 massacre has since shown up in multiple attempts to destroy the community, whether through outright violence, slow dispossession, or narrative suppression—again the silences of Tulsa's history.

But not privileging that violence must be accompanied by appropriate treatment of its foil, which is the narrative of Greenwood's prosperity. *Violent Utopia* has offered both the massacre and the lauded history of Greenwood to help orient the ethics that guide everyday Black North Tulsans' navigation of their circumstances. Their experience is defined by poverty, a lack of commercial activity, and an ever-increasing reliance on nonprofits and state agencies to satisfy everyday needs. In taking this approach, *Violent Utopia* resists reproducing the narrative of North Tulsa and its history as exceptional. The lived reality of daily life in North Tulsa is preoccupied with neither the narratives of historic Greenwood nor the massacre that destroyed it. To be sure, Black life in Tulsa is mediated by this history; however, a comprehensive understanding illustrates the broader process by which thinking with North Tulsa and its history gleans a representative understanding of Black life's condition as the universal operation of racialism in America. Drawing on it can permit those of us committed to Black study and politics to do what Black Tulsans do every day: move forward.

The forces that partly contributed to Black Wall Street's development—racist segregation and isolation—were wholly responsible for its destruction. There is nothing simple about that story, so failing to appreciate that leaves Tulsa's Black narrative to the will of exception. What we see today is a veritable economy of exception developed around Blackness. That economy is invested in the excess value of Blackness. Just as for centuries capitalism demanded that violence extract all available and excess labor value from enslaved Africans, with that excess put to the purpose of profit in the commodity markets of the slave economies, the same attachment to extracting excess Black value can be found in the economies of racial discourses. Those discourses are no less committed to the violence of that extraction, however. As such, Black people become bonded in the markets of meaning, which I identify as the discursive sites of exception. Exceptionally pathological Blackness leaves us with Black deviance, criminality, whose extractive potential is ever present, the kind that the police and the prisons extract. At the other end, Black excellence is the exceptional domain that mandates that Black people remain perpetually productive, accomplished, and ultimately alienated—Black anomie and the community. Exceptional violence and exceptional success both leave everyday Blackness out of the equation of simply living. Exceptions are not representative; exceptions, while productive, are not constructive.

Tulsa's narrative can do so much more than present exceptional Blackness, whether tragic or romantic. The story of North Tulsa tells us about the power of everyday Blackness and, of course, its many challenges. What is exceptional about the story of Greenwood is that it was made possible in a unique geography, during a period of multiple violent, though opportune, transformations that took place in Indian Territory in the period between Reconstruction and Oklahoma statehood. Thus, the history of Greenwood and North Tulsa is one of what Black people do when an opportunity is at hand and their freedoms are unhindered.

This book has been about the narrative of how Greenwood's freedom, pursued and obtained in Indian Territory, became curtailed by state enclosure through Jim Crow. It's also about how the complete dispossession of Greenwood's freedom—though attempted through the exceptional violence of the 1921 race massacre—was accomplished through the mundane but no less violent process of urban renewal.

Through the ongoing articulations of North Tulsans seeking to restore the promise their forebears both sought and attained, this book hopes to follow their path *back* to freedom. They've sought that path through the complicated relationship that North Tulsans have to their material present and the mythic sense of the past. I realized that Greenwood, for many North Tulsans and Black Tulsans generally, but especially for all of those who were directly working to restore and repair it, was a form of utopia.

"Utopia in black," as Alex Zamalin calls Black notions of utopia, "became much more critical and infused by a sense of tragedy. It became defined by unfinished conversations, unresolved debates, critical problematics, which resisted easy resolution."[11] He argues that the "romantic tropes, sense of wholeness, spiritual redemption, and rational teleology that had long been a staple of Western utopia was [*sic*] given a different take in the black tradition."[12] The unreconciled quality inherent in Zamalin's definition gestures toward the sensation around the tragedy of the 1921 race massacre.

Legitimate questions linger around what Greenwood would have been today had it been left alone, untroubled, left in possession of itself. For Zamalin, the ideal notion of a Black utopia is "a future society" where Black people are "imagined to be free from the fetters of white supremacy and racial violence," but for North Tulsans, this is what Greenwood was, irrespective of Jim Crow.[13] In fact, segregation produced a certain sanctuary in Black community that secured the sanctity of Blackness. Black Tulsans know exactly where their utopia was and where it can be again.

This locating is contrary to Jayna Brown's primary articulation of Black utopia, where she takes up the concept as an elsewhere, "rocketed into another dimension."[14] Brown uses speculative methods to define utopia as "the (im)possibilities for forms of subjectivity outside a recognizable ontological framework, and modes of existence conceived of in unfamiliar epistemes." She asserts that "these (im)possibilities open up where the human has abandoned us and onto a much bigger universe, when we jump into the unknowable."[15] Brown's construction of utopia is structured around the seeming inescapability for her of anti-Blackness and its "social formations [that] have denied African diasporans the rights and freedoms associated with being defined as human."[16]

There is much to appreciate about Brown's formula, especially her project's general imperative of destabilizing the notion of human supremacy, which, however, is unable to escape the reference of the denial of Black humanity. But for North Tulsans, even though today they face all the violence that would warrant seeking refuge in an elsewhere, Brown's prescriptions do not apply. Greenwood for North Tulsans is an ontological mooring. It is the "grounds" from which they "imagine the world and more humanly workable geographies."[17] Even though temporally Greenwood the utopia is located in the past, that doesn't quite qualify it as an elsewhere because, for one, its influence as a referent has remained mostly available and thus proximate, and because, second, with the logic of the reparations claim in mind, Greenwood still exists but has undergone a century of assault—a nuisance that needs abatement. Moreover, there has been a continued custodianship of Greenwood in the acts and activism of people like Uwa and Billy Parker.

To be fair, while the notion of an idealized place for North Tulsans isn't entirely an "elsewhere," José Esteban Muñoz's utopian notion of elsewhere is instructive because he grounds it in the effect of desire. Muñoz builds from Ernst Bloch's seminal philosophy of utopia, *The Principle of Hope*, around which most utopian theorists orient their thinking. In *Cruising Utopia*, Muñoz advances queerness as a utopian formation based on "an economy of desire." For him, "this desire is always directed at that thing that is not yet here, objects and moments that burn with anticipation and promise." The "not yet here" doesn't disqualify the utopian "promise" of Greenwood because the past and its pleasures can "stave off the affective perils of the present" to enable desire as the core of utopian futurity.[18] This idea is rooted in Bloch's notion of "concrete utopia," which Ruth Levitas explains as "reach[ing] forward to a real possible future, and involv[ing] not merely wishful but will-full thinking," that is, "simultaneously anticipating and effecting the future."[19]

Desire and willfulness, yes; however, a "real possible future," in the case of North Tulsa's Greenwood utopia, is still in question. Marlon, Kiki, and Clifton would say it is entirely possible because that future is the past. Muñozian desire drives the utopianism of that past, one of burning anticipation and promise. The utopian past is made feasible by what I have called elsewhere a sense of Blackness's "continuity," which "works through Trouillot's notion of 'pastness' where 'the past does not exist independently from the present' but is a position readily available to mobilize history to shape opportunities."[20] Thus, continuity suspends the forward directionality of utopia, which is not to say that utopia cannot be oriented toward the past.

Davina Cooper considers this proposition in relation to what she calls "everyday utopias," or radically different "networks and spaces that perform regular daily life."[21] Cooper recognizes that utopian studies' emphasis is commonly on speculative futures, and she writes that utopias can still "face what is passed and do so in several ways." Cooper argues that "they may pursue a 'cut-off' past, refusing or blocking conceptual lines in order to hand them over to a previous time"; produce "boundaries between what we do now and what they did then"; and seek "to make sense of the utopian present through the norms and knowledge" of the past.[22] Cooper identifies utopia as "experiments in living that necessarily involve prefigurative practice (in the sense of enacting today that other world that is sought, a world that may reside in the future but also may not), [and] everyday utopias assert the importance of maintaining and sustaining what *is*, rendering the pursuit of further change secondary to securing and protecting *existing* forms of innovative practice."[23] Cooper concludes that "it is the making-past of conceptual lines that needs working" and urges us to resist suggestions that "such pasts have been achieved," because "for many sites the production of what is past is an ongoing (and contested) project."[24]

The notion of utopia in Tulsa is that of a Black idealized society but one rooted in the sense of historical time. Utopia is commonly figured as being future oriented, a horizon, an elsewhere, a no-place. Therefore, one might validly discount the application of utopia to the sense of community that North Tulsans seek to have restored. And yet the function of utopia as an imaginary might allow us to fully grasp the anticipatory impulse behind repair. The idea of what one might be, of one's state of having been repaired, is often as impossible as the geographic state of utopia.

The impulse for repair appears across all the approaches to North Tulsa's challenges. Whether through John Perkins's philosophy, Clifton's organizational call for greater collaboration, North Tulsans' desire for better leadership, the churches' and nonprofits' various initiatives, and of course the legal pursuit of reparations, healing the disconnect was imperative. This imperative went beyond bringing resources to a community. It was about that community's reconstitution. To be fair, this is the impetus behind most development philosophies. There is always a "mission," by which I mean a missionary imperative behind them. Philanthropies, the state, the church, and community organizations all have an idealized notion of the community they are serving that they want to see materialized. Too often, these idealized notions serve as sanitizing initiatives, from Greenwood Rising to the memorialization activities and monuments that preceded it. And while this was more than apparent in North Tulsa, it didn't encompass the whole story.

Captured in the statements of these programs, initiatives, and community discourses is the notion that meaningful progress can come only through collective action. Still, even more so, there was a preexisting expectation of this collectivity. In other words, the North Tulsa community didn't need to learn collectivity, which I have noted has been the experience of Black communities elsewhere.[25] Instead, North Tulsa needed to *recover* its collectivity, heal the "disconnect" that was its absence, and bring about reparation.

From the vantage point of everyday discourse, the narrative history of the legacy of Black Wall Street, or even the massacre, is not as stable as it is thought to be. The trouble with history is, as Trouillot notes, that "historical narrative is a particular bundle of silences."[26] In North Tulsa the bundling occurred at the scales of class and generation. The narrative framework could only frame the present as a moment of failure. Thus, the narrative of Greenwood's prosperity put the local community in a peculiar position for both the time and space of its geographic and economic circumstances. It was a devastatingly demanding litmus. For Black Tulsans, it was a horizon, albeit one situated in the past and one that needed to deftly navigate and be reconciled with North Tulsa's contemporary circumstances.

Emphasizing the massacre as a means of seeking reparations for the history of violence a century past elides the impact the massacre has on Tulsa's Black and poor community's contemporary everyday life chances. This narrative of the past subsumes the present moment. In contrast, as discussed in the previous chapters, North Tulsa's residents' current activity and ambitions might provide a basis for determining what repair and reparation might be. Their efforts contend that reparations frameworks do not need to be oriented toward a speculative future. North Tulsans show that there are prior articulations of freedom to which we may look for the answers. This position, as simple as it may be, stands as a radical counter to the narrative that Black life in the United States has always be subjugated and abject.

Undertaking this process, I would learn, was inseparable from the seeking of redress for the massacre itself, and in North Tulsa the repair of reparations would take on much deeper meaning than simple compensation, instead seeking the full realization of restorative justice. The desire for the restoration of Black Wall Street was a latent force behind the desire for reparations. But rather than focusing on compensation or reconciliation, the desire to trace back the past to recover what was left behind was no doubt a more powerful force. This desire was layered in the notion of Tulsa's Black residents as having been dispossessed, as chapter 1 argues. The legal discourse surrounding the conceptualization of Black dispossession in Tulsa was situated in the past and in the framing of Tulsa's history. The accounts I heard all framed the loss of the Black community's institutional and economic strength, the intentional laying waste of the Greenwood District, as today being felt in the rupturing of community. As a result, the efforts to return to some semblance of community in the past were understood as a need to restore what had been lost.

For the community's displaced and resident populations, those who wanted to reverse the effects of displacement or wanted to leave the community behind, this sense of restoration may be what has been intended with the invocation of reconciliation all along. If not taken as a form of interracial conciliation, which, to be sure, was at the heart of the term's meaning in North Tulsa and which had everything to do with quieting and moving past the 1921 race massacre, reconciliation could instead be a means of understanding the working of repair, and a more meaningful and even radical interpretation could be gleaned. Reconciliation could focus less on the event of the massacre itself and more on what North Tulsans thought the event had displaced, that is, the ability to succeed. This view was especially evident among community members who self-described as Black Wall Street's descendants. It became much clearer why various members of the community repeatedly presented cooperation or collaboration as the solution.

The lingering era *before* the race massacre—the specter of Black Wall Street—drove the community's ambitions, but, more important, it points to the Black community's capacity to, absent any "nuisance," bring about their own repair. This, I believe, is what Uwa was trying to tell me. Thus, as Black Tulsans map their way back to freedom *through* Greenwood, they illustrate the power of a sovereign relationship to place. To realize that power requires resisting the narrowing of the imagination of what and where Black lives can be.

Black life, like Black freedom, is capacious; North Tulsa shows us that this fact must simply be remembered.

INTRODUCTION

1   Das, *Life and Words*, 8, 11.

2   McKittrick, "On Plantations," 949.

3   Murphy et al., "Role of Geography," 178.

4   Oklahoma State University–Tulsa, "Center for Family Resilience."

5   Saunt, *Unworthy Republic*, xvii.

6   Saunt, *Unworthy Republic*, 317.

7   Named after Senator Henry L. Dawes of Massachusetts, it was also known as the Dawes Severalty Act of 1887.

8   Emancipation took place in 1866 when the treaties of 1866 between the Five Civilized Tribes and the federal government brought both freedom and tribal incorporation to those formerly enslaved.

9   A. Roberts, "Who Belongs in Indian Territory?," 337.

10 The Homestead Act of 1862 provided that a legal settler could claim 160 acres of public land, and those who lived on and improved the claim for five years could receive a title.

11 Painter, *Exodusters*.

12 Bittle and Geis, "Racial Self-Fulfillment," 250. It was understood that "[Negroes] operated under the same restrictions as did the Whites in their quest for Indian lands, but they had as little difficulty in eventually alienating these lands from the Indians through circumvention of existing statutes."

13 Smallwood, "Segregation."

14 The town was named after John Mercer Langston, a US congressman from Virginia and an advocate of freed Blacks' equal rights.

15 Oklahoma Historical Society, "Langston City Herald."

16 Haynes, quoted in Stuckey, "Boley, Indian Territory," 495.

17 A. Roberts, *I've Been Here*, 6.

18 A. Roberts, *I've Been Here*, 6.

19 A. Roberts, *I've Been Here*, 6.

20 A. Roberts, *I've Been Here*, 5.

21 A. Roberts, *I've Been Here*, 5. In *I've Been Here All the While*, Roberts uses what she calls "a mixture of historical creation and historians' interventions" (3) to elect the gender-neutral *freedpeople* instead of *freedmen*. However, I chose to use

and capitalize the historical reference *Freedmen* as the result of consultation with Freedmen group organizers and members in Oklahoma.

22 National Register of Historic Places Inventory—Nomination Form, September 27, 1974, https://npgallery.nps.gov/NRHP/GetAsset/NHLS/75001568_text.

23 Slocum, *Black Towns, Black Futures*, 17.

24 Field, *Growing Up with the Country*, 146. While not for the same reasons, Kendra Field shows perhaps a different set of challenges to the narrative of all-Black towns, writing that "the vast majority of the celebrated 'all-black' towns of Oklahoma were in fact built upon Indian allotments—and publicized by motivated white railroad investors, who hired African-American men as town promoters to recruit black southerners."

25 *Tulasi* is the same word from which Tallahassee, Florida, takes its name.

26 The St. Louis and San Francisco Railway had entered Indian Territory by 1871. However, owing to Native opposition, the line wouldn't extend to Tulsa until 1882.

27 Madigan, *Burning*, 8.

28 Allen and Leonard, "How Many Rushed?"

29 Krehbiel, *Tulsa, 1921*, 21.

30 The 1907 Oklahoma Constitution did not call for strict segregation out of fear that President Theodore Roosevelt would veto the document. However, once Oklahoma had joined the Union, the Oklahoma Senate's Bill One made segregation the state's official policy.

31 Ellsworth, *Death in a Promised Land*, 108.

32 Krehbiel, *Tulsa, 1921*, 23.

33 Buck Colbert B. C. Franklin, Greenwood leader, lawyer, and father of historian John Hope Franklin, noted, "In the beginning, there was no segregation or apparently any thought of segregating the races" within the city of Tulsa. Franklin, *My Life and an Era*, 199.

34 Tulsa would continue to develop by incorporating surrounding territories to the east, west, and (mainly) south. It was as if the city sought to flee its northern association with Greenwood.

35 Gara, "Baron of Black Wall Street."

36 Hirsch, *Riot and Remembrance*, 45.

37 Hirsch, *Riot and Remembrance*, 44.

38 Quoted in Hirsch, *Riot and Remembrance*, 44.

39 Hirsch, *Riot and Remembrance*, 38.

40 Quoted in Hirsch, *Riot and Remembrance*, 38

41 Marshall, "Tulsa Race Massacre."

42 Tulsa Historical Society and Museum, "The 1921 Tulsa Race Massacre."

CHAPTER 1. VIOLENCE

1 *Tulsa Tribune*, "Nab Negro."

2 Scott Ellsworth notes that what the Tuesday, May 31, 1921, issue of this newspaper said may never be known fully, because when the early issues of the *Tribune*

were later microfilmed, someone removed part of the editorial page. The original bound volumes of the newspaper were destroyed. Ellsworth, *Death in a Promised Land*, 47.

3 Ellsworth, *Death in a Promised Land*, 48.

4 E. Woodson, "Strange Fruit on the Southern Plains," 78.

5 Henry, *Long Overdue*, 80.

6 IWW History Project: Industrial Workers of the World 1905–1935, "Arrests, Prosecutions."

7 Ellsworth, *Death in a Promised Land*, 49.

8 Ellsworth, *Death in a Promised Land*, 52.

9 *New York Times*, "Series of Fierce Combats."

10 White women made some of these "arrests." Ellsworth, *Death in a Promised Land*, 59.

11 Messer and Bell, "Mass Media and Governmental Framing."

12 Hirsch, *Riot and Remembrance*, 144.

13 The nearby towns that refugee Black Tulsans fled to included Bartlesville, Broken Arrow, Claremore, Collinsville, Dewey, Muskogee, Owasso, Sapulpa, and Sperry. White Tulsans mailed riot postcards around the country. Hirsch, *Riot and Remembrance*, 144.

14 Ellsworth, *Death in a Promised Land*, 59.

15 Quoted in Madigan, *Burning*, 174.

16 Regarding air bombings, Ellsworth notes, "There is some confusion over the use of airplanes." He acknowledges that police "took over private airplanes and flew over the city" in order to observe activity in Black neighborhoods, "purportedly because many white Tulsans feared a black counterattack." *Death in a Promised Land*, 63. Ellsworth bases his assessment on reports from the *Chicago Defender* and mine draws from my conversations with a riot survivor, Mary E. Jones Parrish.

17 Messer and Bell show how "in the hope of further reducing the Black population, local railroads supported the Reconstruction Committee by offering fare discounts to those who wished to leave the city: Effective June 10 the Missouri, Kansas & Texas Railway company will put into effect for Tulsa charity half-fare rates to negroes who desire to leave the city. To obtain such concession negroes must have the approval of the Red Cross." Messer and Bell, "Mass Media and Governmental Framing," 866.

18 *Tulsa Tribune*, "It Must Not Be Again."

19 Messer and Bell, "Mass Media and Governmental Framing," 864.

20 *Tulsa Tribune*, "Plan to Move Negroes."

21 The Oklahoma Commission to Study the Tulsa Race Riot of 1921 asserted that less than $100,000 was covered. Oklahoma Commission to Study the Tulsa Race Riot of 1921, *Tulsa Race Riot*, 148.

22 Messer and Bell, "Mass Media and Governmental Framing of Riots," 866. Chris Messer and Patricia Bell note that there is "no evidence to support the belief that these codes were uniformly applied throughout the city."

23 H. Johnson, *Black Wall Street*, loc. 1574 of 5077. According to Hannibal Johnson, this feat was accomplished through the court case of *Joe Lockard v. City of Tulsa*, in which "Joe Lockard sought legal authority to rebuild on his property and, more importantly, to enjoin the post-Riot City of Tulsa fire ordinance. The court declared that the ordinance constituted an invalid taking of property without due process of law."

24 These churches were Mt. Zion Baptist Church, Vernon AME, and First Baptist Church of North Tulsa. H. Johnson, *Black Wall Street*, 103.

25 H. Johnson, *Black Wall Street*, 105.

26 H. Johnson, *Black Wall Street*, 110.

27 Ever since oil was discovered in Red Fork in 1901, Tulsa's residents had seen themselves and their city as headed for prosperity. The big oil strike at Glenpool in 1905 materialized this vision, becoming the world's largest known oil reservoir. The find made the Oklahoma territories the new epicenter of oil speculation and extraction. Within a few years of this strike, over a hundred oil companies would come to populate the Tulsa. With the rise of the oil industry came the tenfold increase of Tulsa's population by 1920. Oil brought related industries to the town but particularly banking, with the current Bank of Oklahoma beginning in 1910 as the Exchange National Bank of Tulsa, formed by four oil investors. Over a hundred years later, maintaining its ties to the industry, Bank of Oklahoma was acquired by oil billionaire George Kaiser in the 1990s.

28 Moynihan, *Negro Family*, 66.

29 H. Johnson, *Black Wall Street*, 113.

30 H. Johnson, *Black Wall Street*, 119.

31 H. Johnson, *Black Wall Street*, 121.

32 Muir, *Approaches to Landscape*.

33 Hirsch, *Riot and Remembrance*, 195.

34 Hirsch, *Riot and Remembrance*.

35 Hirsch, *Riot and Remembrance*, 195.

36 Looney, "Greenwood Fades Away."

37 Connolly, *World More Concrete*, 52.

38 Connolly, *World More Concrete*, 5.

39 Connolly, *World More Concrete*, 137.

40 Connolly, *World More Concrete*, 136.

41 Connolly, *World More Concrete*, 5.

42 Connolly, *World More Concrete*, 261.

43 Connolly, *World More Concrete*, 3, 269.

44 Connolly, *World More Concrete*, 6.

45 Stoler, "Making Empire Respectable," 640.

46 Wells-Barnett, *Red Record*, n.p.

47 Hartman, *Scenes of Subjection*.

48 Du Bois, *Black Reconstruction in America*, 15–16.

49 S. Best, *Fugitive's Properties*, 82. Best refers to this fugitivity of freedom as "opprobrious theft." S. Best, *Fugitive's Properties*, 19.

50 Peter Hudson argues for the notion of "odious debt," in colonial economic processes, which stems from refuting the obligation to repay a debt that was contracted through illicit and therefore odious processes. Hudson, *Bankers and Empire*, 224.

51 McKittrick, *Demonic Grounds*, xxiv. McKittrick takes direct influence from Sylvia Wynter's framework of the demonic in "Beyond Miranda's Meanings: Un/Silencing the 'Demonic Ground' of Caliban's 'Woman'" to identify "the ways in which subaltern lives are not marginal/other to regulatory classificatory systems, but instead integral to them." McKittrick, *Demonic Grounds*, xxv.

52 Mary Douglas wrote of a similar predicament concerning female subjects, identifying their pollution taboos as "related to the attempt to treat women simultaneously as persons and as the currency of male transactions." Douglas, *Purity and Danger*, 188.

53 Du Bois, *Souls of Black Folk*, 89.

54 Du Bois, *Souls of Black Folk*, 3–4.

55 *Purity and Danger* remains a seminal intervention into the long-established anthropological interest in notions of pollution. *Purity and Danger* at the time directly dealt with what we might consider one of the most universally human concerns: the very qualification of pollution, filth, and disorder. In North America today, amid the COVID-19 pandemic, Douglas's work remains as relevant as it was in the 1960s, if not more so. Indeed, the pandemic has made evident multiple American (and Western) anxieties around contagion marked by an obsession with sanitization, the resistance to containment by quarantine, and the securing of epidemiological privilege. But those anxieties have reliably operated in other ways. This point is also apparent when considering the other pandemic of 2020—the anti-Black racism that consumed the year. Though far more enduring and chronic than COVID-19, anti-Blackness became a global concern of unprecedented magnitude through the murder of George Floyd. Its roots, nevertheless, lie in the same fear of pollution that guides the world's anxieties over the coronavirus's spread.

56 Douglas, *Purity and Danger*, xi.

57 Wynter, "Unsettling the Coloniality," 271.

58 Douglas, *Purity and Danger*, 50.

59 Douglas, *Purity and Danger*, xi.

60 Douglas, *Purity and Danger*, 48.

61 Douglas, *Purity and Danger*, 49.

62 Douglas, *Purity and Danger*, 119. For Douglas, the eschewal of unclean foods (however defined), the taboo around menstrual blood, or even the taboo against incest were identifiable examples. There was much anthropological debate about Douglas's claims. Specifically, there were concerns that her argument asserted that human cognitive and cultural aversion to pollution was the foundation of classification. But what Douglas aimed to demonstrate was that "organising requires classifying, and that classification is at the basis of human coordination," a point that many leading social scientists before Douglas and since have come to

accept. Moreover, Douglas did not claim that there was a universal understanding of what constituted pollution but instead that the notion of pollution was universal. And so what matters is the classifications. Douglas, *Purity and Danger*, xvii. Douglas cites *Primitive Classification* by Émile Durkheim and Marcel Mauss as foundational to her argument.

63 Wynter, "Unsettling the Coloniality."

64 Douglas, *Purity and Danger*, xiii.

65 Douglas, *Purity and Danger*, xiii.

66 Douglas, *Purity and Danger*, xiii. Douglas states that complicity is necessary because, taken on an individual basis, "taboo beliefs seem so outlandish that it is difficult to see how a rational person could give them credence."

67 Douglas, *Purity and Danger*, 3–4.

68 Du Bois, *Black Reconstruction in America*, 700.

69 Du Bois, *Black Reconstruction in America*, 700.

70 Roediger, *Wages of Whiteness*.

71 Roediger, *Wages of Whiteness*, 109.

72 Anderson, "White Space," 10, 11.

73 Anderson, "White Space," 13.

74 Anderson, "White Space," 13.

75 Anderson, "White Space," 15.

76 Anderson, "White Space," 13.

77 Lipsitz, *How Racism Takes Place*.

78 Douglas, *Purity and Danger*.

79 Wynter, "Unsettling the Coloniality," 316.

80 Jacobs, "Case in Point."

81 Crutcher's case sadly stands as part of a long procession of police murders of Black citizens. Terence's sister, Tiffany Crutcher, founded the Terence Crutcher Foundation and the Demanding a Just Tulsa Coalition in response to the crisis of police violence in Tulsa.

    Some might suggest that any encounter with the police carries danger because of the ease with which such encounters can escalate. Thus, officers who lack training, overreact, or are threatened by the presence of a weapon might potentially harm or kill anyone, irrespective of race. Some even cite the similarity in actual totals of Black and White victims of police violence, choosing to discount how those numbers differ when compared to those groups' respective percentages of the population.

82 Douglas, *Purity and Danger*, 118.

83 Hartman, *Lose Your Mother*, 88.

84 Douglas, *Purity and Danger*, 119.

85 Moynihan, "Memorandum for the President," 7.

86 Connolly, *World More Concrete*, 52.

87 Moynihan, "Memorandum for the President," 7.

88 D. Thomas, *Exceptional Violence*, 19.

89 Taylor, *Archive and the Repertoire*, 21; D. Thomas, *Exceptional Violence*, 89.

90 D. Thomas, *Exceptional Violence*, 109.
91 D. Thomas, *Exceptional Violence*, 110.
92 D. Thomas, *Exceptional Violence*, 110.
93 D. Thomas, *Exceptional Violence*, 110.
94 University of Richmond Digital Scholarship Lab, "Mapping Inequality."
95 Saunt, *Unworthy Republic*, 317.

CHAPTER 2. INHERITANCE

1 Darrell's zip code has a nearly 70 percent Black population and is also the poorest in Tulsa. Residents in the zip code had an average life expectancy of seventy years.
2 Heath, "Case for Reparations in Tulsa."
3 Livingston, "Contact between Police and People with Mental Disorders," 850. Livingston notes that one in four people with mental disorders have histories of police arrest, that about one in ten individuals have police involved in their pathway to mental health care, and that one in a hundred police dispatches and encounters involve people with mental disorders. These issues have since begun to be addressed in Tulsa. Cosgrove, "Tulsa, Oklahoma Counties Address Jail."
4 Heath, "Case for Reparations in Tulsa."
5 Bureau of Justice Assistance, "Problem-Oriented Drug Enforcement," 45.
6 Tulsa Police Department, *Drug Problem Inventory*, 10.
7 Tulsa Police Department, *Drug Problem Inventory*, ii.
8 Bureau of Justice Assistance, "Problem-Oriented Drug Enforcement," vii.
9 Bureau of Justice Assistance, "Problem-Oriented Drug Enforcement," vii.
10 Wilson and Kelling, "Broken Windows."
11 Center for Evidence-Based Crime Policy, "Broken Windows Policing."
12 Hot spot policing focuses on "specific locations within the larger social environments of communities and neighborhoods, such as addresses, street blocks, or small clusters of addresses or street blocks," with the belief that focusing on smaller geographic units will maximize crime prevention. Center for Evidence-Based Crime Policy, "Hot Spots Policing."
13 Braga et al., "Problem-Oriented Policing," 544.
14 Center for Evidence-Based Crime Policy, "Broken Windows Policing."
15 Bureau of Justice Assistance, "Problem-Oriented Drug Enforcement," 1.
16 Fagan and Davies, "Street Stops and Broken Windows," 462.
17 Kotabe, Omid, and Berman, "Order of Disorder," 1714.
18 Tulsa Police Department, *Drug Problem Inventory*, 4.
19 Tulsa Police Department, *Drug Problem Inventory*, 7–8.
20 Tulsa Police Department, *Drug Problem Inventory*, 8.
21 Oklahoma Center for Nonprofits, "Celebrating 40 Years"; Taylor, "Charity Inc."
22 Rodney, *How Europe Underdeveloped Africa*.
23 Block and Reynolds, "Funding a Peoples' Food Justice," 1709.
24 George Kaiser Family Foundation, "Birth through Eight Strategy."

25 Winkler, "Why Oklahoma."
26 According to the census, growing pockets of Hispanic communities—the only demographic that's growing in the area—are emerging owing to the availability of affordable housing in North Tulsa.
27 Family and Children's Services, "Women in Recovery."
28 Urban Institute, Pay for Success Initiative, "Oklahoma Women in Recovery."
29 The word gap theory comes from the work of Betty Hart and Tod Risley in their *Meaningful Differences in the Everyday Experience of Young American Children.*
30 Nowlain, "Is the 30 Million Word Gap."
31 See Ismail and Kamat, "NGOs, Social Movements"; and Kamat, " Privatization of Public Interest."
32 Ranganathan, "Rule by Difference," 1387.
33 Ferguson, *Anti-politics Machine.*
34 CAP Tulsa, "Who we are."
35 California Evidence-Based Clearinghouse for Child Welfare, "Parents as Teachers."
36 Quandt et al., "Evaluating the Effectiveness."
37 Sacks, *Invisible Visits.*
38 Oklahoma Human Services, "Advantage Administration."
39 Kohl-Arenas, *Self-Help Myth.*
40 Scherz, *Having People, Having Heart,* 140.
41 Graham, "Tulsa Native, Activist Cornel West."
42 H. Johnson, *Black Wall Street,* 103.
43 T. Thomas, *Kincraft,* 5.
44 T. Thomas, *Kincraft,* 5.
45 T. Thomas, *Kincraft,* 15.
46 Center for Community School Strategies, "Framework for TACSI Schools."
47 *Tulsa World,* "Tulsa Area's 20 Largest Churches."

CHAPTER 3. RESTORATION
1   Morgan, "Planned North Tulsa Grocery Store."
2   *News on 6,* "North Tulsa Grocery Store Closes."
3   *News on 6,* "North Tulsa Grocery Store Closes."
4   *News on 6,* "North Tulsa Grocery Store Closes."
5   *The Frontier,* "What Happened to Jack."
6   Harkins, "New North Tulsa Grocery Store."
7   *News on 6,* "Gateway Market Reopens Doors."
8   Duke, "North Tulsa Grocery Store."
9   Duke, "North Tulsa Grocery Store."
10 Clifton Durante, LinkedIn, accessed November 22, 2019, https://www.linkedin .com/in/clifton-durante-iii-2ab97219/.
11 Healthy Community Store Initiative, home page.

12 Rial, "Banal Religiosity." Carmen Rial has noted how a civilizing device promotes better insertion of individuals into modern institutions. Rial argues that this process occurs through neo-Pentecostal beliefs.

13 Sharpe, *In the Wake*, quoted in Garth and Reese, "Black Food Matters," 23.

14 Garth, "Blackness and 'Justice,'" 112.

15 Garth, "Blackness and 'Justice,'" 109.

16 Newman and Yuson, "Good Food," 151, 133.

17 Newman and Yuson, "Good Food," 152.

18 Newman and Yuson, "Good Food," 152.

19 NorthTulsa100, "History."

20 NorthTulsa100, "History."

21 Clifton Durante, LinkedIn, accessed November 22, 2019, https://www.linkedin.com/in/clifton-durante-iii-2ab97219/. See also ESTEEM, accessed November 11, 2021, https://www.esteemcd.org.

22 LEAD North, "About Us."

23 *The Frontier*, "What Happened to Jack?"

24 *The Frontier*, "What Happened to Jack?"

25 Quoted in Vicent, "North Tulsa Moves Closer."

26 Quoted in Vicent, "North Tulsa Moves Closer."

27 Garth, "Blackness and 'Justice,'" 112.

28 Garth, "Blackness and 'Justice,'" 126.

29 D. Thomas, *Political Life in the Wake*.

30 Trouillot, *Silencing the Past*, 29.

31 Christian Community Development Association, "About."

CHAPTER 4. REPAIR

1 In 2019, Brady Street was renamed Reconciliation Way. Tate Brady, whom it honored, was one of the founders of the City of Tulsa. The name was changed due to Brady's racist past and his specific efforts to remove Black Tulsans from Greenwood following the 1921 race massacre.

2 Justice for Greenwood, "Justice for Greenwood Oral History."

3 Fire in Little Africa, Earl Hazard, and Thomas Who?, "Descendants," track 4 on *Fire in Little Africa*, Motown Records, 2021.

4 Justice for Greenwood, "About Us."

5 H. Johnson, *Black Wall Street*, 100.

6 H. Johnson, *Black Wall Street*, 100.

7 H. Johnson, *Black Wall Street*, 100.

8 H. Johnson, *Black Wall Street*, 100.

9 H. Johnson, *Black Wall Street*, 100.

10 Oklahoma Commission to Study the Tulsa Race Riot of 1921, *Tulsa Race Riot*, 72.

11 Trouillot, *Silencing the Past*, 25.

12 Trouillot, *Silencing the Past*, 28.

13 Trouillot, *Silencing the Past*, 26.

14 Trouillot, *Silencing the Past*, 28.
15 Joseph, *Against the Romance of Community*, xxxii.
16 Joseph, *Against the Romance of Community*, viii.
17 Joseph, *Against the Romance of Community*, 172.
18 Joseph, *Against the Romance of Community*, xx.
19 Robinson, *Black Marxism*, 186.
20 H. Johnson, *Black Wall Street*, 128.
21 Greenwood Cultural Center, "About Us."
22 1921 Tulsa Race Massacre Centennial Commission, "About the Commission."
23 Greenwood Rising, "About."
24 Greenwood Rising, "About."
25 Osborne, "Bynum's Administration."
26 Krehbiel, "John Hope Franklin Reconciliation Park Opens."
27 Summers, *Black in Place*, 174.
28 Nakassis, "Brands and Their Surfeits," 112.
29 Newell, "Brands as Masks," 141.
30 Bureau of Justice Assistance, "Problem-Oriented Drug Enforcement," 45.
31 Oklahoma Commission to Study the Tulsa Race Riot of 1921, *Tulsa Race Riot*, 27.
32 See Nagata, Kim, and Wu, "Japanese American Wartime Incarceration"; and Skewes and Blume, "Understanding the Link."
33 Kelley, "Tulsa Race Massacre."
34 Parrish, *Race Riot 1921*; *Sixty Minutes*, "Tulsa Burning."
35 Kelley, "Tulsa Race Massacre."
36 Oklahoma Commission to Study the Tulsa Race Riot of 1921, *Tulsa Race Riot*, 31.
37 Oklahoma Commission to Study the Tulsa Race Riot of 1921, *Tulsa Race Riot*, 25.
38 Oklahoma Commission to Study the Tulsa Race Riot of 1921, *Tulsa Race Riot*, 26.
39 Oklahoma Commission to Study the Tulsa Race Riot of 1921, *Tulsa Race Riot*, 27.
40 Lowenthal, *Past Is a Foreign Country*, 8.
41 Black Wall Street Chamber of Commerce, "About Us."
42 Degruy, *Post-traumatic Slave Syndrome*.
43 Nakassis, "Brands and Their Surfeits," 123.
44 Lindelof, *Watchmen*.
45 Greenwood Bank, "Why We Exist" (emphasis added).
46 Watts, "The Art of Hope."
47 Bloomberg Philanthropies, "Greenwood Initiative."
48 Bloomberg Philanthropies, "Greenwood Initiative."
49 Bloomberg Philanthropies, "Greenwood Initiative."
50 Humphrey and Verdery, *Property in Question*, 7.
51 M. Brown, *Who Owns Native Culture?*, 86.
52 Simone, "Urbanity and Generic Blackness," 188.
53 Build in Tulsa, home page.
54 Oklahoma Commission to Study the Tulsa Race Riot of 1921, *Tulsa Race Riot*, viii, 19.
55 Oklahoma Commission to Study the Tulsa Race Riot of 1921, *Tulsa Race Riot*, viii.
56 Oklahoma Commission to Study the Tulsa Race Riot of 1921, *Tulsa Race Riot*, viii.

57 Oklahoma Commission to Study the Tulsa Race Riot of 1921, *Tulsa Race Riot,* 21.

58 Oklahoma Commission to Study the Tulsa Race Riot of 1921, *Tulsa Race Riot,* 21.

59 Henry, *Long Overdue,* 86.

60 Henry, *Long Overdue,* 86.

61 Quoted in Henry, *Long Overdue,* 87.

62 Henry, *Long Overdue,* 90.

63 Henry, *Long Overdue,* 90.

64 Henry, *Long Overdue,* 90.

65 Oklahoma Commission to Study the Tulsa Race Riot of 1921, *Tulsa Race Riot,* viii.

66 Ogletree and McDougall, "Petition Alleging Violations."

67 Ogletree and McDougall, "Petition Alleging Violations."

68 Darity and Mullen, *From Here to Equality,* 243.

69 Solomon-Simmons, "Reparations Are the Answer."

70 H.Res.398, "Recognizing the Forthcoming Centennial."

71 50 OK Stat § 50-2 (2019).

72 Fussell, "Dead Men Bring No Claims," 1919.

73 Daniel, *Dispossession,* 6.

74 The crop-lien system was a credit system that became widely used by cotton farmers in the US South from the 1860s to 1930. "Partition sales" are one cause of the dispossession crisis. Property developers entice faraway relatives who may never have visited their family's land to sell their share for a fraction of its market value.

75 Darity and Mullen, *From Here to Equality,* 209.

76 Darity and Mullen, *From Here to Equality,* 221.

77 Darity and Mullen, *From Here to Equality,* 222.

78 Lewis, *Scammer's Yard.*

79 Fire in Little Africa, Earl Hazard, and Thomas Who?, "Descendants," track 4 on *Fire in Little Africa.*

80 Lewis, *Scammer's Yard,* 168.

81 Trouillot, *Silencing the Past,* 28.

82 Trouillot, *Silencing the Past,* 25.

83 Davis, *Are Prisons Obsolete?,* 20.

CHAPTER 5. TERRITORY

1 Scott, *Omens of Adversity,* 13.

2 Franke, *Repair,* 61.

3 Lipsitz, *How Racism Takes Place.*

4 As advanced by Cedric Robinson in *Black Marxism.*

5 McKittrick, "Plantation Futures," 4.

6 McKittrick, "On Plantations," 951.

7 Johnson, *Shadow of the Plantation,* 6, 12.

8 Robinson, *Black Marxism.*

9 McKittrick, "On Plantations," 947.

10 Wynter, "Unsettling the Coloniality," 268.

11 Wynter, "Unsettling the Coloniality," 272.

12 Asaka, *Tropical Freedom*, 3, 5.

13 Madera, *Black Atlas*, 109.

14 Madera analyzes texts that include Martin Delany's serialized *Blake*, James Pierson Beckwourth's *The Life and Adventures of James P. Beckwourth*, Pauline Hopkins's *Contending Forces*, multiple works by Alice Dunbar-Nelson, and William Wells Brown's *Clotel*.

15 Madera, *Black Atlas*, 70.

16 Madera, *Black Atlas*, 11.

17 Madera, *Black Atlas*, 18.

18 Madera, *Black Atlas*, 19.

19 Madera, *Black Atlas*, 23.

20 Madera, *Black Atlas*, 101.

21 Madera, *Black Atlas*, 101.

22 Madera, *Black Atlas*, 71, 73.

23 Madera, *Black Atlas*, 73.

24 Madera, *Black Atlas*, 3.

25 Madera, *Black Atlas*, 77.

26 Madera, *Black Atlas*, 109.

27 Field, "'No Such Thing as Stand Still,'" 696.

28 Kelley, *Freedom Dreams*, 16.

29 Field, "'No Such Thing as Stand Still,'" 696.

30 Ellison, *Going to the Territory*, 131.

31 Wynter, "Unsettling the Coloniality," 268.

32 Wolfe, "Land, Labor, and Difference," 887.

33 Chang, *Color of the Land*, 144.

34 Chang, *Color of the Land*, 145.

35 Chang, *Color of the Land*, 144.

36 Wolfe, "Land, Labor, and Difference," 887.

37 Chang, *Color of the Land*, 156.

38 Quoted in Bittle and Geis, "Racial Self-Fulfillment," 249.

39 Chang, *Color of the Land*, 158.

40 Chang, *Color of the Land*, 162.

41 Lewis, "So Black People Stay," 333.

42 Quoted in Chang, *Color of the Land*, 162.

43 Reese, "Freedmen."

44 A. Roberts, "Different Forty Acres," 219.

45 Stuckey, "Boley, Indian Territory," 498.

46 As discussed in Sampson, "Debate on individualism"; and Sampson, "Reinterpreting Individualism and Collectivism."

47 Strathern, *Gender of the Gift*, 13.

48 Slocum, *Black Towns, Black Futures*, 17.

49 Day, *Alien Capital*, 26.

50 Wolfe, "Land, Labor, and Difference," 887.

51 Englert, "Settlers, Workers, and the Logic of Accumulation," 1649.

52 King, *Black Shoals*, 16.

53 Miles and Holland, *Crossing Waters, Crossing Worlds*, 3.

54 Miles and Holland, *Crossing Waters, Crossing Worlds*, 4.

55 Miles and Holland, *Crossing Waters, Crossing Worlds*, 5, 7.

56 Byrd, *Transit of Empire*, xiv.

57 Miles and Holland, *Crossing Waters, Crossing Worlds*, 7.

58 Byrd, *Transit of Empire*, xx.

59 Byrd, *Transit of Empire*, 40.

60 Byrd, *Transit of Empire*, 54.

61 Byrd, *Transit of Empire*, xxx.

62 Byrd, *Transit of Empire*, 138.

63 In January 2011 a Cherokee Nation district court judge overruled the 2007 vote and reaffirmed that the Treaty of 1866 granted Freedmen and their descendants full citizenship rights. But the Nation waited to restore Freedmen's rights until the federal case was decided in 2017.

64 King, *Black Shoals*, xi.

65 King, *Black Shoals*, xi.

66 King, *Black Shoals*, xi, xii.

67 A. Roberts, *I've Been Here All the While*, 2–3.

68 A. Roberts, *I've Been Here All the While*, 2.

69 Murray, *Atlantic Passages*, 7.

70 Murray, *Atlantic Passages*, 8.

71 A. Roberts, *I've Been Here All the While*, 11.

72 Quoted in Chang, *Color of the Land*, 150.

73 Miles, "Beyond a Boundary," 418.

74 Miles, "Beyond a Boundary," 420.

75 Miles, "Beyond a Boundary," 419.

76 Miles, "Beyond a Boundary," 423.

77 Miles, "Beyond a Boundary," 420.

78 Miles, "Beyond a Boundary," 421.

79 Miles, "Beyond a Boundary," 422.

80 Miles, "Beyond a Boundary," 423.

81 Miles, "Beyond a Boundary," 425.

82 Amadahy and Lawrence, "Indigenous Peoples and Black People in Canada," 121.

83 Miles, "Beyond a Boundary," 425.

84 Miles, "Beyond a Boundary," 426, 418.

85 Miles, "Beyond a Boundary," 426.

86 Miles, "Beyond a Boundary," 426.

87 Miles, "Beyond a Boundary," 425.

88 Miles, "Beyond a Boundary," 425.

89 A. Roberts, *I've Been Here All the While*, 11.

90 King, *Black Shoals*, 68.

91 King, *Black Shoals*, 69–70.
92 King, *Black Shoals*, 31, 33.
93 King, *Black Shoals*, xii.
94 King, *Black Shoals*, xv.
95 Lambek, *Ordinary Ethics*, 2, 4.
96 Rifkin, *Beyond Settler Time*, 11.
97 Rifkin, *Beyond Settler Time*, 12.
98 Karuka, *Empire's Tracks*, 2.
99 Walcott, *Long Emancipation*, 1.
100 Walcott, *Long Emancipation*, 2.
101 Walcott, *Long Emancipation*, 3.
102 Walcott, *Long Emancipation*, 2.
103 Du Bois, *Black Reconstruction*, 30.
104 D. Thomas and Joseph Masco, "Sovereignty Unhinged."
105 Getachew, "Limits of Sovereignty as Responsibility," 226.
106 Getachew, "Limits of Sovereignty as Responsibility," 226.
107 Rifkin, *Beyond Settler Time*, 3.
108 D. Thomas, *Political Life in the Wake of the Plantation*, 2, 13.
109 D. Thomas, *Political Life in the Wake of the Plantation*, 13.
110 D. Thomas, *Political Life in the Wake of the Plantation*, 18.
111 D. Thomas, *Political Life in the Wake of the Plantation*, 18.
112 Quoted in Gara, "Baron of Black Wall Street."
113 S. Best, *None Like Us*, 39.
114 S. Best, *None Like Us*, 39.
115 S. Best, *None Like Us*, 40.
116 Wynter, "Pope Must Have Been Drunk," 27, 19.
117 Stuart Banner's "Why Terra Nullius-Anthropology and Property Law in Early Australia" shows how terra nullius was initially not how British colonists in North America viewed Native land. Given my discussion, that changed to justify the movement for allotment.
118 Franke, *Repair*, 15.
119 Franke, *Repair*, 15.
120 Franke, *Repair*, 19.
121 Franke, *Repair*, 19.
122 Franke, *Repair*, 19.
123 Franke, *Repair*, 61.
124 Franke, *Repair*, 21.
125 Franke, *Repair*, 22.
126 Franke, *Repair*, 17.
127 Franke, *Repair*, 61.
128 Stuckey, "Boley, Indian Territory," 494.
129 Stuckey, "Boley, Indian Territory," 494.
130 A. Roberts, *I've Been Here All the While*, 90.
131 Field, *Growing Up with the Country*, 162.

132 Chang, *Color of the Land*, 150.
133 Ellison, *Going to the Territory*, 131.
134 Chang, *Color of the Land*, 156.
135 C. Woodson, "Century of Negro Migration," 144.
136 Miles and Holland, *Crossing Waters, Crossing Worlds.*
137 Field, *Growing Up with the Country*, 139.
138 Field, *Growing Up with the Country*, 141.
139 Quoted in Field, *Growing Up with the Country*, 138.
140 Field, *Growing Up with the Country*, 138.
141 It didn't help that owing to a boll weevil invasion, agriculture profits, specifically in cotton, had taken a hit.
142 Field and Coletu, "The Chief Sam Movement," 116.
143 Field and Coletu, "The Chief Sam Movement," 109.
144 Field and Coletu, "The Chief Sam Movement," 116.
145 Field, *Growing Up with the Country*, 5.
146 Field, *Growing Up with the Country*, 115.
147 Field, *Growing Up with the Country*, 5.
148 Slocum, *Black Towns, Black Futures.*
149 It is, however, critical to continue to recognize that all-Black towns succeeded largely because of the treaty rights and activism of Freedmen, whose interactions with the American government through the settler colonial process had given them land and a degree of rights within Indian nations. See A. Roberts, *I've Been Here All the While*, 90.
150 Miles and Holland, *Crossing Waters, Crossing Worlds*, 4; and Slocum, *Black Towns, Black Futures*, 11.
151 Slocum, *Black Towns, Black Futures*, 18.
152 Singh, *Black Is a Country*, 171.
153 Asaka, *Tropical Freedom*, 202.
154 Asaka, *Tropical Freedom*, 202, 203, 138.
155 Asaka, *Tropical Freedom*, 138.
156 Painter, *Exodusters.*
157 Kelley, *Freedom Dreams*, 17.
158 Field, *Growing Up with the Country*, 4.
159 Kelley, *Freedom Dreams*, 18.
160 Kelley, *Freedom Dreams*, 18.
161 Kelley, *Freedom Dreams*, 18.
162 Kelley, *Freedom Dreams*, 29.
163 Kelley, *Freedom Dreams*, 16.
164 Field, "'No Such Thing as Stand Still,'" 696.
165 Miles, "Beyond a Boundary," 426.
166 Hartman, *Lose Your Mother*, 88.
167 N. Roberts, *Freedom as Marronage*, 171.
168 N. Roberts, *Freedom as Marronage*, 11.
169 N. Roberts, *Freedom as Marronage*, 11.

CONCLUSION

1   Scott, *Omens of Adversity Tragedy*, 131.

2   Fire In Little Africa, Hakeem Eli'juwon, and St. Domonick, "P.O.D.," track 14 on *Fire in Little Africa*, Motown Records, 2021.

3   The song's BMX reference refers to the building of the $23 million BMX racing facilities at the city-owned Evans-Fintube industrial site in Greenwood. The mayor argued that the facility would revitalize the historic Greenwood District. Of the funding for the facility, $15 million came from tax-supported Vision Tulsa revenue, with $6.5 million from city funds, and $1.5 million donated by the Hardesty Family Foundation to USA BMX. Canfield, "Massive."

4   In Murphy et al., "Role of Geography," 178. Gilmore in this forum was asking this question concerning the role of scholar-activists in the geography discipline.

5   In Murphy et al., "Role of Geography," 178.

6   In Murphy et al., "Role of Geography," 178.

7   Gilmore, "Abolition Geography," 226.

8   In Murphy et al., "Role of Geography," 178.

9   Siddiqui, "Freedom Is a Place," 171.

10 Slocum, *Black Towns, Black Futures*, 38.

11 Zamalin, *Black Utopia*, 12.

12 Zamalin, *Black Utopia*, 12.

13 Zamalin, *Black Utopia*, 12.

14 J. Brown, *Black Utopias*, 6

15 J. Brown, *Black Utopias*, 6.

16 J. Brown, *Black Utopias*, 7.

17 McKittrick, *Demonic Grounds*, xxv.

18 Muñoz, *Cruising Utopia*, 26.

19 Levitas, "Educated Hope," 15.

20 Lewis, *Scammer's Yard*, 44; Trouillot, *Silencing the Past*, 15.

21 Cooper, *Everyday Utopias*, 2.

22 Cooper, *Everyday Utopias*, 222.

23 Cooper, *Everyday Utopias*, 223.

24 Cooper, *Everyday Utopias*, 222.

25 Lewis, "So Black People Stay."

26 Trouillot, *Silencing the Past*, 27.

Allen, Douglas W., and Bryan Leonard. "How Many Rushed during the Oklahoma Land Openings?" *Cliometrica* 14, no. 2 (2019): 397–416.

Amadahy, Zainab, and Bonita Lawrence. "Indigenous Peoples and Black People in Canada: Settlers or Allies?" In *Breaching the Colonial Contract*, edited by Arlo Kempf, 105–36. Dordrecht, Netherlands: Springer, 2009.

Anderson, Elijah. "The White Space." *Sociology of Race and Ethnicity* 1, no. 1 (2015): 10–21.

Asaka, Ikuko. *Tropical Freedom: Climate, Settler Colonialism, and Black Exclusion in the Age of Emancipation*. Durham, NC: Duke University Press, 2017.

Banner, Stuart. "Why Terra Nullius-Anthropology and Property Law in Early Australia." *Law and History Review* 23, no. 1 (2005): 95.

Beckwourth, James Pierson. *The Life and Adventures of James P. Beckwourth*. New York: A. A. Knopf, 1931.

Best, Stephen M. *The Fugitive's Properties: Law and the Poetics of Possession*. Chicago: University of Chicago Press, 2010.

Best, Stephen M. *None Like Us: Blackness, Belonging, Aesthetic Life*. Durham, NC: Duke University Press, 2019.

Bittle, William E., and Gilbert L. Geis. "Racial Self-Fulfillment and the Rise of an All-Negro Community in Oklahoma." *Phylon Quarterly* 18, no. 3 (1957): 247–60.

Black Wall Street Chamber of Commerce. "About Us." Accessed April 6, 2021. https://www.bwschamber.com/about-us.

Bloch, Ernst. *The Principle of Hope*. Cambridge, MA: MIT Press, 1986.

Block, Daniel R., and Kristin Reynolds. "Funding a Peoples' Food Justice Geography? Community-Academic Collaborations as Geographic Praxis." *Annals of the American Association of Geographers* 111, no. 6 (2021): 1705–20.

Bloomberg Philanthropies. "The Greenwood Initiative." Accessed April 1, 2021. https://www.bloomberg.org/founders-projects/the-greenwood-initiative/.

Braga, Anthony A., David L. Weisburd, Elin J. Waring, Lorraine G. Mazerolle, William Spelman, and Francis Gajewski. "Problem-Oriented Policing in Violent Crime Places: A Randomized Controlled Experiment." *Criminology* 37 no. 3 (1999): 541–80.

Brown, Jayna. *Black Utopias: Speculative Life and the Music of Other Worlds*. Durham, NC: Duke University Press, 2021.

Brown, Michael F. *Who Owns Native Culture?* Cambridge, MA: Harvard University Press, 2009.

Brown, William Wells. *Clotel.* Charlottesville: University of Virginia Press, 2006.

Browne, Simone. *Dark Matters: On the Surveillance of Blackness.* Durham, NC: Duke University Press, 2015.

Build in Tulsa. Home page. Accessed June 6, 2021. https://www.buildintulsa.com.

Bureau of Justice Assistance. *Problem-Oriented Drug Enforcement: A Community-Based Approach for Effective Policing.* Washington, DC: U.S. Department of Justice, 1993.

Byrd, Jodi A. *The Transit of Empire: Indigenous Critiques of Colonialism.* Minneapolis: University of Minnesota Press, 2011.

California Evidence-Based Clearinghouse for Child Welfare. "Parents as Teachers." Accessed June 6, 2020. https://www.cebc4cw.org/program/parents-as-teachers /detailed.

Canfield, Kevin. "Massive open-air, free-span BMX arena nearly 50% completed." May 29, 2021. https://tulsaworld.com/news/local/massive-open-air-free-span-bmx -arena-nearly-50-completed/article_f8915248-85cc-11eb-a7dc-3ff4d4ad9cb5.html.

CAP Tulsa. "Who We Are." Accessed June 6, 2020. https://captulsa.org/who-we-are.

Center for Community School Strategies. "Framework for TACSI Schools." October 1, 2020. https://www.csstrategies.org/wp-content/uploads/2016/04/1TACSI -Framework_2014-2015.pdf.

Center for Evidence-Based Crime Policy. "Broken Windows Policing." Accessed November 27, 2021. https://cebcp.org/evidence-based-policing/what-works-in -policing/research-evidence-review/broken-windows-policing.

Center for Evidence-Based Crime Policy. "Hot Spots Policing." Accessed November 27, 2021. https://cebcp.org/evidence-based-policing/what-works-in-policing/research -evidence-review/hot-spots-policing.

Center for Family Resilience, Oklahoma State University–Tulsa. Accessed April 29, 2021. https://education.okstate.edu/research/centers/center-family-resilience/index.html.

Chang, David A. *The Color of the Land: Race, Nation, and the Politics of Landowner-ship in Oklahoma, 1832–1929.* Chapel Hill: University of North Carolina Press, 2010.

Christian Community Development Association. "About." Accessed August 6, 2020. https://ccda.org/about/.

Connolly, N. D. B. *A World More Concrete: Real Estate and the Remaking of Jim Crow South Florida.* Chicago: University of Chicago Press, 2014.

Cooper, Davina. *Everyday Utopias: The Conceptual Life of Promising Spaces.* Durham, NC: Duke University Press, 2014.

Cosgrove, Jaclyn. "Tulsa, Oklahoma Counties Address Jail Changes, Mentally Ill Inmates." *Oklahoman,* January 22, 2017. https://newsok.com/article/5535086/tulsa -oklahoma-counties-address-jail-changes-mentally-ill-inmates.

Daniel, Pete. *Dispossession: Discrimination against African American Farmers in the Age of Civil Rights.* Chapel Hill: University of North Carolina Press, 2013.

Darity, William A., and A. Kirsten Mullen. *From Here to Equality: Reparations for Black Americans in the Twenty-First Century.* Chapel Hill: University of North Carolina Press, 2020.

Das, Veena. *Life and Words: Violence and the Descent into the Ordinary*. Berkeley: University of California Press, 2006.

Davis, Angela Y. *Are Prisons Obsolete?* New York: Seven Stories, 2003.

Day, Iyko. *Alien Capital: Asian Racialization and the Logic of Settler Colonial Capitalism*. Durham, NC: Duke University Press, 2016.

DeGruy, Joy. *Post Traumatic Slave Syndrome: America's Legacy of Enduring Injury and Healing*. Portland, OR: Joy DeGruy Publications, 2005.

Delany, Martin R. *Blake; Or, The Huts of America*. Cambridge, MA: Harvard University Press, 2017.

Douglas, Mary. *Purity and Danger: An Analysis of the Concepts of Pollution and Taboo*. 1966. London: Routledge, 2002.

Du Bois, W. E. B. *Black Reconstruction in America: Toward a History of the Part Which Black Folk Played in the Attempt to Reconstruct Democracy in America, 1860–1880*. London: Routledge, 2017.

Du Bois, W. E. B. *The Souls of Black Folk*. New Haven, CT: Yale University Press, 2015.

Duke, Cori. "North Tulsa Grocery Store, Gateway Market, Closing Permanently." 2 *News Oklahoma*, November 1, 2017. https://www.kjrh.com/news/local-news/north-tulsa-grocery-store-gateway-market-closing-permanently.

Dunbar-Nelson, Alice. "People of Color in Louisiana." In *Creole: The History and Legacy*, edited by Sybil Kein, 3–41. Baton Rouge: Louisiana State University Press, 2000.

Dunbar-Nelson, Alice. *The Works of Alice Dunbar-Nelson*. 3 vols. Edited by Gloria T. Hull. New York: Oxford University Press, 1988.

Durkheim, Émile, and Marcel Mauss. *Primitive Classification*. Chicago: University of Chicago Press, 1963 [1903].

Ellison, Ralph. *Going to the Territory*. Westminster, UK: Knopf Doubleday, 2011.

Ellsworth, Scott. *Death in a Promised Land: The Tulsa Race Riot of 1921*. Baton Rouge: Louisiana State University Press, 1992.

Englert, Sai. "Settlers, Workers, and the Logic of Accumulation by Dispossession." *Antipode* 52, no. 6 (2020): 1647–66.

Fagan, Jeffrey, and Garth Davies. "Street Stops and Broken Windows: Terry, Race, and Disorder in New York City." *The Fordham Urban Law Journal* 28, no. 2 (2000): 457–504.

Family and Children's Services. "Women in Recovery." Accessed June 3, 2020. https://www.fcsok.org/services/women-in-recovery.

Fanon, Frantz. *Black Skin, White Masks*. New York: Grove, 2008.

Ferguson, James. *The Anti-politics Machine: "Development," Depoliticization, and Bureaucratic Power in Lesotho*. Cambridge: Cambridge University Press, 1990.

Field, Kendra Taira. "'No Such Thing as Stand Still': Migration and Geopolitics in African American History." *Journal of American History* 102, no. 3 (2015): 693–718.

Field, Kendra T. *Growing Up with the Country: Family, Race, and Nation after the Civil War*. New Haven, CT: Yale University Press, 2018.

Field, Kendra Taira, and Ebony Coletu. "The Chief Sam Movement, a Century Later: Public Histories, Private Stories, and the African Diaspora." *Transition: An International Review*, no. 114 (2014): 108–30.

Franke, Katherine. *Repair: Redeeming the Promise of Abolition*. Chicago: Haymarket Books, 2019.

Franklin, Buck Colbert, John Hope Franklin, and John Whittington Franklin. *My Life and an Era: The Autobiography of Buck Colbert Franklin*. Baton Rouge: Louisiana State University Press, 1997.

The Frontier. "What Happened to Jack? Voters Explain Why They Voted against Long-time Councilor Jack Henderson." November 10, 2016. https://www.readfrontier.org/stories/happened-jack-voters-explain-voted-longtime-councilor-jack-henderson/.

Fussell, Melissa. "Dead Men Bring No Claims: How Takings Claims Can Provide Redress for Real Property-Owning Victims of Jim Crow Race Riots." *William and Mary Law Review* 57, no. 5 (2016): 1913–48.

Gara, Antoine. "The Baron of Black Wall Street." *Forbes*, June 18, 2020. https://www.forbes.com/sites/antoinegara/2020/06/18/the-bezos-of-black-wall-street-tulsa-race-riots-1921.

Garth, Hanna. "Blackness and 'Justice' in the L.A. Food Justice Movement." In *Black Food Matters: Racial Justice in the Wake of Food Justice*, edited by Hanna Garth and Ashanté M. Reese, 107–30. Minneapolis: University of Minnesota Press, 2020.

Garth, Hanna, and Ashanté M. Reese. "Black Food Matters: An Introduction." In *Black Food Matters: Racial Justice in the Wake of Food Justice*, edited by Hanna Garth and Ashanté M. Reese, 1–28. Minneapolis: University of Minnesota Press, 2020.

George Kaiser Family Foundation. "Birth through Eight Strategy for Tulsa (BEST): Disrupting Intergenerational Poverty by Acting Early, When It Matters Most." Accessed April 4, 2020. https://www.gkff.org/what-we-do/birth-eight-strategy-tulsa.

Getachew, Adom. "The Limits of Sovereignty as Responsibility." *Constellations* 26, no. 2 (2019): 225–40.

Gilmore, Ruth W. "Abolition Geography and the Problem of Innocence." In *Futures of Black Radicalism*, edited by Gaye Theresa Johnson and Alex Lubin, 225–40. London: Verso Books, 2017.

Graham, Ginnie. "Tulsa Native, Activist Cornel West Says 'Market-Driven Morality' Will Kill Democracy." *Tulsa World*, October 6, 2017. https://tulsaworld.com/news/local/tulsa-Native-activist-cornel-west-says-market-driven-morality-will-kill-democracy/article_408dbd92-a462-5e99-8198-abfaba606cb0.html.

Greenwood Bank. "Why We Exist." Accessed April 1, 2021. https://bankgreenwood.com/about.

Greenwood Cultural Center. "About Us." Accessed April 1, 2021. https://greenwoodculturalcenter.com/about-us.

Greenwood Rising. "About." Accessed April 1, 2021. https://www.greenwoodrising.org/about.

Harkins, Paighten. "New North Tulsa Grocery Store Will Help Shrink Area's Food Desert." *Tulsa World*, December 18, 2016. https://tulsaworld.com/news/local/new-north-tulsa-grocery-store-will-help-shrink-areas-food-desert/article_fb1e3f0d-de3e-5465-89e3-a248dc6a6917.html.

Hart, Betty, and Todd R. Risley. *Meaningful Differences in the Everyday Experience of Young American Children*. Baltimore: Paul H. Brookes, 1995.

Hartman, Saidiya V. *Lose Your Mother: A Journey along the Atlantic Slave Route.* New York: Farrar, Straus and Giroux, 2008.

Hartman, Saidiya V. *Scenes of Subjection: Terror, Slavery, and Self-Making in Nineteenth-Century America.* New York: Oxford University Press, 1997.

Haynes, Thomas. *Boley Progress,* April 19, 1906.

Healthy Community Store Initiative. Home page. Accessed July 3, 2020. http://www.tulsarealgoodfood.org/home.

Heath, Dreisen. "The Case for Reparations in Tulsa, Oklahoma: A Human Rights Argument." Human Rights Watch, May 29, 2020. https://www.hrw.org/news/2020/05/29/case-reparations-tulsa-oklahoma.

Henry, Charles P. *Long Overdue: The Politics of Racial Reparations.* New York: New York University Press, 2007.

Hirsch, James S. *Riot and Remembrance: The Tulsa Race War and Its Legacy.* Boston: Houghton Mifflin, 2002.

Hopkins, Pauline E. *Contending Forces: A Romance Illustrative of Negro Life North and South.* New York: Oxford University Press, 1988.

H.Res.398 Recognizing the Forthcoming Centennial of the 1921 Tulsa Race Massacre. *Congressional Documents and Publications.* Washington: Federal Information and News Dispatch, 2021.

Hudson, Peter James. *Bankers and Empire: How Wall Street Colonized the Caribbean.* Chicago: University of Chicago Press, 2017.

Humphrey, Caroline, and Katherine Verdery. *Property in Question: Value Transformation in the Global Economy.* Oxford: Berg, 2004.

Ismail, Feyzi, and Sangeeta Kamat. "NGOs, Social Movements and the Neoliberal State: Incorporation, Reinvention, Critique." *Critical Sociology* 44, no. 4–5 (2018): 569–77.

IWW History Project: Industrial Workers of the World 1905–1935. "Arrests, Prosecutions, Beatings, and Other Violence 1906–1920." Accessed March 23, 2021. https://depts.washington.edu/iww/persecution.shtml.

Jacobs, David. "Case in Point: Four Holes in Officer Betty Shelby's Defense." NAACP Legal Defense and Educational Fund. Accessed November 29, 2021. https://www.naacpldf.org/naacp-publications/ldf-blog/case-in-point-four-holes-in-officer-betty-shelbys-defense/.

Johnson, Charles Spurgeon. *Growing Up in the Black Belt.* Washington, DC: American Council on Education, 1941.

Johnson, Charles Spurgeon. *Shadow of the Plantation.* 1934. Somerset, UK: Routledge, 1996.

Johnson, Hannibal. *Black Wall Street: From Riot to Renaissance in Tulsa's Historic Greenwood District.* Fort Worth, TX: Eakin, 2000. EPub.

Joseph, Miranda. *Against the Romance of Community.* Minneapolis: University of Minnesota Press, 2002.

Justice for Greenwood. "About Us." Accessed August 1, 2021. https://www.justiceforgreenwood.org/about-us.

Justice for Greenwood. "The Justice for Greenwood Oral History Project." Accessed August 1, 2021. https://www.justiceforgreenwood.org/descendants.

Kamat, Sangeeta. "The Privatization of Public Interest: Theorizing NGO Discourse in a Neoliberal Era." *Review of International Political Economy* 11, no. 1 (2004): 155–76.

Karuka, Manu. *Empire's Tracks: Indigenous Nations, Chinese Workers, and the Transcontinental Railroad.* Oakland: University of California Press, 2019.

Kelley, Robin D. G. *Freedom Dreams: The Black Radical Imagination.* Boston: Beacon, 2002.

Kelley, Robin D. G. "Robin D. G. Kelley: The Tulsa Race Massacre Went Way beyond 'Black Wall Street.'" Interview by George Yancy. *Truthout*, June 1, 2021. https:// truthout.org/articles/robin-kelley-business-interests-fomented-tulsa-massacre-as -pretext-to-take-land/.

King, Tiffany Lethabo. *The Black Shoals: Offshore Formations of Black and Native Studies.* Durham, NC: Duke University Press, 2019.

Kohl-Arenas, Erica. *The Self-Help Myth: How Philanthropy Fails to Alleviate Poverty.* Oakland: University of California Press, 2015.

Kotabe, Hiroki P, Omid Kardan, and Marc G. Berman. "The Order of Disorder: Deconstructing Visual Disorder and Its Effect on Rule-Breaking." *Journal of Experimental Psychology*: General 145, no. 12 (2016): 1713–27.

Krehbiel, Randy. "John Hope Franklin Reconciliation Park Opens to the Public." *Tulsa World*, October 27, 2010. https://tulsaworld.com/news/local/racemassacre/john -hope-franklin-reconciliation-park-opens-to-the-public/article_ccd6b797-0e17-561f -8de8-87a2fo4b3foa.html.

Krehbiel, Randy. *Tulsa, 1921: Reporting a Massacre.* Norman: University of Oklahoma Press, 2019.

Lambek, Michael. *Ordinary Ethics: Anthropology, Language, and Action.* New York: Fordham University Press, 2010.

LEAD North, "About Us." Accessed November 22, 2021. http://leadnorthtulsa.org /about-us/history/.

Levitas, Ruth. "Educated Hope: Ernst Bloch on Abstract and Concrete Utopia." *Utopian Studies* 1, no. 2 (1990): 13–26.

Lewis, Jovan Scott. "A So Black People Stay: Bad-Mind, Sufferation, and Discourses of Race and Unity in a Jamaican Craft Market." *Journal of Latin American and Caribbean Anthropology* 20, no. 2 (2015): 327–42.

Lewis, Jovan Scott. *Scammer's Yard: The Crime of Black Repair in Jamaica.* Minneapolis: University of Minnesota Press, 2020.

Lewis, Jovan Scott. "Subject to Labor: Racial Capitalism and Ontology in the Postemancipation Caribbean." *Geoforum*, available online June 13, 2020. https://doi.org /10.1016/j.geoforum.2020.06.007.

Lindelof, Damon, creator. *Watchmen.* Burbank, CA: Warner Bros. Home Entertainment, 2019.

Lipsitz, George. *How Racism Takes Place.* Philadelphia: Temple University Press, 2011.

Livingston, James D. "Contact between Police and People with Mental Disorders: A Review of Rates." *Psychiatric Services* 67, no. 8 (2016): 850–57.

Looney, Joe. "Greenwood Fades Away before Advance of Expressway." *Tulsa Tribune*, May 4, 1967. http://www.batesline.com/archives/2017/07/greenwood-expressway -demolition-1967.html.

Lowenthal, David. *The Past Is a Foreign Country—Revisited*. Cambridge: Cambridge University Press, 2015.

Madera, Judith. *Black Atlas: Geography and Flow in Nineteenth-Century African American Literature*. Durham, NC: Duke University Press, 2015.

Madigan, Tim. *The Burning: Massacre, Destruction, and the Tulsa Race Riot of 1921*. New York: Thomas Dunne Books/St. Martin's, 2001.

Marshall, Kendrick. "Tulsa Race Massacre: For Years It Was Called a Riot. Not Anymore. Here's How It Changed." *Tulsa World*, May 31, 2020. https://tulsaworld .com/news/local/racemassacre/tulsa-race-massacre-for-years-it-was-called-a -riot-not-anymore-heres-how-it/article_1c09be68-a46d-11eb-994b-432bf923c904 .html.

McKittrick, Katherine. *Demonic Grounds: Black Women and the Cartographies of Struggle*. Minneapolis: University of Minnesota Press, 2006.

McKittrick, Katherine. "On Plantations, Prisons, and a Black Sense of Place." *Social and Cultural Geography* 12, no. 8 (2011): 947–63.

McKittrick, Katherine. "Plantation Futures." *Small Axe: A Caribbean Journal of Criticism* 17, no. 3 (2013): 1–15.

Messer, Chris M., and Patricia A. Bell. "Mass Media and Governmental Framing of Riots: The Case of Tulsa, 1921." *Journal of Black Studies* 40, no. 5 (2010): 851–70.

Miles, Tiya. "Beyond a Boundary: Black Lives and the Settler-Native Divide." *William and Mary Quarterly* 76, no. 3 (2019): 417–26.

Miles, Tiya, and Sharon Patricia Holland, eds. *Crossing Waters, Crossing Worlds: The African Diaspora in Indian Country*. Durham, NC: Duke University Press, 2020.

Morgan, Rhett. "Planned North Tulsa Grocery Store Builder Asks for Up to $1.5 Million in TIF Funding." *Tulsa World*, January 10, 2020. https://tulsaworld.com /business/planned-north-tulsa-grocery-store-builder-asks-for-up-to-1-5-million-in -tif/article_6fc09b2b-5c85-59b5-bc77-2216b7846003.html.

Moynihan, Daniel Patrick. "Memorandum for the President." The White House, July 2, 1970. https://www.nixonlibrary.gov/sites/default/files/virtuallibrary /documents/jul10/53.pdf.

Moynihan, Daniel Patrick. *The Negro Family: The Case for National Action*. No. 3. Washington, DC: US Government Printing Office, 1965.

Muir, Richard. *Approaches to Landscape*. Basingstoke, UK: Macmillan, 1999.

Muñoz, José Esteban. *Cruising Utopia*. New York: New York University Press, 2019.

Murphy, Alexander B., H. J. De Blij, B. L. Turner, Ruth Wilson Gilmore, and Derek Gregory. "The Role of Geography in Public Debate." *Progress in Human Geography* 29, no. 2 (2005): 165–93.

Murray, Robert. *Atlantic Passages: Race, Mobility, and Liberian Colonization*. Gainesville: University Press of Florida, 2021.

Nagata, Donna K., Jacqueline H. J. Kim, and Kaidi Wu. "The Japanese American Wartime Incarceration: Examining the Scope of Racial Trauma." *American Psychologist* 74, no. 1 (2019): 36–48.

Nakassis, Constantine. "Brands and Their Surfeits." *Cultural Anthropology* 28, no. 1 (2013): 111–26.

Newell, Sasha. "Brands as Masks: Public Secrecy and the Counterfeit in Côte d'Ivoire." *Journal of the Royal Anthropological Institute* 19, no. 1 (2013): 138–54.

Newman, Andrew, and Yuson Jung. "Good Food in a Racist System: Competing Moral Economies in Detroit." In *Black Food Matters: Racial Justice in the Wake of Food Justice*, edited by Hanna Garth and Ashanté M. Reese, 131–57. Minneapolis: University of Minnesota Press, 2020.

News on 6. "Gateway Market Reopens Doors in North Tulsa." October 4, 2014. https:// www.newson6.com/story/5e362b832f69d76f6204c7ab/gateway-market-reopens -doors-in-north-tulsa.

News on 6. "North Tulsa Grocery Store Closes Doors Early." July 28, 2014. https://www .newson6.com/story/5e362e412f69d76f6204e749/north-tulsa-grocery-store-closes -doors-early.

New York Times, "Series of Fierce Combats," June 2, 1921. https://www.nytimes.com /1921/06/02/archives/series-of-fierce-combats-angered-whites-surround-negro -quarterand.html.

Ngai, Mae M. *Impossible Subjects: Illegal Aliens and the Making of Modern America*. Politics and Society in Twentieth-Century America. Princeton, NJ: Princeton University Press, 2004.

Nir, Sarah Maslin. "White Woman Is Fired after Calling Police on Black Man in Central Park." *New York Times*, May 26, 2020. https://www.nytimes.com/2020/05/26 /nyregion/amy-cooper-dog-central-park.html.

1921 Tulsa Race Massacre Centennial Commission. "About the Commission." Accessed April 1, 2021. https://www.tulsa2021.org/about.

NorthTulsa100. "History of NorthTulsa100." Accessed February 10, 2021. http://www .northtulsa100.com/about-us.html.

Nowlain, Lisa. "Is the 30 Million Word Gap a Stat We Should Be Using?" *ALSC Blog*, November 27, 2015. https://www.alsc.ala.org/blog/2015/11/is-the-30-million-word -gap-a-stat-we-should-be-using.

Ogletree, Charles, and Gay J. McDougall. "Petition Alleging Violations of the Human Rights of John Melvin Alexander et al. by the United States of America." October 26, 2005. Available on *SSRN*, https://papers.ssrn.com/sol3/papers.cfm?abstract _id=993646.

Oklahoma Center for Nonprofits. "Celebrating 40 Years of Nonprofit Leadership." Accessed November 27, 2021. https://okcnp.org.

Oklahoma Commission to Study the Tulsa Race Riot of 1921. *Tulsa Race Riot: A Report by the Oklahoma Commission to Study the Race Riot of 1921*. Oklahoma City: Oklahoma Historical Society, 2001. https://www.okhistory.org/research/forms/freport.pdf.

Oklahoma Historical Society. "The Langston City Herald (Langston City, O.T.)." Accessed March 21, 2020. https://gateway.okhistory.org/explore/collections/LANGHD/.

Oklahoma Human Services. "*Advantage* Administration." Accessed April 29, 2020. https://oklahoma.gov/okdhs/services/aging/advantageadmin.html.

Oklahoma State University–Tulsa. "Center for Family Resilience." Accessed November 20, 2021. https://education.okstate.edu/research/centers/center-family-resilience /index.html.

Osborne, Deon. "G.T. Bynum's Administration Rushes to Rebury 1921 Massacre Victims despite Vote to Postpone." *Black Wall Street Times*, July 30, 2021. https://theblackwallsttimes.com/2021/07/30/g-t-bynums-administration-rushes-to-rebury-1921-massacre-victims-despite-vote-to-postpone/.

Painter, Nell Irvin. *Exodusters: Black Migration to Kansas after Reconstruction*. New York: W. W. Norton, 1992.

Parrish, Mary E. Jones. *Race Riot 1921: Events of the Tulsa Disaster*. Tulsa, OK: Out on a Limb Publishing, 1998.

Quandt, Sara A., Joseph G. Grzywacz, Jennifer W. Talton, Grisel Trejo, Janeth Tapia, Ralph B. D'Agostino Jr., Maria C. Mirabelli, and Thomas A. Arcury. "Evaluating the Effectiveness of a Lay Health Promoter-Led, Community-Based Participatory Pesticide Safety Intervention with Farmworker Families." *Health Promotion Practice* 14, no. 3 (2013): 425–32.

Ranganathan, Malini. "Rule by Difference: Empire, Liberalism, and the Legacies of Urban 'Improvement.'" *Environment and Planning A: Economy and Space* 50, no. 7 (2018): 1386–406.

Reese, Linda. "Freedmen." Oklahoma Historical Society. Accessed April 3, 2021. https://www.okhistory.org/publications/enc/entry.php?entry=FR016.

Rial, Carmen. "Banal Religiosity: Brazilian Athletes as New Missionaries of the Neo-Pentecostal Diaspora." *Vibrant: Virtual Brazilian Anthropology* 9, no. 2 (2012): 128–59.

Rifkin, Mark. *Beyond Settler Time: Temporal Sovereignty and Indigenous Self-Determination*. Durham, NC: Duke University Press, 2017.

Roberts, Alaina E. "A Different Forty Acres: Land, Kin, and Migration in the Late Nineteenth-Century West." *Journal of the Civil War Era* 10, no. 2 (2020): 213–32.

Roberts, Alaina E. *I've Been Here All the While: Black Freedom on Native Land*. Philadelphia: University of Pennsylvania Press, 2021.

Roberts, Alaina E. "Who Belongs in Indian Territory?" *Journal of the Gilded Age and Progressive Era* 20, no. 2 (2021): 334–37.

Roberts, Neil. *Freedom as Marronage*. Chicago: University of Chicago Press, 2015.

Robinson, Cedric J. *Black Marxism: The Making of the Black Radical Tradition*. 1983. Chapel Hill: University of North Carolina Press, 2000.

Rodney, Walter. *How Europe Underdeveloped Africa*. Rev. ed. Washington, DC: Howard University Press, 1981.

Roediger, David R. *The Wages of Whiteness: Race and the Making of the American Working Class*. London: Verso, 1999.

Sacks, Tina K. *Invisible Visits: Black Middle-Class Women in the American Healthcare System*. New York: Oxford University Press, 2019.

Sampson, Edward E. "The Debate on Individualism: Indigenous Psychologies of the Individual and Their Role in Personal and Societal Functioning." *American Psychologist* 43, no. 1 (1988): 15–22.

Sampson, Edward E. "Reinterpreting Individualism and Collectivism: Their Religious Roots and Monologic versus Dialogic Person-Other Relationship." *American Psychologist* 55, no. 12 (2000): 1425–32.

Saunt, Claudio. *Unworthy Republic: The Dispossession of Native Americans and the Road to Indian Territory.* New York: W. W. Norton, 2020.

Scherz, China. *Having People, Having Heart: Charity, Sustainable Development, and Problems of Dependence in Central Uganda.* Chicago: University of Chicago Press, 2014.

Scott, David. *Omens of Adversity: Tragedy, Time, Memory, Justice.* Durham, NC: Duke University Press, 2013.

Sharpe, Christina Elizabeth. *In the Wake: On Blackness and Being.* Durham, NC: Duke University Press, 2016.

Siddiqui, Tasneem. "Freedom Is a Place: Black Self-Determination in the Low Country and Sea Islands, 1865–1900." PhD diss., University of Southern California, 2015.

Simone, AbdouMaliq. "Urbanity and Generic Blackness." *Theory, Culture and Society* 33, no. 7–8 (2016): 183–203.

Singh, Nikhil Pal. *Black Is a Country: Race and the Unfinished Struggle for Democracy.* Cambridge, MA: Harvard University Press, 2005.

Sixty Minutes. "Tulsa Burning." Last modified June 14, 2020. https://www.youtube .com/watch?v=EgUrsmzFAd4.

Skewes, Monica C., and Arthur W. Blume. "Understanding the Link between Racial Trauma and Substance Use among American Indians." *American Psychologist* 74, no. 1 (2019): 88–100.

Slocum, Karla. *Black Towns, Black Futures: The Enduring Allure of a Black Place in the American West.* Chapel Hill: University of North Carolina Press, 2019.

Smallwood, James. "Segregation." Oklahoma Historical Society. Accessed March 22, 2020. https://www.okhistory.org/publications/enc/entry.php?entry=SE006.

Snorton, C. Riley. *Black on Both Sides: A Racial History of Trans Identity.* Minneapolis: University of Minnesota Press, 2017.

Solomon-Simmons, Damario. "Reparations Are the Answer to Protesters' Demands for Racial Justice." *Los Angeles Times,* June 8, 2020. https://www.latimes.com /opinion/story/2020-06-08/racial-protest-tulsa-massacre-reparations.

Stafford, Charles. "The Punishment of Ethical Behavior." In *Ordinary Ethics: Anthropology, Language, and Action,* edited by Michael Lambek, 187–206. New York: Fordham University Press, 2010.

Stoler, Ann L. "Making Empire Respectable: The Politics of Race and Sexual Morality in 20th-Century Colonial Cultures." *American Ethnologist* 16, no. 4 (1989): 634–60.

Strathern, Marilyn. *The Gender of the Gift: Problems with Women and Problems with Society in Melanesia.* Berkeley: University of California Press, 1988.

Stuckey, Melissa N. "Boley, Indian Territory: Exercising Freedom in the All-Black Town." *Journal of African American History* 102, no. 4 (2017): 492–516.

Summers, Brandi Thompson. *Black in Place: The Spatial Aesthetics of Race in a Post-chocolate City.* Chapel Hill: University of North Carolina Press, 2019.

Taylor, Diana. *The Archive and the Repertoire: Performing Cultural Memory in the Americas.* Durham, NC: Duke University Press, 2003.

Taylor, Marnie. "Charity Inc.: Potts Honored for 30 Years of Changing Lives." *Journal*

Record, November 30, 2011. https://journalrecord.com/2011/11/30/charity-inc-potts
-honored-for-30-years-of-changing-lives-opinion.

Thomas, Deborah A. *Exceptional Violence: Embodied Citizenship in Transnational Jamaica*. Durham, NC: Duke University Press, 2011.

Thomas, Deborah A. *Political Life in the Wake of the Plantation: Sovereignty, Witnessing, Repair*. Durham, NC: Duke University Press, 2019.

Thomas, Deborah A. "Time and the Otherwise: Plantations, Garrisons and Being Human in the Caribbean." *Anthropological Theory* 16, no. 2–3 (2016): 177–200.

Thomas, Deborah A., and Joseph Masco, eds. "Sovereignty Unhinged: An Illustrated Primer for the Study of Present Intensities, Disavowals, and Temporal Derangements." Unpublished manuscript, April 8, 2021. Typescript.

Thomas, Todne. *Kincraft: The Making of Black Evangelical Sociality*. Durham, NC: Duke University Press, 2021.

Trouillot, Michel-Rolph. *Silencing the Past: Power and the Production of History*. Boston: Beacon, 1995.

Tulsa Democrat. "Shall Tulsa Be Muskogeeized?" April 4, 1912.

Tulsa Historical Society and Museum. "The 1921 Tulsa Race Massacre." Accessed September 3, 2020. https://www.tulsahistory.org/exhibit/1921-tulsa-race-massacre.

Tulsa Police Department. *Drug Problem Inventory: Problem-Oriented Approach to Drug Enforcement*. Tulsa, OK: Tulsa Police Department, 1989.

Tulsa Tribune. "It Must Not Be Again." June 4, 1921.

Tulsa Tribune. "Nab Negro for Attacking Girl in an Elevator." May 31, 1921.

Tulsa Tribune. "Plan to Move Negroes into New District." June 3, 1921.

Tulsa World. "Tulsa Area's 20 Largest Churches." Updated February 26, 2019. https://tulsaworld.com/archive/tulsa-areas-20-largest-churches/article_70168225-b51a-5566-a0f4-b977f3d5012e.html.

Urban Institute, Pay for Success Initiative. "Oklahoma Women in Recovery PFS Project." Accessed June 3, 2020. https://pfs.urban.org/library/pfs-projects-glance/content/oklahoma-women-recovery-pfs-project.

University of Richmond Digital Scholarship Lab. "Mapping Inequality: Redlining in New Deal America." Accessed July 15, 2020. https://dsl.richmond.edu/panorama/redlining/#loc=12/36.138/-96.052&city=tulsa-ok.

Vicent, Samantha. "North Tulsa Moves Closer to Having an 'Oasis' in a Food Desert." *Tulsa World*, June 29, 2020. https://tulsaworld.com/news/local/north-tulsa-moves-closer-to-having-an-oasis-in-a-food-desert/article_387e7e10-7402-55ba-9707-23c11dbffie8.html.

Walcott, Rinaldo. *The Long Emancipation: Moving toward Black Freedom*. Durham, NC: Duke University Press, 2021.

Watts, James D., Jr. "The Art of Hope: Exhibit Brings Artists Together to Examine Past, Future of Greenwood." *Tulsa World*, updated May 29, 2021. https://tulsaworld.com/entertainment/the-art-of-hope-exhibit-brings-artists-together-to-examine-past-future-of-greenwood/article_ec9b2c58-924b-11eb-8f1c-b7019757fe69.html.

Wells-Barnett, Ida B. *The Red Record: Tabulated Statistics and Alleged Causes of Lynching in the United States*. Project Gutenberg. 2005. https://www.gutenberg.org/ebooks/14977.

Wilson, James Q., and George L. Kelling. "Broken Windows." *Atlantic Monthly*, March 1982. https://www.theatlantic.com/magazine/archive/1982/03/broken-windows/304465/.

Winkler, Elizabeth. "Why Oklahoma Has the Most Women per Capita in Prison." *Wall Street Journal*, January 2, 2018. https://www.wsj.com/articles/why-oklahoma-has-the-most-women-per-capita-in-prison-1514898001.

Wolfe, Patrick. "Land, Labor, and Difference: Elementary Structures of Race." *American Historical Review* 106, no. 3 (2001): 866–905.

Woods, Clyde. *Development Arrested: The Blues and Plantation Power in the Mississippi Delta*. London: Verso Books, 2017.

Woodson, Carter Godwin. *A Century of Negro Migration*. New York: AMS Press, 1970.

Woodson, Evan. "Strange Fruit on the Southern Plains: Racial Violence, Lynching, and African Americans in Oklahoma, 1830–1930." PhD diss., Oklahoma State University, 2015.

Wynter, Sylvia. "Afterword: Beyond Miranda's Meanings: Un/Silencing the 'Demonic Ground' of Caliban's 'Woman.'" In *Out of the Kumbla: Caribbean Women and Literature*, edited by Carole Boyce Davies and Elaine Savory, 355–72. Trenton, NJ: Africa World Press, 1990.

Wynter, Sylvia. *No Humans Involved: An Open Letter to My Colleagues*. Stanford, CA: Institute NHI, 1994.

Wynter, Sylvia. "The Pope Must Have Been Drunk, the King of Castile a Madman: Culture as Actuality, and the Caribbean Rethinking Modernity." In *The Reordering of Culture: Latin America, the Caribbean, and Canada in the Hood*, edited by Alvina Ruprecht, 17–41. Montreal: McGill-Queen's University Press, 1995.

Wynter, Sylvia. "Unsettling the Coloniality of Being/Power/Truth/Freedom: Towards the Human, after Man, Its Overrepresentation—an Argument." *Centennial Review* 3, no. 3 (2003): 257–337.

Zamalin, Alex. *Black Utopia: The History of an Idea from Black Nationalism to Afrofuturism*. New York: Columbia University Press, 2019.

Note: numbers in italics refer to figures in the gallery following chapter 3.

poverty cycle, 69–71, 82
Prayer Wall for Racial Healing, 90
professionals, community and, 129–30
Project Oasis, 121–22
Promotora program, 3–4
property insurance, 28–29
property seizure, 40
prosperity. *See* wealth
public nuisance law, 164–66, 168–69
purity, 41, 227n55
Purity and Danger (Douglas), 43

race: Black Indians and, 182–83; class and, 183; life expectancy and, 55; reconciliation and, 129; unemployment and, 56. *See also* Blackness
racialization, 7, 34, 49, 93, 181, 184–85
racism, 2, 13, 26, 30, 32, 34–36, 39–40, 46, 48, 54, 94, 104, 125, 132, 156, 168–70, 184, 186, 203, 214–15, 227n55. *See also* anti-Blackness; Jim Crow
Randle, Lessie Benningfield, 162–63, *G.17*
Ranganathan, Malini, 70
Rastafarianism, 206
Reagan, Ronald, 35
recidivism, 139
reconciliation, 17, 107, 112, 125–26, 128–29, 141–42, 145, 159–60, 170–72, 173,193, 210–12, 220–21, *G.15*
Reconstruction, 3, 6, 17, 182, 201, 205
redlining, 36–37, 54, 130
Red Record, The (Wells), 41
Reese, Ashanté M., 103
religion, 83, 89, 106, 123–26
Repair (Franke), 176
reparations, 157–60, 174–76, 178, 199, 210, 220, *G.12, G.13, G.15, G.16*
Republic of New Africa, 206
"Residential Security" maps, 36
restitution, 159
restoration, 174–75, 178
Reynolds, James, 139
R&G Family Grocers, 98–99
Rial, Carmen, 231n12
Rifkin, Mark, 193–94, 196
riot vs. *massacre* (as terms), 18–19
Risley, Tod, 230n29
Roberts, Alaina, 10, 188, 223n21

Roberts, Neil, 207–8
Roberts, Oral, 124
Rodney, Walter, 63
Roediger, David, 46
Roosevelt, Franklin D., 36
Roosevelt, Theodore, 224n30
Rosewood massacre, 1, 152, 159–60
Rowland, Dick, 1, 21–24, 26, 45, 48–49, 51, 62
Royce, Josiah, 107

Sam, Alfred, 202–3
Sampson, Edward, 185
Sapulpa, Oklahoma, 225n13
Saunt, Claudio, 7, 54
schools, 33–35, 55, 68–69, 71, 84, 91, 127
Schusterman Foundation, 90, 122
Scott, David, 174, 211
Sea Islands, 199–200
segregation, 33–34, 39, 49, 55, 134. *See also* Jim Crow
Seminole, 7, 182
sense of place, 2, 6, 177, 185, 192, 208
settler Blackness, 188, 207
settler colonialism, 185–94, 207
Sharpe, Christina, 104
Shaw, Lester, 171, 211
Sherman, William Tecumseh, 175–76
Shumate, Jabar, 108
Siddiqui, Tasneem, 214
Sierra Leone, 206
Simone, AbdouMaliq, 156–57
Singh, Nikhil Pal, 204
60 Minutes, 147
slavery, 7, 50, 125, 136, 174–77, 194–95, 199. *See also* plantation
Slocum, Karla, 185, 203, 214–15
Smitherman, A. J., 13
social order, 40–42, 51–52, 61–64, 215
Solomon-Simmons, Damario, 133, 162, 167, 211
Souls of Black Folk, The (Du Bois), 42–43
Spears, Franklin and Chappelle (law firm), 29
Sperry, Oklahoma, 225n13
St. Andrew Baptist Church, *G.5*
staying vs. *living* (as terms), 50
Stoler, Ann, 40
Stradford, J. B., 12–13
Strathern, Marilyn, 185
Stuckey, Melissa, 184

www.ingramcontent.com/pod-product-compliance
Lightning Source LLC
Chambersburg PA
CBHW071734270326
41928CB00013B/2670